IMAGINING SPAIN

HENRY KAMEN

IMAGINING SPAIN

HISTORICAL MYTH & NATIONAL IDENTITY

YALE UNIVERSITY PRESS
NEW HAVEN AND LONDON

For information about this and other Yale University Press publications, please contact:
U.S. Office: sales.press@yale.edu   www.yalebooks.com
Europe Office: sales@yaleup.co.uk   www.yaleup.co.uk

Set in Adobe Garamond by SX Composing DTP, Rayleigh, Essex
Printed in Great Britain by St. Edmundsbury Press Ltd, Bury St. Edmunds, Suffolk

Library of Congress Cataloging-in-Publication Data

Kamen, Henry.
    Imagining Spain: historical myth and national identity/Henry Kamen.
        p. cm.
    Includes bibliographical references and index.
    ISBN 978-0-300-12641-9 (alk. paper)
    1. Spain—History. 2. Spain—Civilization. 3. Nationalism—Spain. I. Title.
    DP48.K36 2008
    946—dc22

                                                            2007031678

A catalogue record for this book is available from the British Library.

10 9 8 7 6 5 4 3 2 1

Our past is the seed-ground for creating our future. We shall find again in the past the future that we lost. History points the way to the future. The past bears the imprint of the ideals that we were going to realize in ten thousand years.

Ramiro de Maeztu, *Defensa de la Hispanidad* (1934)

Ernest Renan was right when he wrote over a century ago: 'Forgetting, even getting history wrong, is an essential factor in the formation of a nation, which is why the progress of historical studies is often a danger to nationality.' We historians today are the first line of defence against the advance of dangerous national myths.

Eric Hobsbawm

CONTENTS

PREFACE

Nearly all the ideas on the country's past presently lodged in the minds of Spaniards are rudimentary and frequently bizarre. This fund of beliefs is undoubtedly one of the big obstacles to improving our way of life.

José Ortega y Gasset, *Invertebrate Spain* (1921)

One of the most extraordinary aspects of Spain's sixteenth century is that many Spaniards are still living in it. In a sense, they have never left it. The sixteenth century has dictated a good part of their ideas and aspirations, their vision of the past and of the future. Pick up any newspaper, any novel, and you will find echoes of the sixteenth century somewhere. When politicians wish to make sense of their policies, they look backwards to it for inspiration. When the public buys historical novels, they tend to be about the sixteenth century.[1] Not without reason did Franco choose emblems – the yoke and the arrows – that belonged to that epoch. Not without reason did Gerald Brenan, in *The Spanish Labyrinth*, find clues to Spanish socialism and Spanish anarchism in the ideas of the Golden Age. It was an age that created, and is creating, Spain, not only because of those who still yearn for it but also on account of those who feel they must reject it passionately. For that reason its myths deserve our attention: the present book is an outline of the part played by myths about the early modern period in the formation of contemporary Spanish attitudes.

What is a historical myth? The first and most obvious definition is that it is not based on reality, and is in essence a product of the imagination. In that sense, it lacks any empirical evidence to support it. It is, historically speaking, false. The present book is not about false myths. Even if unreal, a myth always has a point of origin, and that origin is related to our human consciousness and experience. The myths of world history are born out of perceptions and hopes that have formed our lives. They therefore reflect reality, even if they are not real or truthful. One evening after dinner in his Cambridge college in 1931, the literary scholar C. S. Lewis went for a walk with his guest J. R. Tolkien and talked about myths. Lewis claimed that myths were 'lies'. 'No, they are not', said Tolkien, and went on to explain his view. Myths, Tolkien felt, are an expression of reality and therefore not entirely false. Some myths are even partial versions of a truth that lies behind them. The conversation changed Lewis' perception of the problem.

Years later, Lewis – whose thinking about the matter led him to become a Catholic – observed that 'myth is not truth but reality, and therefore every myth becomes the father of innumerable truths on the abstract level. Myth is the mountain whence all the different streams arise which become truths down here in the valley.' He was restating, but from a different perspective, the views of many European thinkers, among them the German writer Herder, who considered that myths were the foundation of national culture. The myths with which we are concerned in this book are historical fictions that appear to lack evidence in support of their veracity. But they also reflect reality for those who have created them and continue to believe in them. The myths cease to be merely historical imaginings, they enter the real world, become accepted and begin to influence the way we think. Claude Lévi-Strauss commented on this: 'myth always refers to events alleged to have taken place long ago. But what gives the myth an operational value is that the specific pattern described is timeless; it explains the present and the past as well as the future.'[2]

This book is not about what are conventionally called 'historical myths', that is, specific stories that came to form part of the narrated past, such as the story of the presence of the apostle St James in Spain. Nor is it about unverifiable events that historians have had to decide whether to accept or reject, in the way that Juan de Mariana in the sixteenth century had to decide when he was writing his narrative of Spain. Rather, it is about broad presuppositions that have affected the way Spaniards write or think about the past. To some extent, it is not important whether these presuppositions are based on fact. Whether they are true or not is less relevant than the purpose and intention they serve. All the myths touched on in this essay are, in their origin, ideological strategies with identifiable political motives. The political motives can be seen most clearly in the case of myths that have been systematically invented in order to undermine observed historical fact. In that respect, they fly in the face of fact and are intentional fallacies. I do not discuss the fallacies in detail, for that would have plunged me into twentieth-century polemic, whereas my intention has been merely to outline how they relate to the sixteenth century.

That century had its own myths, both sacred and secular. For example, popular rebels in all countries looked back to a mythical age of freedom from oppression, while ruling elites clung to a multitude of traditions that served to affirm their social position and political superiority.[3] Myths about the sixteenth century dealt with in these pages tended to evolve very much later, mainly in the nineteenth century. Intellectual leaders of the period, like the writer José Ortega y Gasset, helped to contribute substantially to them. Those ideas were 'myths' in the sense that Plato understood this notion, that is, they were deliberately created because they answered a positive need, and can be construed as true because they represent a certain (even if imagined) perception of the past. When considering the myths in this book, we need to address ourselves not only to the historical roots but also to the reasons why they came into existence and the part they still play today in politics.

Since the early nineteenth century, liberals, conservatives and subsequent ideologues of both left and right have relied heavily on the early modern period because it was the most fertile ground for the construction of myths. The past was a territory that, once conquered and defined, would serve to construct the present. In the same way the communist regime in East Germany attempted to acquire historical legitimacy by constructing an ideological myth based on the sixteenth century.[4] In consequence, ideologues never ceased to write with passion about what had happened long ago, and in doing so they also made a significant contribution to the thought processes of the age in which they lived. Spain's historical literature and artistic heritage would be much poorer, for example, had progressives of the nineteenth century not created a long-lasting myth about the Comuneros of Castile in 1520 as being the first in the peninsula to defend the cause of liberty.[5] The creation of myths helped to rescue events, ideas and personages from obscurity, and made it easier to identify the heroes and villains of the past with political programmes of the present. In brief, much of the present book is inevitably concerned with the nineteenth and twentieth centuries, when what we may call the 'founding myths' of modern Spanish politics took shape. Those myths – which concerned a multitude of issues, ranging from the idea of a nation to the greatness of the empire and the onset of decline –

were shared equally by conservatives and progressives. In time, of course, these groups disagreed over exactly what the founding myths represented, and they went on to elaborate other political principles, which had little to do with the themes touched on here.

The early modern period became a relevant point of reference because it was, for many, the age when Spain had achieved everything: riches, pride, influence, empire, cultural hegemony. That established an immovable peak, which contrasted with subsequent epochs. The recurrent idea of a 'decline' viewed anything which came after that period as disastrous and unworthy of emulation. The seventeenth and eighteenth centuries, whatever their intrinsic merits, were for example viewed with little admiration. The eighteenth century contributed in many ways to a revival of interest in the past among thinking Spaniards,[6] but it also split them firmly down the middle over politics, culture and ideals, offering them in the end little to hold on to that was solid. If they wanted roots, identity and security, they had to forget about the age they lived in and to burrow farther back into their past. Because it dwells mainly on the early modern period, this book touches only in a perfunctory way on developments after the late eighteenth century. For example, the idea of a failed monarchy gathered enormous force in the period after Napoleon's armies occupied the peninsula; it helped to inspire a powerful anti-monarchist movement, and on two occasions it led to the substitution of monarchy by a republic. In the same way, Catholic ideology within its nineteenth-century context drew on fertile ideas that did not base themselves exclusively in an idealization of the past. The sixteenth century, in short, had a crucial part to play in evolving the major 'founding myths', but the nineteenth and twentieth centuries inevitably drew on many additional sources in order to arrive at their political ideologies. The Golden Age of the sixteenth century was only one part of the image that sustained fascist ideologues in the 1930s.

The process of re-creating the past led, unfortunately, to an intense politicization of the main features of its history. Concentration at a later period on the ideological relevance of the sixteenth century created an interminable confrontation among Spaniards, because every key statement made about that century had a direct effect on the way they viewed the present. This deep ideological antagonism, which is as passionate today as it always has been, often goes unperceived by non-Spaniards, who imagine that it is little more than a polite difference of opinion, when in reality it is an enormous chasm that can bar the way to any tranquil discourse.[7] The present volume, as a reader will quickly realize, does not attempt any historical revisionism, nor try to present any provocative novelty; it merely summarizes conflicting points of view and underlines the reasons why those points of view came into being, always within the context of the early modern period.

From the outset, we need to eliminate from consideration what is often termed a 'myth' but in reality is nothing more than an ideological label. I refer to the so-called 'black legend', a term invented by a conservative writer, Julían Juderías. The summary given by one of his contemporaries, the writer Ramiro de Maeztu,[8] is much to the point:

> Don Julían Juderías published the first edition of his *The Black Legend* early in 1914, inspired by purely patriotic sentiment. He had arrived at the conclusion that Protestant prejudices, first, and revolutionary prejudices, after, created and sustained the legend of 'an inquisitorial, ignorant, fanatical Spain, incapable of forming part of civilized peoples, always unchanging, predisposed always to violent repression and an enemy of progress and innovation'. Since this viewpoint offended his patriotism, Sr Juderías wrote his book with the modest intention of showing that we were intolerant and fanatical only when the other nations of Europe were also 'intolerant and fanatical', and that since 'we deserved the respect of others' we had a right to be studied seriously 'without foolish zeal and unfair preconceptions'.

According to Juderías, the admirable achievement of Spain in Europe and America in the sixteenth century invited a flood of hostile propaganda from Spain's enemies, who distorted the truth into a negative 'black legend' about Spain and the Spaniards. Since then, Juderías' book has gone through endless printings in Spanish, and various writers have written numerous books on the same theme. The basic premise of these works has been that propaganda by foreigners was false and presented a wholly distorted picture of the truth. Since then, anything critical of Spain's historical role has come to be termed a 'black legend', with the obvious implication that it is not true. Since our concern here is not with the subjective notions of 'true' or 'false' but, more specifically, with the way Spaniards – rather than foreigners – have contemplated their past, the term 'black legend' is for our purposes both misleading and irrelevant. There are good reasons for leaving Juderías and his devotees out of our picture: his book was distorted by nationalist ideology and a sense of victimization, it tended to blame foreigners rather than Spaniards (though it also denounced, logically, all liberals), and it assumed that any criticism of Spain's past was malicious and false. Juderías failed to realize that criticism of a world power by other nations in early modern Europe had a justifiable logic. Recently, a fine scholarly study has looked at crucial aspects of the ideas that foreigners in that period held about Spain.[9] The present short study, by contrast, considers some of the myths that Spaniards held and still hold about themselves, on seven specific themes. The myths may be regarded as true because they have played a real part in the thinking and evolution of Spaniards down to this day. They have been used, above all, as a way of defining the identity that Spaniards wished to have.

An earlier version of this book was published in Spain in 2006, and I am fortunate in being been able to profit from observations made about it at the time. Many of my arguments can be explored more fully in other studies, notably my recent volume on *Empire* (2003). All translations of texts and quotations are my own. Titles of works are usually given in English, even if the work never appeared in this language. Book references are kept to a minimum; works frequently cited appear in the Notes only with the name of the author, but the full title is given in the Select Bibliography. Because the following account covers a broad range of themes and concepts, it has been impossible to avoid a certain looseness in the use of terms, most notably when I keep referring to 'Spaniards' even while assuming that there was no coherent entity called 'Spain'. The treatment of mythology is also necessarily brief, and, for example, I have not ventured into the field of existential myths, which for American authors such as Thoreau and Emerson offered a profound key to understanding human culture. In sum, this is a short essay, in which I hope to share the same sentiments as Descartes professed when he wrote his *Discours de la Méthode*: 'ne proposant cet écrit que comme une histoire ou, si vous l'aimez mieux, une fable, j'espère qu'il sera utile à quelques-uns sans être nuisible à personne'.

Lake Oconee, Georgia
2007

CHAPTER ONE

THE MYTH OF
THE HISTORICAL NATION

If we define the concept of nation by today's criteria, then one cannot say there was a Spanish nation before the end of the fifteenth century. I would go further and say that, if by nation we understand a single state with a single political body, we have not yet become a nation and perhaps will never be one.

Juan Valera, 1887, *Complete Works*, (1958)

All our ills derive from one alone: the loss of our national idea.

Ramiro de Maeztu, *Defence of Spanishness* (1934)

Birth of a nation

Spanish historians are agreed that the myth of Spain as a nation was born around 1808 or 1812. The exact date is not important, for there is general accord about the significance of that decade. The army of revolutionary France had occupied the peninsula and eventually dethroned its king, setting up Napoleon's brother Joseph as the new ruler. On 2 May – celebrated by some as the beginning of Spain's 'independence' – the people of Madrid and other towns rose against the foreign troops.

If a common enemy can help people to bond together and form a nation, then Spain had a good opportunity to emerge as one when it faced the occupying French army that kept Joseph Bonaparte on the throne. The anti-French riots in various towns in 1808, immortalized in Goya's paintings on the theme (done five years later and never exhibited in his lifetime, so that they also form part of a distant memory rather than a direct testimony), seemed to promise that all Spaniards would rally to a common cause and create a bright new future, based on liberty from the foreigner. The riots of the Second of May were later presented as a popular uprising against the French and symbol of a 'national' resistance. As it happened, the chief victims of the rioters were not Frenchmen but Spaniards, leading supporters of the government who were attacked, murdered and had their property destroyed. The spark of revolt, however, did ignite a struggle against the French. Raymond Carr observes that 'modern Spanish nationalism of a type comparable to nationalism in other European countries was created by the fact of resistance to Napoleon. A myth of enormous potency, available to radicals and traditionalists alike, grew out of Spain's unique and proud resistance.'[1]

An essential component of the myth was the unexpected victory achieved by Spanish forces over French troops at Bailén (July 1808). A scholar who has studied the battle concludes that it was 'lost by the French rather than won by the Spaniards',[2] a view that explains the subsequent saga of (in the words of Carr) 'defeat after defeat, justifying Napoleon's judgement that the Spanish army was the worst in Europe'.[3] In the end, it was the British army under Wellington, rather than any Spanish army, that drove the French out after the battle of Vitoria (1813). But Bailén came to be presented, in the excited patriotic press of the time, as a victory of enormous dimensions.[4] In practical terms, continuous and effective military pressure against the French came not so much from a 'national' upsurge among Spaniards, or even from the British army, as from the guerrillas who were more interested in their own local priorities than in the patriotic cause.[5]

The 1808 risings were only the beginning of a dream that went sour, creating a new and powerful mythology that has lingered into our own day. The French forces withdrew to areas of Spain they could more easily control, while the Spanish 'patriots' summoned to Cadiz in 1810 a Cortes aimed at unifying the national effort. Among its memorable acts were the agreement of a new national charter, the Constitution of 1812, and a decree of 1813 abolishing the Inquisition. When the deputy Agustín Argüelles presented the text of the Constitution, he exclaimed: 'Spaniards, you now have a *patria*!' In reality, there was no *patria* nor any feeling of national solidarity, and the measures of 1812 and 1813 were not the healing measures they appeared to be. Quite the reverse: they had a devastating effect on Spanish public life for the next hundred years. Moreover, they created an illusion of national unity that had little foundation in reality.

The notion of a 'national' cause in the uprising of Spaniards in 1808 was, in perspective, pure myth, invented by political groups at the time and transmitted repeatedly down to our own day. Far from uniting national forces, the Cortes of Cadiz divided Spaniards. It divided them through its debates, its legislation and its famous 1812 Constitution, a piece of paper which – in the view of perhaps the most level-headed Spaniard of that moment, Joseph Blanco White – was founded on fantasy and never had the opportunity to translate itself into reality. The Constitution began by announcing that it was speaking for 'the Spanish Nation', that 'sovereignty resides essentially in the Nation' and that 'love of the *patria* is one of the principal obligations of all Spaniards'. It also declared that 'the Spanish Nation is free and independent' and that 'the objective of Government is the Nation's happiness'. It went on to proclaim that 'the religion of the Spanish Nation is and shall forever be the Catholic, Apostolic and Roman, the only true one. The Nation protects it and prohibits the exercise of any other.' Fine studies have recently analysed the enthusiasm with which the new mythology was adopted by the deputies, their excitement after the successful incident at Bailén and their optimism at the new gospel which they believed they were bringing to the world. They pinned their hopes on an entity called 'the people', by which they meant, specifically, those who had risen against the French in Madrid and other cities on 2 May 1808. That 'people', they proclaimed, was the 'honour and glory of the Nation'.

To explain how the very shaky concept of a 'nation' had now emerged, deputies in the Cortes with a feeling for history presented an idealized version of the past in which, as they saw it, a free people had struggled for centuries against a despotic tyranny, from which they were now liberating themselves.[6] It was, a leading scholar has pointed out, the 'mythical construction of a legendary past'.[7] This theme took them back to the medieval and early modern periods, which were unashamedly given a face-lift. In the beginning, wrote one deputy, Argüelles, 'Spaniards were in the period of the Goths a free and independent nation'. The Spanish were visualized as a great people who had developed fully in the Middle Ages, but after the year 1516 were ruined by despotic foreign rulers from whom they were not rescued until the nineteenth century, when the patriotic forces of the newly liberated nation emerged. Did this mean that the nation was always in existence as a nation, aspiring always to the fulfilment of its liberties? Of course, claimed the 'Liberals', the political tendency that supported the Constitution and only years later evolved into the political grouping known by that name. One of their number, Francisco Martínez Marina, published in 1813 his *Theory of the Cortes*, in which he explained confidently that, as far back as the eleventh century, Castile 'began to be a nation' – a nation that was among 'the most cultured and civilized of Europe', in which the monarchy was democratic, the Cortes functioned and the people were free. The point of greatest glory in the nation, he argued, was achieved under Ferdinand and Isabella. However, immediately afterwards there came foreign monarchs who dissipated Spain's resources, spent its immense wealth, and wasted the blood of its sons on foreign battlefields. The foreign despots crushed Spain's liberties, in Castile 'when Padilla died at Villalar in a shameful condemnation, in Aragon when Lanuza was beheaded at Saragossa, in Catalonia when Pau Claris died'.[8] For three hundred years, since the succession to the throne of a foreign absolutist dynasty, the democratic traditions of the nation had been abolished, its representative institutions (the Cortes) had been silenced, and the people had been left without a voice. Now at last, thanks to the 'people', who could protest against all the corrupt foreign rulers, Spain could become once more the nation that it had been.

Liberal history and the nation

The political groups that opposed the regimes both of Bonaparte and of Ferdinand VII evolved later, as we have noted, into what were known generally as the 'Liberals'. They were opposed by persons who very much later evolved into a Conservative political party. In practice there was often little difference between the groupings, since both had the same social background and political outlook. Their work (above all, that of the Liberals) in creating a radically different vision of Spain's past affects all the myths referred to in this book and therefore merits attention from the very beginning. The opening decades of the nineteenth century were the age when Europeans became conscious of the need to understand their national identity. It was the age when Ranke and Burckhardt in Germany, Macaulay, Gibbon and Acton in England wrote their classic studies. Spain, by contrast, lacked any researched survey of its past and few writers ventured into the field. As late as 1887, the writer Juan Valera was still lamenting that, 'since a very long time ago and certainly since the fashion for it grew, in Spain little has been written about anything, least of all History. Histories are written mainly in France, England, Germany and Italy, nations that are more advanced and mentally more productive than we are.' He was exaggerating, for in his own generation some important steps had been taken to fill the gap, not least through his own writings. The first significant progress was made by the deputies in the Cortes of Cadiz, who set about inventing their own version of what the past signified, conjuring up fictitious information about medieval origins and fifteenth-century glory to suit the tone of their speeches. In the years that followed, writers who had been driven into exile were influenced by foreign models and began to produce what has been referred to as Romantic history. Romanticism's taste for medieval history created a school of narrative in which everything associated with the medieval era was idealized and accepted into the cultural heritage of the nation.

Political refugees in England were among the pioneers of the new history. A romanticized version of Spain's history was offered to the English public in 1830, when the Liberal exile Telesforo de Trueba published in London *The Romance of History: Spain*, a collection of fictional narratives in the style of the American writer Washington Irving. Fortunately, not all such historical production was literary fiction. A key figure was the Liberal politician Antonio Alcalá Galiano (1798–1865), an aristocrat who helped to bring about the Revolution of 1820 in Spain and entered the Cortes, but in 1823 was obliged to seek exile in England at the onset of the so-called 'ominous decade', when the French army invaded the country and restored the absolutist monarchy of Ferdinand VII. He spent the next eleven years as a refugee, seven of them in London. Fascinated by history, he devoted his leisure hours in exile to translating into Castilian works of history from English and French, languages in which, thanks to his elitist education, he was completely at home. He was serious about giving the Spaniards their own history books, but, since they had none of their own, he translated and published (1844) an English textbook,[9] adding annotations by himself, his friend, the Liberal poet and politician Martínez de la Rosa, and the diplomat Donoso Cortés. Until that period, the only authoritative history of their country known to Spaniards was by the sixteenth-century Jesuit Juan de Mariana (see below), which had the advantage of being a work open to Liberal interpretation, but also the disadvantage of covering only the period down to the year 1516. This did not deter nineteenth-century writers, who re-published the text of Mariana, then 'completed' it down to their own time.[10] A typical work of this type was published in ten volumes in Valencia in 1839. However, no researched surveys by Spaniards appeared. A French scholar who published his own *History of Spain* in 1839 commented that, while there were modern authorities one could cite for the histories of other nations, 'there is unfortunately no Spanish name that can be cited'.[11]

Partly as a result of the Peninsular War, foreigners established a virtual monopoly over Spain's early modern history. The pioneer was the American Washington Irving (1783–1859), whose visit to Spain in 1815 inspired him so greatly that he remained in Europe for seventeen years. From 1826 to 1829 he was attached to the American legations in Madrid; then he had another long stay in Spain from 1842 to 1846, as minister plenipotentiary of the United States. The Spanish years produced a pioneering life of *Columbus* (1828, translated into Spanish in 1834) and a history of the *Conquest of Granada* (1829). In 1829 he moved to London and published *Alhambra* (1832), a narrative of the alleged history and legends of Moorish Spain. Irving's work happened to coincide with a vogue in Europe for 'Orientalism' – a fashion for Arabic themes that exercised a strong influence on several British, German and French writers and artists during this active phase of European imperial expansion.[12]

The definitive historical work of those years, however, was by the American W. H. Prescott, a *History of the Reign of Ferdinand and Isabella* (3 vols, Boston 1838), a study that was eventually published in Spanish in Madrid in 1845. It has recently been observed that Prescott's history helped to create the perspective that some readers in the United States still have about Spain.[13] What has never been remarked is that, through the 1845 Spanish translation, Prescott had an even more important impact on Spaniards themselves, by affording them a carefully documented and fully comprehensive historical account which they had hitherto lacked. When Francisco Martínez de la Rosa wrote a *Short History of Spanish Politics* in the 1840s,[14] the sources he cited when narrating the history of his country were principally Prescott, Ranke, Coxe and Watson. Spaniards were also able to draw on the life of Philip II by Robert Watson (first published in English 1777 and translated into Spanish several years later), on Leopold von Ranke's survey of Spain, which had been published in French in Paris in 1839 and was therefore accessible to Spanish intellectuals, and on the Spanish translation (1846, with a prior French translation in 1827) of William Coxe's 1815 masterly survey of the house of Bourbon in Spain. The proliferation and quality of these studies (Prescott and Coxe, for example, are still essential reading) certainly influenced the way Spaniards approached their past.

Despite the reiterated appeals to *patria*, it seemed that Spaniards were little interested in studying their own past. A push was given them by perhaps the greatest scholar of his time, the Frenchman Louis-Prosper Gachard, who served as archivist of the new Kingdom of Belgium from 1831 to 1885 (see Chapter 2). In 1843 Gachard presented himself at the medieval castle at Simancas, just outside Valladolid; there the Spanish archives of state had been growing and gathering dust since the sixteenth century, when Philip II established the collection. He was the first foreign researcher ever to work at Simancas, and diligently began arranging to copy hundreds of documents relating to the history of Belgium. When the dignitaries of the Academy of History in Madrid heard that someone was doing the unthinkable and consulting historical documents, they sent someone to investigate and found that the foreigner was, indeed, doing research on the papers. Greatly alarmed at this novelty, they sent a team of men to the archive to record meticulously every document that Gachard copied. The researcher today can still follow the course of this drama since every document used by Gachard was faithfully annotated 'copied for Mr Gachard', so that the Madrid scribes would know exactly which bits of paper had to be recopied. Gachard was both irritated and amused by this, but in the process he managed to harvest a rich amount of original information relating to the struggle of the Netherlands for independence from Spain. The Academy of History, at a loss as to what to do with their great store of recopied documents, finally decided to publish them as a collection (the famous multi-volume *Collection of Unpublished Documents on the History of Spain*), then forgot about the value of what they had copied.

Fortunately, there were Spaniards who concerned themselves with their history. An authentic native account was at last supplied by a Liberal writer and member of parliament whose work began to emerge in the 1850s. Modesto Lafuente (1806–66), son of a doctor from the province of Palencia, never lived outside the peninsula. He entered the priesthood at an early age but left it when he was thirty in order to plunge into the world of writing and politics in Madrid. He got married in 1843, became a prosperous writer of articles for the Madrid press, and in 1854 successfully obtained a seat in the Cortes. His contribution to the new Spanish historiography took the form of a thirty-volume *History of Spain* (1850–67) that ranks as the most impressive one-man history ever written in Spain, a work which, after a century and a half, is still valuable to consult and a pleasure to read. It immediately became a classic, which subsequent Liberal writers 'completed' to bring up to date. Lafuente undertook careful research in the archives and attempted to be both informative and impartial. He was obviously influenced by the authors writing in the wake of the Cortes of Cadiz, and he also picked up valuable information from foreign scholars. His political views lay at the core of the work, offering the most complete expression of the way Liberals viewed the past of their country. He placed emphasis on the political unity of Spain, on the role of constitutionalism and on the fundamental value of freedom as a prerequisite to a healthy political life. Probably the most striking aspect of his view of early modern Spain, to which we shall refer later (Chapter 2), was his formulation of the myth of a free Castile, whose liberties were eroded by the foreign dynasties that followed Ferdinand and Isabella. His approach was scholarly enough to win applause from most actors on the political stage but it also hallowed views that were later seen to be partisan and divisive.

Thanks to Lafuente, Spaniards were in possession of an informed, native and apparently impartial history of their country. For the first time since the work of Mariana, they could read about the past with confidence. Above all, they could understand what factors had served to create the nation in which they lived. 'Throughout the first half of the nineteenth century,' Álvarez Junco reminds us, 'the most important efforts to build a Spanish national mythology were made by the Liberal elites.'[15] Lafuente's work remained the standard history of Spain until at least the 1890s, when it had to compete with the publication of the multi-volume *History of Spain* master-minded by the conservative statesman Antonio Cánovas del Castillo, but it continued to be used long after that by those who appreciated its scholarship and its viewpoint. Reading through Lafuente, one could grasp the dimensions and the character of the Spanish nation. In the last quarter of the nineteenth century, this new perception of the past was transmitted through the medium of the educational system, which directed the preparation of textbooks and the way the past had to be taught.[16] Schoolchildren who had never heard of Lafuente imbibed his views as received wisdom.

Lafuente began his history by asking the same question that Tolstoy asked himself when he was writing (in those same years) his novel *War and Peace*: What is it that moves nations?[17] He accepted that history brought progress: 'like Vico, we believe in the guidance and order of Providence, and like Bossuet we accept the advance of mankind towards Progress'. But the story he had to tell was not an encouraging one. True to his principles as a Liberal, he described a nation that achieved greatness by the end of the fifteenth century, and then had fallen into precipitous decay for three hundred years. In order to understand Lafuente, we need to grasp the fundamental fact that he created a vision of the past on the basis of the political struggles of the present. Behind him lay the story of Spain at the point where Mariana had left off (in 1516, the year of the death of Ferdinand the Catholic), a Spain that seemed to be at the peak of its glory. Before him lay the Spain of the present, a Spain in tatters, recently overrun by foreign armies, ruled by foreign kings who destroyed parliamentary government and favoured the power of the Inquisition: a country that had once controlled an empire but was now reduced to ignorance and misery. What had happened to transform the former into the latter?

There was no doubt in Lafuente's mind that a momentous change had taken place. This change affected three crucial themes, all of them within the ambit of the early modern period. First, liberty and greatness: they had once been achieved in the person of Isabella of Castile, but they were now in peril because of royal absolutism. The word 'absolutism', invented by the Liberals of the Cortes of Cadiz, was never defined and came to denote, quite simply, those political policies of which they disapproved.[18] The concept was meaningless, for absolutism as a doctrine did not exist; but the word served a convenient polemical purpose and therefore continued to be used in a moralizing sense by subsequent historians. Second, the bright promise of worldwide empire had been betrayed by foreign rulers, who proved indifferent to the country's interests. The one ruler directly identified was Joseph Bonaparte, but the condemnation extended to all of Spain's monarchs after Queen Isabella, since they were all foreigners. Third, the possibility of material well-being and culture had been destroyed by the activities of the Inquisition and the Church. The three themes identified the Liberals' principal enemies: 'absolutism', foreign ideas and the Church. The Liberals applied these categories to the way they wrote Spain's early modern history. Liberal politicians of the mid-nineteenth century also used the three themes as central and active components of the government programme, through which they offered solutions to the canker that had been eating into the heart of Spain. Their political outlook developed in several other directions, but at its core was the conviction that they were putting their country back on the road from which it had been diverted in the sixteenth century.

Was there a nation before the nineteenth century?

Political leaders of the early nineteenth century were certain that their nation existed, but they had difficulty defining its antecedents. The problem, as one views it today, was one of creating historical myths and using words and language that would tone in with them. The criteria used by scholars in judging nations usually derive – and this is also the case with Spain – from the way the countries in question evolved in the period following the French Revolution (1789). Influential studies in English invariably commence their narrative of 'nationalism' around the year 1800. The immensely fertile discussions of the subject available to the reader fail, however, to give much help on the question of the character of the 'nations' and of 'nationalism' that may have existed prior to that period.[19] Indeed, it is – arguably – a mistake to restrict the rise of nations to the nineteenth century, because this arbitrarily excludes from our consideration a vast span of previous history in which the theme was certainly a relevant one and had an indisputable importance.

The Liberals expended much effort in demonstrating that their country had its own character as a nation already in the nineteenth century. Some of them insisted on going further back in time when they looked for a national character, and the habit stuck. A Castilian nationalist writer has recently maintained that 'Spain was the first society to constitute itself into a nation' in late medieval times.[20] Historians would find it difficult to agree with him, since, without citing any evidence or making any attempt to explain what constitutes a 'nation', he appears to assume that an entity called 'Spain' already existed in the far distant past. The refusal to define the meaning of words lies at the heart of the problem of deciding when 'Spain' began to exist in a form that we would recognize. However, the practice of identifying nations well before the nineteenth century is certainly not limited to Spain. Very recently, an expert on England's history claimed that 'England was clearly a nation state in the fifteenth century', and another has no doubt in picking out sixteenth-century England as 'the first nation in the world, and the only one, with the possible exception of Holland, for about two hundred years'.[21] A somewhat more detached outlook can be found in other historians, who are willing to concede that England, as a nation, formed part of Great Britain, which was developing in the nineteenth century, but that Britain also included three other nations, namely the Scots, the Welsh and the Irish.[22]

Few political concepts have aroused more passion than that of the 'nation'. The term has always defied explanation, but since at least the fifteenth century it has been called upon repeatedly by European writers and politicians to define the vague *je ne sais quoi* that binds people together and gives them something to be proud of. What is it that binds? Of what are they to be proud? A specific answer to these questions was never supplied, and in the present essay no attempt will be made to arrive at a definition of what appears

10

to be indefinable. However, the word was certainly used everywhere. In Germany, the writer Conrad Celtis, in 1492, called for his 'nation' of 'Germany' to free itself from slavery, and Sebastian Brant in 1494, in his well-known *Ship of Fools*, referred specifically to 'the German nation'.[23] Yet, as we know, at that date Germany did not exist either politically or culturally; many centuries would pass before it came into being. For Machiavelli in *The Prince* (1514), Ferdinand of Aragon was 'King of Spain'[24] yet as we know Ferdinand was not king *of* Spain. Machiavelli was using 'Spain' in the same spirit in which he wrote of 'Italy': as a broad geopolitical concept, which in reality corresponded only to a combination of small states. In the same way, 'Spain' referred not to a real entity but to a relationship between the various kingdoms to be found in the Iberian Peninsula. The word did not figure in the official titles of its rulers. These called themselves 'King of Castile, King of Aragon' and so on; 'King of Spain' was used only informally, with 'Spain' functioning as a shorthand term, because that entity had no legal existence. But the fact did not stop writers from using it because 'Spain', like 'Germany', was obviously a convenient way to refer to the shared experiences of those who lived in the territories of those kingdoms.

All European countries were, in pre-industrial times, made up of endless diversity: a never-ending variety of peoples, customs, languages, foods, drinks, dress, weights and measures, attitudes, religious practice, soil, plants, animals, climate. In a brilliant book that has received little attention in Spain, the French historian Fernand Braudel – who used to talk to me of these things when he encouraged me in the first steps of what became my doctoral thesis for the University of Oxford – set out to 'explain France's diversity, if it can be explained'.[25] In his book he begins by talking about the incredible variety of economic character, localized political life, dialects and family structure in a country that was so dismembered that only a mythical unity, an 'invented' identity, could be given to it. The same incredible diversity, more fundamental and real than any idea of a 'nation', could be found everywhere, in Italy, Germany, the Low Countries, the British Isles.[26] Those local experiences were, far more than the unreal concept of 'Spain', the real substance of social, political and religious life. 'In the Spanish monarchy,' wrote Baltasar Gracián in 1640, 'where there are many provinces, different nations, diverse languages, dissimilar attitudes and varying climates, great capacity is required in order to preserve and to unite.'[27] Long before Spain began to emerge as a reality, the local communities had their own identity, their indubitable bonds and their unquestionable pride.[28] There is now a large literature on what 'community' meant at the time, and as an example we may note the definition given by a writer in the early seventeenth century, that 'communities are four in number: the household, the neighbourhood, the city and the realm'.[29] It was these communities that could represent a sort of 'nation' for those who lived in them.

The word 'nation' (*nación*) can be found in documents of a very early period, but had a wide variety of meanings, just as it still has today. In the sixteenth century it referred mainly to one's place of birth (in Spanish, *nacer* to be born, hence *nación*). For example, in the trading centres of northern Europe the various colonies of merchants were identified according to 'nation' (the 'Genoese nation', the 'Spanish nation', the 'Portuguese nation'); at the Cortes in Valladolid in 1548 a speaker called attention to 'the strength of this nation',[30] meaning the people of Castile; and the troop units serving in the imperial armies in Italy were each identified by their 'nation', or place of origin. The word applied to companies within an army (most armies were at that time made up of units from different countries), to define their origins and shared language. The soldiers of the Castilian *tercios* in Flanders, absent for years from their homes and desperate to identify the cause for which they were sacrificing their youth and their lives, seemed to be using the term, 'Spanish nation', in a broader, more collective sense. 'We are from the same nation as you, all Spaniards,' wrote the soldiers serving in Holland to the mutineers in the town of Alost in 1576.[31] When the duke of Alba tried to placate mutinous troops in Flanders, he told them: 'Whom else would I do more for than you, who are of my nation?'[32]

But 'nation' was not the only word they used to refer to the things that bonded them together. Other such words also came into common usage, for instance, the word 'country', which had strong geographical overtones, signifying one's place of origin. Political leaders were also concerned to cultivate words associated with 'loyalty'. Of these, the most important was the word *patria*, which was widely used in Italy to refer to the city to which one belonged, and was also found in Spain. Love of *patria* was seen as a fundamental sentiment.[33] All too often, such words were used very loosely. There was certainly a broadly accepted idea of the territory of Spain as *patria* and *nación*, but this usage did not signify any political reality. 'There was', a scholar rightly reminds us, 'no united Spain' in the time of Ferdinand and Isabella.[34] However, when chroniclers came to describe the territory in which they lived, they often used the word 'Spain'. A Catalan historian was capable of writing, in 1547, a history of Catalonia with the title *Chroniques de*

Espanya, even though Catalonia was politically autonomous of the rest of Spain. The existence of 'Spain' did not imply any political unity, but that was no obstacle to writing about it. 'The first modern history of Spain was, undoubtedly, that written by Esteban de Garibay.'[35] Garibay dedicated his *Forty Books of the Compendium of Chronicles and Universal History of all the Realms of Spain* to Philip II, and published it at Antwerp in 1571. He described the work as an 'advanced history of our Spanish nation and of our native kings'. The first half of the volume was on Castile, but the rest of the work dealt also with Navarre, the crown of Aragon and Islamic Spain, so that it covered all the relevant kingdoms that made up 'Spain' and, significantly, included the Muslims as a nation within Spain.

Some writers of that time gave a bit more emphasis to their definition of Spain. At the end of the reign of Philip II, a Madrid magistrate, Gregorio López Madera, published a work in which he praised Spain as his *patria*, then insisted that it was a united nation ('the kingdom of Spain is truly one') and that it had existed forever. Possibly the first authentic nationalist of Castile, he insisted that Spain had always been Christian (he dismissed the Moors as passing invaders) and that its language had been given directly by God and was not a mere derivation from Latin.[36] His work tended to fall into the category of laudatory writings rather than historical narrative. The first truly general history of Spain as a nation, ample in scope, well informed and impressively objective, was that by the Jesuit Juan de Mariana, written first in Latin, then translated by him and published in two volumes in 1601, as a *General History of Spain*.[37] For over three centuries it remained the history most consulted by Spaniards.

One could also define belonging to a nation by explaining who it was that did *not* belong. In opposition to the idea of *nación* or place of origin, people were also aware of the *extranjero* ('foreigner'), the person who did not belong to their *nación*. In the preface to his 1492 *Grammar*, for example, Nebrija spoke of 'foreign nations'. Over the centuries, people became increasingly aware of the differences between themselves and others: others spoke differently, lived differently, ate differently. But what was it that they themselves had in common, inside their own lands? That was far more difficult to decide. On the whole, the decision tended to be made not by the people but by the authorities, which used criteria such as law, order and tax-paying (very much the same criteria that we use today) in order to identify those who belonged to, or were 'natives' of, the territory. Those who were not 'natives', or 'citizens', were classified as foreigners and excluded from certain rights. In Aragon in the seventeenth century, therefore, a resident of neighbouring Valencia might be a foreigner, and vice versa. This meant that a political criterion was being adopted, and so the emergence of what was called a 'state' began to give identity to what had been thought of, vaguely, as a 'nation'. The power of the 'state', in other words, began to define the persons it controlled (the 'nation'), and to exclude others.

It is easy to get confused by the use of words. In the Middle Ages, people already spoke of 'Spain' even though no such political or cultural entity existed. As we have noted, writers referred to concepts such as 'Italy', 'Germany' or 'France', and in the Renaissance there were hopes that these words might become political realities. They did not. A recent scholar has put the matter precisely. 'There was no legal concept of a Spanish nationality in Spain during the early modern period. There were "subjects" of the Spanish king. But the different political entities which made up Spain were composed of different "nationalities": Navarrese, Aragonese, Castilians, Catalans, Portuguese. In Spain there was no national monarchy, and peripheral provinces were juridically distinct nations.'[38] This statement limits itself only to the historical regions of the peninsula.

In fact, the regions were not the only nations within Spain. The kingdom of Granada up to the year 1492 was evidently a nation, in which a common government, culture, loyalty and history – a history of far greater duration than that shared by the Christian kingdoms – bound the Muslim inhabitants together. As late as the year 1568, the leader of the Moriscos, who rose in rebellion, claimed that 'we are no band of thieves, but a kingdom!' The Jews, who also suffered a grievous blow on their expulsion in 1492, were a small group but laid claim to be a nation too. During the centuries they had lived in Spain, they gradually came to develop the idea that they formed a distinct socio-cultural group, based not on territory or government, because they had neither, but on religion and place of origin. The Christians among whom they lived were undoubtedly irritated by the Jews' claim to a separate identity.[39] Already a powerful minority in southern Castile by the midfifteenth century, converted Jews (the *conversos*) were secure in their social position and proud to be both Christian and of Jewish descent. As many of their own writers affirmed, they were a *nación*. They had their own individuality and took pride in it. The chronicler Andrés Bernáldez reported that 'they entertained the arrogant claim that there was no better people in the world than they'. The writer Alonso de Palencia reported complaints by Old Christians that the *conversos* acted 'as a nation apart, and nowhere would they agree to act together with the Old Christians; indeed, as though they were a people of totally opposed ideas, they openly and brazenly favoured whatever was contrary to the Old Christians'.[40] By the later seventeenth century, the exiled Jewish writer Isaac Cardoso, who was living in Italy, commented: 'In a nation like Spain there are many nations, so intermingled that the original one can no longer be recognized. Israel, by contrast, is one people among many, one even though scattered, and in all places separate and distinct.'[41] He was arguing that Spain was simply a community of nations, whereas Israel was something much greater, a nation that could be found within other peoples. The exiled Jews, in other words, may have come from Spain and been scattered, but they still formed a coherent 'nation'. Iberia, despite the echoes of the Inquisition, gave to Jewish and *converso* exiles a common bond, which made them all 'men of the nation'. Even those who were no longer practising Jews felt a profound kinship, based less on religion than on origin, with the *converso* world from which they had emerged.[42]

If we ask ourselves, then, whether there was a nation in Spain before the nineteenth century, the answer is (as Gracián stated) that there were many, for Spain existed as a community of nations. The evidence is irrefutable. No one was more conscious of it than the kings of Spain. Around 1650, Juan de Palafox, an Aragonese who was bishop first of Puebla (Mexico) and then of Osma in Aragon, commented that in preceding centuries the rulers had always recognized the multinational character of Spain. Ferdinand and Isabella, he emphasized, had never tried to create a united Spain: 'Queen Isabella even changed her clothes according to the nation she was in; in Castile she was a Castilian, in Aragon an Aragonese, in Catalonia a Catalan.' Spain, he felt, would succeed only through the recognition of its variety: 'in all Vizcaya you will not find an orange, in all Valencia not a chestnut'. The government must tolerate linguistic diversity, 'governing Castilians in Castilian, Catalans in Catalan'. As we know, Spain's rulers did not use the word 'Spain' in their titles and knew that the countries they ruled each had a special character. Philip II was fully aware of this. When pressing his claims to the throne of Portugal just prior to his invasion of that country in 1580, he explained in a message to the Portuguese: 'Uniting some realms with others does not follow from having the same ruler, since, though Aragon and Castile have a single ruler, they are not united, but as separate as they were when they had different rulers'.[43] In other words, if Portugal accepted him as king, it would not lose its right to be an autonomous nation. When he eventually took over Portugal, he respected that right fully.

With time, inevitably, the nations within Spain became aware that their privileges were being eroded. The classic cases were those of the Muslims and Jews. This situation prevailed until Philip V eventually unified most of the Spanish autonomous realms under one political administration in the first decade of the eighteenth century. For the first time, in 1712, a session of the Cortes in Madrid represented not only Castile, but also the whole of Bourbon Spain, and included two deputies from Valencia and five from Aragon.[44] From that period on, Spain existed as a political unit, that is to say, as a state occupying most of the peninsula. But was the new state a *nación*, superseding the nations within it? 'Spaniards' certainly existed, but was there a 'Spanish nation'? – a question that takes us outside the scope of the present essay, which is limited to the early modern period.

The identities of Castile and Spain

Anyone who tries to identify a 'nation' is automatically trying to impose criteria with which others will always disagree. A leading expert on the subject, Hugh Seton-Watson, wrote thus, after many years of studying the small nations of Eastern Europe:[45] 'no "scientific definition" of a nation can be devised; yet the phenomenon has existed and exists'. In the same work, he went on to say: 'a nation exists when a significant number of people in a community consider themselves to form a nation, or behave as if they formed one. It is not necessary that the whole of the population should so feel, or so behave, and it is not possible to lay down dogmatically a minimum percentage of a population which must be so affected. When a significant group holds this belief, it possesses "national consciousness".' He also warned, however, that if only a small proportion of citizens claim the description of nation for their community, the so-called nation may be little more than a fiction. These observations, applied to Spain, help us to arrive at the important conclusion that 'Spain' may have existed as a 'nation' long before it existed as a state, because there were enough people, both at an elite and at a popular level, who shared the feeling that they belonged to something called Spain. We should not, however, misunderstand what this meant. Spain in the early modern period was a real 'nation' in much the same way as Germany, neither more nor less. That is to say, although Spaniards shared many things, around 1700, on the eve of Philip V's political reforms, they did not have a common way of life, common aspirations, a common language, a common culture, or a common government. Those barriers to unity would, as in Germany, take nearly two centuries to break down. The essential step towards forming a modern-type nation was political, that is, it consisted in the creation of a state that could define more specifically what did and did not constitute a nation.

However, within that so-called nation there were many other local loyalties that took precedence, and therefore impeded the forming of general loyalties. It is habitual to cite the Catalans as an obstacle to the emergence of a united Spain, but we forget that Castile was also, at times, a barrier to unity. The Comuneros of Castile in 1520, in revolt against the government of Charles V, were firm supporters of their own special privileges against those of other peninsular realms.[46] They were, I. A. A. Thompson reminds us, not just anti-Flemish and anti-imperialist, but also anti-Spanish and separatist. There was nothing new about this intense regionalism. Immediately after the death of Queen Isabella in 1504, many Castilians favoured separation from Aragon, 'since Castilians have been pushed around long enough by the Aragonese'.[47] They resented the rule of King Ferdinand. During the centuries of Habsburg rule, when the crowns of Castile and Aragon coexisted as fully autonomous neighbours within the Spanish community, there were numerous occasions when Castilians expressed and demonstrated their impatience with the Aragonese. In the Castilian Cortes of the sixteenth century, the deputies were quite firm in distinguishing between 'these realms' (Castile) and 'those' (Aragon). The phrase 'these realms' almost never came to mean 'Spain', it usually meant 'Castile and León'. The natives of Aragon continued to be considered as outsiders and foreigners by Castilians. In the same way, the Aragonese considered other subjects of the Spanish empire to be foreigners. In the seventeenth century Juan de Solorzano, author of the *Politics of the Indies*, stressed that 'we should classify the Aragonese as foreigners, just as we do the Portuguese, Italians, Flemish and others'.[48]

Among the different nationalities of Spain, the most significant was clearly the nation of Castile. The problem is that even 'Castile' is difficult to define, for it was certainly not the political entity that historians know as the 'crown of Castile'. The latter included areas such as Galicia, Andalusia and Asturias, where the way of life was substantially different, especially in culture and dialect, from that of the Castilians. Moreover, chroniclers and writers based in Castile began to adopt a special variety of regionalism, by referring in their writings to 'Spain' when they really meant 'Castile'. They wrote about 'our Spain' when their theme was only Castile, and increasingly they referred to their language as 'Spanish'. These usages did not mean that Spain had suddenly become united; they simply signified that, in the Castilian mind, a fundamental fusion of two distinct concepts was taking place. It was a very long process, of which non-Castilians were well aware. But many Castilians were (and are) normally unimpressed by objections to this fusion (or confusion).

Critics of Castile's role in the history of the peninsula have always maintained that Castile hijacked Spain's identity. The claim is not wholly without foundation, and it is easy to understand why this happened. Castile's land mass was nearly four times the area of the kingdoms in the crown of Aragon, with a corresponding superiority in natural resources and wealth. Around 1500 Castile contained nearly 80 per cent of the population of peninsular Spain. The three largest cities of Spain at that time were in Castile: Seville, Granada and Toledo. Castile, unlike the crown of Aragon, had many of the essentials of a united government: it had one Cortes, one tax structure, one language, one coinage, one administration, and no internal customs barriers. It also had larger and more powerful trading structures (most notably, the sheep-traders guild, the *Mesta*), which managed the bulk of Spain's external trade and guaranteed Castile's preponderance in any economic association with Aragon. Spain's military initiatives in Europe would have been impossible without Castile's soldiers. In the first decade of the sixteenth century, voices were raised in Barcelona criticizing the leading role adopted by Castile in the affairs of Naples, which had just recognized Ferdinand the Catholic as its king. Ferdinand silenced his critics by reminding them that the troops which had made possible the annexation of Naples had not been Catalan, but Castilian.

The age of empire was also pioneered by Castile. The majority of emigrants to the colonies were from the crown of Castile, and their language was Castilian. For them, Castile and Spain were perceived as identical. Because of the dominant role played by Castilians in foreign enterprises, the history of voyage, discovery, conquest and war was written up by official historians in a way that gave all the glory to Castile. In a sense this was not new, for other European nations, too, were in that same epoch trying to discover their own identity through an exploration of their past. Today, reading the stirring historical accounts that have come down to us, it is easy to forget that they were essentially works of propaganda by Castilians who on the one hand were delighted by the achievements of their citizens and on the other were anxious to please their sponsors, who were normally the government.

Historians writing in the sixteenth century were the first to confuse, no doubt deliberately, the identities of Castile and Spain. The official historian

Antonio de Herrera went so far as to present the entire imperial enterprise, both in Europe and in the New World, as exclusively a history of the deeds of Castilians. In his pages the Portuguese explorer Magellan was transformed into a Castilian, and the 1525 battle of Pavia in Italy, fought against the French army by an international imperial force (mainly Germans, with a strong contingent of Italians and Spaniards), became a conflict between French and Spaniards alone, in which the capture of the King of France was a consequence of the victory of the 'Spanish army'.[49] Herrera's contemporary, Prudencio de Sandoval, introducing his narrative of the life of Charles V, declared 'I am going to write about the kingdoms of Castile', a phrase that four lines later became 'this history of Spain'.[50] The part played by non-Castilians in the task of discovery and settlement was in no way glossed over by the chroniclers, but non-Castilians were invariably given an identity as 'Spaniards', which obscured their nationality and origins. The chroniclers described, for example, the sponsors of Sebastian Cabot's 1525 expedition to North America simply as merchants of Seville, omitting the detail that they were Genoese.[51] The work of the Castilian historians became perhaps the most powerful tool in the creation of the desired image of empire. Subsequent historians in their turn quoted the earlier writers. The contribution of non-Castilian allies was not forgotten, but simply lost from sight. During the twentieth century, this lapse, if we may term it so, became transformed into a firm ideological tenet of Castilian nationalists, in which the achievements of the past had to be attributed only to 'Spaniards', without reference to regional origins. The myth of an eternally united Spain, in which there were no nations except that of Castile, was in this way projected back onto the past.

To a twentieth-century Castilian like the writer José Ortega y Gasset, it seemed logical that Castile should always take primacy over Aragon. 'The clever Aragonese vixen understood that Castile was right, that it was necessary to tame the surliness of its people and incorporate them into a bigger Spain. Its higher flights of imagination could only be carried out by Castile. That was when the unity of Spain came about.'[52] Ortega dated the 'unity' to the fifteenth century. This Castile-centred reading of the past, which runs through all Ortega's writings, does little justice to what really happened. Castile of course had the largest population in the peninsula, and therefore there were more Castilians visible in every type of activity, but the essential fact was that a nation began to take shape because all Spaniards worked together and contributed to it, not because Castilians were the sole or the superior contributors.

The best testimony we have for Spaniards working together is in military activity. One small example may suffice. When the final stages of the ten-year campaign against Muslim Granada were under way, an Italian eyewitness, Pietro Martire d' Anghiera, expressed in 1489 his admiration for the sense of common purpose in the Christian army:

> Who would have thought that the Asturians, Galicians, Basques, and the rude inhabitants of the Pyrenees would be mixing freely with Toledans and the jealous Andalusians, living together in harmony in one military camp and obeying the orders of their leaders and officers to the extent that you would think they had all been raised in the same language and were subject to one common discipline?[53]

The collaboration among Spaniards – and the significant reliance on a common language, Castilian – set an important precedent for subsequent cooperation in wars, explorations and settlements. Spaniards fought side by side in the struggle for Granada and would continue to fight together in Italy and, later, in America. Writers of the time were quick to accept the feeling of a common identity – among them Diego de Valera, who dedicated his 1493 *Chronicle of Spain* to 'the lady Ysabel, queen of Spain'. The nation began to form because this was a shared experience, to which all had contributed in some measure. It did not, evidently, come into being exclusively because of the efforts of Castilians.

It took a long time for the various nations of the peninsula to react against the supremacy that Castile had built in the sixteenth century. Their consciousness of regional identity – which today is a major issue in the political arrangements that take place in Spain – did not begin to assume a secure form until counter-myths could be created to back them up. From the 1860s on, various accounts came into existence about the historical origins of the regions. Local writers in Galicia, for example, began to develop the idea that the Galicians were a nation of European stock, who had evolved separately from Castilians. The Catalans tried to put forward similar ideas, based on separate origins and a wholly separate political background. The Basque writer Sabino Arana was the first to develop the theory of a Basque 'race', whose origins were in Europe and not in the peninsula. The sixteenth century remained, therefore, the focal period for all those who accepted the preponderance of Castile within Spain, but the nineteenth century supplied a new dimension by producing the regional writers who would lay claim to a distinct nationhood and even to what (pro-Castilian) Spaniards would later denounce passionately as 'separatism'.

The empire helps to create the nation of Spain

If we look at the issue only from inside the peninsula, there are many reasons for doubting whether sixteenth-century Spain – or any other similar country in Europe – had the attributes of a nation. The natives of the peninsula, however, also looked at it from the outside, for when they travelled through the worldwide empire they could not fail to start longing for the land they came from. Once they crossed the Atlantic and the Pacific, or passed to other lands in Europe, emigrants from the peninsula were able to recognize that they came from a common home, after which they still hankered. The Valladolid writer Cristóbal Suárez de Figueroa (*d.*1644), who spent half his life in Italy, saw that 'even spirits that are most opposed in the *patria* become reconciled when they are outside it, and learn to appreciate each other'. He expressed forcefully the desires of those who had left Spain and, with it, the 'skies, rivers, fields, friends, family and other pleasures that we look for in vain when we are away'.[54] Being abroad was a powerful influence in creating sympathy for 'Spain', and helped to give substance to what had been merely an idea. The word began to take on echoes of yearning in referring to the homeland from which all peoples of the peninsula came. The most obvious example is that of the emigration to the New World. Settlers writing home to their loved ones habitually referred to the peninsula as 'Spain', and even when they were content with their new lives did not cease to long for the things that 'Spain' represented for them. For generations of Spaniards, there was a permanent pull between their adopted homeland and the one they had left behind. Spain existed as a nation because absence made it real.

But, although the word 'Spain' appears repeatedly in the correspondence of émigrés, the specific yearning was always regional, for the specific area, city or province from which they came. Spain meant, above all, the region they came from, especially when it was one with very special characteristics. Hundreds must have found themselves in the position of the settler in Cajamarca who wrote in 1698 that, 'though my body is in America, my soul is in Navarre'.[55] The homeland, the *patria*, was experienced as a firm sentiment, but its point of reference was usually regional, not national. The *tierra* ('land') of origin was the fundamental source of their identity. 'This territory', a settler in Mexico wrote to his wife in Madrid in 1706, 'is made up entirely of people from Spain, and those who are from the same *tierra* esteem each other even more highly than if they were relatives.'[56] This was a phenomenon that could be found in most Spanish emigration, down to our own day. In early twentieth-century Mexico, for example, the Spanish communities used to hold interminable feasts to celebrate *mi tierra* (my land) and *mi país* (my country), but they were celebrating only their regions, never their nation.[57] Prominent among emigrants from the *tierras* of Spain were the Basques, who played an important role during the sixteenth century in the push towards northern New Spain, where a province was named New Biscay. The feeling of separateness might often, even in distant America, lead to conflict between Spaniards. There were cases of tension between the Basques and other settlers, especially Andalusians, who were sometimes perceived as 'Moriscos'.[58] In many cases, living abroad helped the settlers to consolidate ties with their native region in the peninsula, rather than promoting a greater consciousness of the whole of 'Spain'. In the eighteenth century, short-term emigrants to America from the Basque village of Oiartzun in the Pyrenees brought back riches that helped to develop the local community and gave it a stronger identity.[59]

Fortunately, the perspective imposed by living outside the peninsula contained other aspects which contributed to giving reality to the idea of a Spanish nation. When Spaniards acted in a political or military capacity outside the homeland, they used the word 'Spain' to identify the country they came from. In the nascent empire of Ferdinand and Isabella, a common bond was created by the sense of participation in an enterprise led and pioneered by Castilians, who formed four-fifths of the population ruled by the crown in the peninsula. At the same time, the growth of the empire bestowed on 'Spain' a significance, a role and an ethic which helped the peoples of the peninsula to realize that they now shared a common enterprise which gave them an unprecedented new identity. Perhaps the most powerful contribution to this identity was made by aggressive warfare. From the wars of Granada onwards, both soldiers and officers in the army absorbed a war ethic in which military values transcended the level of mere personal valour and were placed at the service of prince and state. All soldiers in the pay of Spain, whether Castilians or not, were encouraged to identify themselves directly with the nation. They were told to shout for Spain. The use of a standard battle-cry helped concentrate their zeal. During the Italian wars around the year 1500, all soldiers serving in the *tercios* were under *the obligation* to use the battle-cry 'Santiago, España!'. Castilian chroniclers reported how the soldiers chanted 'España, España!' and 'España, Santiago!' as they hurled themselves at their enemies. They may not even have identified fully with the meaning of the words, but it was a phrase that served to concentrate their ferocity.

Over the next half century the war-cry 'Santiago, España!' began to be heard throughout Europe. It was used by all soldiers – whether Castilian, Italian, German or Flemish – who were fighting on behalf of Spain. The point is worth emphasizing because of the common misapprehension that the troops shouted for Spain because they were Spaniards. Given the international composition of Spain's armies, the truth is that very often they were not. The battle-cries of 'Santiago!' or 'Charge, España!' were no proof that the troops felt any emotion for the Spanish nation. Even troops not in Spain's service were known to use such invocations. At the battle of Mühlberg in Germany in 1547 the crack Hungarian cavalry in the emperor's army had to choose between the official German or Spanish battle-cries, and in view of their antipathy for Germany they had no hesitation in opting to cry 'España!'.[60] Considering that over half of the men in a *tercio* might have been non-Castilian Spaniards, the cohesive effect of this essentially Castilian war-cry was indubitable. All soldiers of the peninsula were encouraged to feel that their cause was the cause of Spain. It was significant that the battle-cry could not, except in the Granada wars, be used within the peninsula. One could not shout 'Spain!' when fighting a battle against other Spaniards. The proclamation of an identity, of a loyalty to Spain, was always directed at outsiders and associated with imperial enterprise. Just as Basques, Extremadurans and Aragonese might feel they had a common cause against the Muslim enemy at Granada, as Pietro Martire had observed, so their joint experience outside the peninsula gave them a common bond. Long before there was any political reality to the concept within Iberia, 'Spain' became a vivid reality for the soldiers outside it, which determined their aspirations. In the year 1500, a military commander trying to mollify four thousand Castilian soldiers in Naples, who were mutinying over the non-payment of their wages, is said to have used the following words to them: 'the whole of that kingdom of Spain, of which we are sons, has its eyes fixed on you'.[61] There was, of course, no 'Kingdom of Spain', for even the king in the peninsula did not usually call himself 'king of Spain'. But the fiction had its purpose. Hundreds of miles away, the scattered towns and isolated villages from which the soldiers came took on the lineaments of a great new identity, the 'Kingdom of Spain', to which they could return if they fought successfully.

The continuing emphasis on the reality of 'Spain' certainly helped the peoples of the peninsula to become aware of their role in the making of the empire. From the wars of Granada onwards, they usually took part together in military enterprises that had a common purpose. But, although 'Spain' became a more palpable concept both to Spaniards and to outsiders, very little changed in the immediate perception of daily life in the peninsula, where the loyalties of hearth and home, of local culture and language, kept their primacy until well into the nineteenth century. From at least the beginning of the sixteenth century there were writers who were using the term *patria* for the community – usually the home town – for which people felt an instinctive loyalty.[62] In colonial Latin America, many writers mentioned the *patria* of their origin as a matter of habit, but the word always referred to a specific town or region, never the national entity of Spain.[63] 'Spain', whether for those who lived in the peninsula or in the colonies, existed in political terms, but it remained an abstract entity that seldom penetrated down to the most intimate local level. In the early eighteenth century, the Asturian monk and scholar Feijoo roundly affirmed that 'Spain is the authentic object of a Spaniard's love', but his definition of 'Spain' referred to little more than its existence as an administrative body, 'that body of state where, under a civil government, we are united by the bonds of the same laws'.[64]

Was Catalonia a nation?

Of all the nations that constituted Spain, the Catalans were the most forceful in asserting their identity. They persisted mainly because others (especially the Count Duke of Olivares in 1640) threatened their privileges and eventually, as a consequence of the War of the Spanish Succession, abolished them (in 1714). From that period, the Bourbon regime attempted to create a political unity that included both Castile and the provinces of the old crown of Aragon. After the 1700s, 'Spain' began to be interpreted by its defenders as a political concept, not simply a cultural one. In reality, the changes imposed by the Bourbons were largely in the area of taxation, that is, they developed control and administration in those sectors which could produce an income to support public policy and warfare. Instead of contributing to a cultural nation, they were contributing to the growth of the 'state'. As is normal, the absorbed territories resented this development. The reaction was strongest in Catalonia, which never gave up its claim to its own character. In the 1700s, when the Catalans were deprived of their regional privileges (the *fueros*, or, in Catalan, *furs*), they did not give up. A century and a half later, a section of their social elite began the process of creating a new identity to replace the one they had lost. The movement, known as the Renaixença, was primarily cultural, not political; it had no regionalist or separatist aspirations. Half a century after the Renaixença, an openly political Catalanism took on a life of its own. This affected the definition of the word nation. In the earlier phase, the refrain among Catalanists had been 'Catalonia is the *patria*, Spain is the nation'. In the later phase, the refrain was: 'Catalonia is the nation, Spain is the state'.

Although both the Renaixença and the political movement were evolving new ideas that had their roots in the conditions of the time, they did not fail to rely heavily on the past in order to justify the present.[65] The central question which has dominated debate in the year 2006, when the new Statute of autonomy (an agreement between the central and the regional governments over the sharing of responsibilities and income) was proposed for Catalonia, was whether Catalonia can be formally described as a nation. As we have seen from the comments of Seton-Watson noted above, the word 'nation' lacks any precise meaning and is often a wholly subjective and fictional concept. Many young nations start out with the disadvantage that they have no past. They therefore have to manufacture it, or at least to establish respectable roots. This is a normal process of myth-making, and the Catalans managed remarkably well, because they had one of the most outstanding histories possessed by any small people in Europe. The course of European history was full of populations who had seen their autonomy destroyed, and the Catalans were not alone in trying to rebuild their identity after the 1700s. One hundred years before, the Spaniards themselves had helped to destroy the 'Czech nation'; Catalans were therefore aware of precedents affecting their case. It is significant that after 1714 many of the refugees from Catalonia drifted to Central Europe and sought support there from the Habsburg monarchy.

The Catalans drew confidence from the economic upturn at the end of the nineteenth century and began to construct a new attitude to their past. There was nothing unique about this, for other peoples in Europe were doing the same thing at the same time. But, because they had been deprived of their autonomy in early modern times, much of the myth-making centred on the sixteenth and seventeenth centuries. Two levels of national myth began to emerge. The first, manufactured in the mid-nineteenth century by the upper-class promoters of the Renaixença, went back to the medieval past, to rescue out of it the fundamental elements of what it was to be Catalan in terms of religion, language and daily customs. At the same period, the regionalists in Catalonia began (like others elsewhere in Europe) to create new symbols for themselves. They picked out traditional folk songs which were now given the status of 'national' songs, and in 1899 they created a somewhat sombre 'national' anthem, *Els Segadors* ('The reapers'), using music composed seven years previously. One other type of music, the late medieval *sardana* dance, was now formalized, cleaned up of any possible sensuality and adopted as a very Catholic and 'national' dance. Then, from 1901 on, the regionalists arbitrarily chose a day in September as a 'national' day (see below).[66] On 11 September of that year, a small group of young men decided to lay a wreath at the memorial to one of the heroes of the siege of Barcelona of 1714. The most important task was to re-interpret the past so as to make it consonant with the new aspirations. If necessary, a past could be invented, in the sense that fragments of events could be pieced together to produce the desired picture. The most interesting aspect of this programme was the systematic renaming of streets, especially in the newly constructed quarter of the Eixample in Barcelona. With professional advice from the historian Victor Balaguer, from 1864 onwards the city council began giving appropriate historical names to streets in order to keep permanently visible those names that were deemed to form part of the reality of Catalonia.[67]

The second level of myth was a recasting of the circumstances that had led to the loss of the *fueros*. A central event in Catalan political history was the loss of its political independence in the early eighteenth century, at the end of the War of the Succession. One of the most influential histories of that past, by the writer Salvador Sanpere i Miquel, was titled *The End of the Catalan Nation* (1903) and concentrated on the details of the 1714 siege of Barcelona. The title was significant, for it stated a nationalist programme. Although the volume described the end of a historic nation, in the author's eyes there was no 'end', and the 'nation' would survive. In opposition to the Castilian view, therefore, Catalans developed an alternative version – that is, 'a continuing aspiration' – to the effect that they were still a nation, with a character distinct from that of the Spain of which they formed a part. The tension between Spain and Catalonia led to a process of myth-making which is still active today.

Two centuries later the conflict embodied by the War of the Spanish Succession was presented by the regionalist political movement of the crown of Aragon as the consequence of a heroic struggle of a united people in defence of liberty and against Castilian absolutism. The Valencians in 1705, a regionalist writer of 1930 argued, were moved by 'the spirit of their country, attached to its liberties, and hostile to the regime of absolutism'.[68] The Valencian myth took the form it possesses today, of commemorating the loss of the *fueros* that resulted from the battle of Almansa in 1707. At Almansa, ran the argument, the Valencian people struggled to defend their liberties but lost. The unfortunate aspect of this specific myth is that no Valencians took part in the battle, and no Valencians lifted a finger to defend their liberties. The battle was exclusively an affair between French and Castilians (on the winning side), and English, Germans and Dutch (the losers). A similar heroic image of Catalonia was deployed by Catalan writers around the year 1900, when the most energetic nationalist leader was the young Enric Prat de la Riba. In his discussion of *Catalan Nationality* (1906), he maintained that 'Catalonia had a language, a law, an art of its own, a national spirit, a national character, a national thought: Catalonia was therefore a nation'. He was, evidently, talking about the past as he saw it, not about the present in which he lived.

In short, the way we view the early modern past of Catalonia has been profoundly affected by the myths that were invented in the 1900s.[69] It is one of the few regions of Europe – Northern Ireland is another – where groups of people come to blows in the streets because they differ in opinion over what happened in the seventeenth century. The issues at stake in that earlier period were, from a regionalist perspective, quite clear.

First, the enemy could be identified. Even though they were writing in the 1900s, the regionalists borrowed the vocabulary of the previous century's Liberals and pinpointed Castilian 'absolutism' as the great enemy of their *fueros*. They suggested that Philip V was inspired by a wish to impose 'absolutism', or that he was influenced by his great grandfather Louis XIV in that direction. The fact that neither Philip V nor his ministers possessed any theory of absolutism was deemed irrelevant. The nineteenth-century concept of 'absolutism', born amid the struggles of constitutionalists against the regime of Ferdinand VII, was transposed back to the events of 1714, and has remained the obligatory text-book explanation of the motives of the King of Spain.

Second, the solidarity of all Catalans was assumed to be indisputable. The conflict of the 1700s was presented as the struggle of a united people against outside aggression. It was a replication of the Liberal image of the 'people' resisting the French. By default, 'the Catalans' were seen as unanimous defenders of liberty against military force. The fact that a substantial part of the population of Catalonia – maybe half, maybe more – supported Philip V was assiduously omitted from the history books.

Third, an emotional issue had to be identified. The oppressors were denounced as enemies of the Catalan language, which they were supposed to have systematically prohibited and eliminated. Even though every historian writing about early modern Catalonia (Catalan historians among them) has insisted that no such prohibition ever occurred, regionalist political parties continue to repeat the fiction in campaign speeches today. The close parallel between the regionalist argument and the standard Liberal position enables us to understand why most Liberal historians in the nineteenth century backed the Catalan version of events and treated the Catalan leader Pau Claris as one of the victims of 'absolutism'.

From the viewpoint of a patriotic Catalan around the year 1900 there was much that was valid in this threefold perspective. As stated by the first spokesman of the new nationalist tendency in the 1890s, one Prat de la Riba who had just emerged from his teens, the Catalans continued to be a nation because they had 'one language, one common history, and live bound together by one same spirit'.[70] The problem, he argued, was that they were unhappy with Castile, or Spain, as the 'state' that governed them, because it threatened them as a nation. This form of discourse, in which the nation (or *patria*) was seen as distinct from the state, endowed the word 'nation' with a special significance – which it still has – for Catalans. The unhappiness is not our primary concern here. However, it led Prat de la Riba and others to some interesting musings on the distant historical past. Though in principle they enjoyed the support of Liberal historians, the nationalists turned an important aspect of the Liberal interpretation of the past on its head. Instead of idealizing the reign of the Catholic Monarchs (see Chapters 2 and 7), Prat saw that period as the beginning of Spain's decline. Everything that had been promising in Spain in the 1480s came, he said, not from Castile but from the crown of Aragon: commercial enterprise, naval power, the Mediterranean empire, money to finance Columbus' voyages. The union of the crowns tilted the balance in favour of the crown of Castile, and the result was decline. Much of the blame was laid at the door of Ferdinand, who had taken his realms into alliance with Castile and had used Castilian troops to enforce his most unpopular measures. Castile gained the initiative thanks to the cooperation of Ferdinand, and destroyed what was best in Spain. It monopolized control, it established the Inquisition, it installed uniformity and absolutism (the concept, put to good use in order to denounce Philip V, was now conveniently dated back to the fifteenth century), and it ruined the overseas colonies.[71] It dragged Catalonia down into the disaster which 1898 represented (when Spain lost its empire to the United States) and from which the Catalans would otherwise have been free. This was a highly important as well as original interpretation of Spain's great age, and by no means a far-fetched one. It linked the sixteenth century directly to the nineteenth, and allowed one to draw crucial political conclusions. The only hope for Catalonia, then, was to create its own 'state'. For the next one hundred years, Catalan politicians would debate what form that 'state' might assume.

One of the most intriguing, but also most relevant, aspects of the Catalan myth was the choice of a national day. Nations that take shape after a period of crisis attempt to choose as their national day a symbolic moment in their history (as the French did with the storming of the Bastille during the Revolution). However, long after the loss of the *fueros*, the Catalans were unable to pick on any crucial moment that could be remembered with emotion. Nearly two hundred years after 1714, when Sanpere published his book in 1903, he singled out no special day as being worthy of mention. The memorable event was simply the defeat, because only the emotion of defeat and repression could serve to animate the spirit. In a pioneering and influential lecture, 'Qu'est-ce qu'une nation?' ('What is a nation?'), given at the Sorbonne in 1882, the writer Ernest Renan (quoted more fully below, in Chapter 7) commented that in the memory of peoples 'griefs are of more value than triumphs, for they impose duties, and require a common effort', an observation that was put into literal effect by nationalist leaders every-where in Europe. The difficulty lay, however, in identifying that defeat with a single day. Around 1900 a small group of regionalists seems to have decided to invent that day, which they chose (as we have seen above) to be 11 September 1714. Support for the day took seventy long years to develop. When the Franco dictatorship ended, a mass-meeting at the town of Sant Boi de Llobregat in 1976 indicated support for a *Diada* (national day) to be identified with 11 September, and the plan was confirmed by a mass demon-stration held in Barcelona on 11 September 1977. The first law approved by the new regional Parliament of Catalonia in 1980, under the presidency of Jordi Pujol, was a decree of 12 June establishing 11 September as the *Diada* of the Catalans. The text supporting the law stated that the proposal 'represents the painful memory of the loss of our liberties on 11 September 1714, and protest and active resistance to oppression'. There was, unfortunately, one fundamental error in choosing this date: Catalonia did not lose its 'liberties' ('liberty' carried a medieval meaning and referred to specific administrative privileges, not to the concept of freedom) on 11 September. That event, according to Sanpere, did not happen until several days later. When they realized that an error had been made in the dating, some officials tried to suggest other interpretations. According to a prominent nationalist politician writing in a newspaper in 2004, 'on the 11 of September 1714, after over a year resisting a harsh and painful siege, at the end of a long war in defence of the liberties of Catalonia, the city of Barcelona surrendered to the Franco–Spanish troops of the Bourbon king, Philip V'.[72] Once again, this was mistaken. The surrender took place not on 11 September but shortly after midday on 12 September. Perhaps the only correct description of what happened on that day is given in the official web page of the regional government of Catalonia: 'The final assault on the city took place on the 11th of September.' The widespread lack of awareness, still to be found among most Catalans, about exactly what happened on that day is a pointer to the problems involved in inventing a historical identity.

The error over the national day, however, is perhaps irrelevant, since ideological history, whether Castilian, Catalan or of any region in Europe, tends to be fictitious and often bears little relation to fact. A sociologist has argued that 'communities are to be distinguished, not by their falsity/genuineness, but by the style in which they are imagined'.[73] The 11 September may not have happened as the type of historical fact commonly represented, but it really happened as an attempt to give substance to a nationalist myth. In that sense, the truth of the date is less meaningful than its role, which is to give citizens of Catalonia a moment in time with which they can identify. 'Once we discover that national identities contain elements of myth,' another sociologist has pointed out, 'we should ask what part these myths play in building and sustaining nations. For it may not be rational to discard beliefs, even if they are, strictly speaking, false, when they can be shown to contribute significantly to the support of valuable social relations.'[74]

The central issue for Catalan nationalism, and with many other national-isms of the twenty-first century, is whether it has a serious historical and social programme, based on recovering a real lost identity and on expressing a valid present identity. The issue is a crucial one, for some would-be nationalisms have no valid past and an often questionable present. Three hundred years have passed since the *fueros* disappeared in 1714 and very many factors have changed, including frontiers, population, outlook and culture. If one is to define a nation as a people living in the same area, sharing a common racial origin, a common cultural heritage, a common language and a common sense of binding loyalty, then it may be necessary to conclude that Catalonia today is no longer the 'nation' that it was in early modern times. Immigration and change in culture and language have for some time been undermining the solidity of Catalan society. The principal language spoken in Catalonia is now Castilian, used preferentially, according to the most recent figures, by just over half the population. However, public acts of the Catalan authorities are normally carried out only in Catalan, sometimes with the addition of English and (reluctantly) of Spanish. Regionalist groups prefer not to accept the proven figures for language use. The regional government affirms on its web page, with a notable indifference to reality, that Catalan is spoken by something between seven and a half and ten million people (the actual population of Catalonia, according to figures available for the year 2007, being seven million of whom over a third are wholly unable to speak Catalan).

Without the standard characteristics of nationhood, the idea of Catalonia as a nation today necessarily has to fall back on myth, which means in practice that it has to appeal constantly to the past it believes it lost in 1714. The official attitude today, for example, is to pay little attention to the Treaty of the Pyrenees (1659)[75] and to continue to publish maps that depict the south of France as a part of Catalonia. The television weather forecast regularly gives weather conditions for the south of France, but not for the rest of the Iberian Peninsula. These little details make the medieval and early modern period a fundamental one for the development of official Catalan ideology, and inevitably provoke bitter debates among those who hold divergent views about that historical epoch. In any case, the real debate has never been, of course, over whether Catalonia is or is not a nation. Most residents of Catalonia feel that they share in a common culture and heritage that makes them Catalans. The real debate has been over the aspiration of some politicians to create a Catalan state, on the premise that every nation has a right to be a state. The attitude of the population of Catalonia to the issue of regional autonomy was made clear in the results of a referendum held in Catalonia in June 2006, when only 36 per cent of the electorate gave their support to the new regional charter (*Estatut*).[76] The remaining 64 per cent, who either abstained or voted 'No', consisted for the most part of the indifferent and hostile, but also included a small proportion of nationalists who did not consider the *Estatut* radical enough. These are issues which arguably confound regionalism with nationalism. They take us well beyond the confines of this essay, which seeks to limit itself to the way in which the early modern period has contributed to the formation of historical and political myths.

Myth and the problem of Spain's identity

One of the crucial factors in the emergence of nations has been the need to define their character in terms of, first, their identity, and second, their historic memory. Two decades after the Cortes of Cadiz, Alcalá Galiano in 1834 emphasized the need to 'create the new nation of Spaniards'. But that nation, despite immense efforts by politicians and above all by the army, did not materialize. Everyone knew that 'Spain' existed, but what was it? A state, a nation, a people, an amalgam of everything, with no clear identity or direction? Historians specializing in the nineteenth century have offered a variety of views as to why no Spanish nation took shape.[77] No national flag evolved until the mid-nineteenth century and, when it did, its use did not become obligatory until the beginning of the twentieth. Most crucially, no national anthem emerged.[78] The absence of a national hymn with unambiguous wording, along the lines of those used by France, Germany and America, was unmistakable evidence of the lack of shared emotions among Spaniards, and in its turn dampened any possible development of such emotions. In the early twentieth century the state was forced to adopt the monarchy's royal march as its anthem, but the piece had two capital defects: it belonged to the royal family, not to the nation, and it had no words to it, so that there was no possibility of identifying with it psychologically.

We have seen, then, that the word *nación* lost its cultural meaning in favour of a political one. That change of use was happening, of course, all over Europe. It was an extremely complicated process, always accompanied by more myth-making, because it was difficult, as it still is, to agree on the real components of a nation. Castilian historians agreed, certainly, that a form of 'nation–state' was formed in the peninsula. As one of them has written enthusiastically, 'the Spanish state which emerged from the traumatic Iron Century,[79] and which was to experience abnormally long periods of peace in the century of the Enlightenment and a difficult adaptation to the new Liberal political regime in the nineteenth century, was a state in no doubt of its identity, practically unquestioned as a national state, and as such frequently envied by other Europeans'.[80] The problem with this statement is that many other historians will disagree whether the alleged 'national state' was 'unquestioned' and whether it was 'envied' by anybody.

At the dawn of the twentieth century, Ortega y Gasset defined Spain as a possibility rather than a fact. He was not, evidently, denying that Spain existed. Rather, he was concerned that it was not taking the form he had hoped for. Most subsequent commentators were faced with the same problem. They could see and touch Spain, but they were never sure what it consisted of and had to continue re-inventing the nation. Like the Liberals of the nineteenth century, the historians of the Franco dictatorship reinterpreted history and pushed the existence of a 'Spanish nation' far back into the past. As we have stressed above, Spain clearly existed. However, insistence in the 1900s on its existence as a nation usually followed a specific political agenda, designed to emphasize that all the peripheral communities of the peninsula were inseparably linked to Castile and could not be separated from it. This agenda was by no means Francoist in origin – little or nothing produced by the regime was original – but merely a borrowing from the fund of nineteenth-century Liberal myths. Because of the primacy which the Liberals gave to the reign of Ferdinand and Isabella, partisans of the 'Spanish nation' argument inevitably have to rely on the historical evidence of the early modern period. The way in which historical 'proof' from the period is cited can be seen in arguments which, like the one below, concentrate on at least three basic affirmations: that Spain has always existed; that it was a harmonized unit with a capital city; and that it had a homogeneous culture with little ethnic instability (that is, all Spaniards were one people).

A fundamental assertion is that 'Spain always existed'. The writer Julián Marías, in 1978, affirmed that Spain is 'the oldest nation in the world':[81]

Spain is the first *nation*, in the modern sense of the word, ever to have existed. It was the creator of a new form of human community and political structure, just over five hundred years ago. If we want to give it a date, it would be 1474.[82] There were no nations before that, either in Antiquity or in the Middle Ages or outside of Europe. There had been cities, empires, kingdoms, counties, lordships, caliphates, but no nations. Shortly after Spain became one, so too did Portugal, France, and England, with Spain as the pioneer. Later on came Holland, Sweden, Prussia, then in a special way Austria, and from the end of the seventeenth century something resembling a nation began to germinate in Russia. Italy and Germany became nations only a century ago (although they had for a long time before, both socially and politically, felt that they were, and in reality they were). Politically the terms 'Spanish monarchy' and 'Spanish nation' came long before 'Spain' did. The *Treasury of the Castilian and Spanish tongue* of Sebastián de Covarrubias (1611) gives this definition: 'NATION: From the Latin *natio, nationis*, which means a kingdom or a large province, such as the Spanish nation'.

This intensely nationalist declaration, based on fragile historical evidence, is an accurate reflection of a widely held opinion. Another writer of similar views, Gustavo Bueno, who has produced a book declaring that *Spain is not a Myth* (2005), identifies Spain as 'the limits of the kingdom of Spain in the time of the Catholic Monarchs. That is what is termed a nation.'[83] Elsewhere, he believes that 'Spain was the first society to become a nation in a political sense', and dismisses disagreement with this view as 'ignorance and pedantry'. Within that Spain, he argues, there is no room for local identities: 'it is much more important for us to be concerned about upholding the identity of Spain, than about disputing the identity of Catalonia'. Following a fashion set by writers in the 1890s, Bueno feels that the quintessential symbol of the nation is Don Quixote, but a Quixote who will defend Spain by force if necessary: 'Don Quixote obliges us to affirm that if Spain exists, if it can resist threats to it, if Spain is a nation and wishes to continue being one, none of this will survive or be maintained solely through culture, laws or constitution. Force of arms is necessary.'

Basic to the argument that Spain was a nation lay the claim that it was inhabited by a population which felt itself to be Spanish and shared a single political centre, the capital at Madrid. A Spanish historian who is an expert on the early modern period affirms that Philip II made Madrid the 'capital of the nation'.[84] It became easy for travellers at the time, and for subsequent historians, to take for granted the idea that Madrid was the capital. The city seemed to fall into the role adopted by Paris for France and London for England. Because Madrid existed, it must follow that Spain existed. That may have been true from the nineteenth century on, but was certainly not true in preceding ages. Philip II chose Madrid as the seat of his court and administration, but had no intention of making it capital of 'Spain'. That was politically impossible, and Madrid under the Habsburgs never became 'capital of the nation'. In his visits to Barcelona, Valencia and Saragossa, for example, Philip II fully recognized that those cities were capitals of their respective regions.[85] After 1580, indeed, he even toyed with the idea of making Lisbon into his administrative capital. In reality, the status of Madrid was enhanced not because it was the capital of Spain, which in early modern times it was not, but because it was the centre of a worldwide monarchy.

Finally, Spain was seen by nationalists as a homogeneous society where all lived in harmony. This interesting idea, usually expressed through use of the word *convivencia* ('living together') is often viewed by its critics as a relatively harmless misreading of the evidence. In reality, it is not an innocent misreading but a politically loaded concept with a very specific intention, to maintain that Spain possessed one of the basic characteristics of a nation, namely national cohesiveness. A recent proponent of this approach leaves us in no doubt as to the way he, in 2003, sees the nation in its great imperial age.[86] Towards the Muslims, he suggests, Spain maintained 'an attitude of understanding and respect, demonstrated by eight centuries of *convivencia*'. This astonishing declaration (which ignores the fact that Spain drove into exile its entire Muslim population of a quarter of a million citizens) is followed by the conclusion that the country had 'a national culture founded on solidarity and integration'. Spain, the author goes on to say, had a unique position in the world, with 'a cultural identity that has marked us out as a Mediterranean people that ended up becoming a crossroads of cultures and civilizations, where cultural syncretism has made us take on the role of a bridge between continents'. If these words mean anything, it must be that Muslims and Jews, not to mention Catalans and Basques, shared in a national culture and lived peacefully with each other. No harm was done to any of them, but all participated contentedly in the nation of which they formed a part.

This interpretation of *convivencia* has become part of the official myth of all Spain's central governments in the twentieth century. Its latest manifestation was the campaign in 2007 pursued by the government for an 'Alliance of Civilizations', based fundamentally on a political *rapprochement* between the socialist party in Spain and the conservative regimes in Morocco and Turkey, as being symbolic of the way in which Spaniards and Muslims lived together in an imagined harmony in the medieval peninsula.

These and similar readings of national history which focused on the sixteenth century were of enormous influence in creating the conviction that Spain was a cohesive reality, eternal and unchanging. By using imprecise and flowery language, the conservative outlook (exemplified for instance in the numerous essays of Gustavo Bueno) has avoided any attempt at defining specifics, least of all the meanings of words or the reality of what happened in the past, and has elevated the discussion to a metaphysical level where no details are cited, no evidence is used, and only vague concepts (such as 'the problem of Spain') are resorted to – their objective being to create further vagueness. Ironically, it was a cultural conservative, the scholar Menéndez Pelayo (see Chapter 3), who seems to have firmly got to grips with the issue. Though often cited as a supporter of ultra-traditionalist positions, Menéndez Pelayo was a clear-headed thinker who always attempted to study history dispassionately and did not close his eyes to social reality. In the mid-nineteenth century, he was already quite firm about the fact that nationalist jargon stood on shaky ground. He stated: 'the ideal of a perfect and harmonious nationality is little short of utopian. We need to approach the nationalities in the way that the centuries approached them, with unity in some things and variety in many more, above all in language and literature.'[87]

The difficulty of defining what is or is not a nation normally derives from two basic sources: the conceptual problem of distinguishing what 'nation' implies, as against other terms such as 'state' or 'country'; and the task of finding a historical basis for, or a historical entity corresponding to, the kind of definition eventually adopted. In the case of many modern states, these two problems have never been solved (sovereign states such as Yugoslavia, for example), or have simply been ignored (as in the example of India) in favour of the more pressing task of bringing the nation into existence. Some Spaniards, it seems, lay claim to having contributed a third basic issue that no other country has had. As Gustavo Bueno proudly points out:

> The genre of the 'philosophical essay on Spain' has no parallel in other nations. No list can be cited of 'philosophical essays on France', 'philosophical essays on England' or 'philosophical essays on Sweden' in the way one can cite the many 'philosophical essays on Spain', written usually by Spaniards but occasionally also by foreigners.

Almost without exception, however, the 'philosophical essays' on a perceived Spanish problem, written by well-known names such as Unamuno and Ortega y Gasset, have been based less on historical evidence than on metaphysical reflection. This was a trend that vitiated any serious approach to the national question, and it continued well into the 1970s. One of my historian colleagues, Jacques Lafaye, writing about the way an imaginary past used to be conjured up in the writings of most Spanish historians in the

1970s, rightly observed in 1977: 'The utopian vision of the glorious national past is a permanent ingredient of ideological currents in the peninsula, whether progressive or conservative.'[88]

CHAPTER TWO

THE MYTH OF
THE FAILED MONARCHY

A king in power, a kingdom oppressed
Or, more exactly, fleeced.

Madrid satire (1621)

The fragility of monarchy

In a bizarre ceremony outside the city of Avila on 5 June 1465, at the height of the civil wars which then raged in Castile, noble opponents of the reigning King Henry IV placed an effigy of the monarch on a stage and then proceeded to divest him ritually of his robes and, by implication, of his royal office.[1] To the accompaniment of groans from the shocked public, the effigy was then thrown off the platform to the ground. The degradation and deposition were complete.

In one way or another, most rulers of modern Spain had to suffer a similar fate. Opposition to the institution of monarchy in Spain is (strange to say) older than the monarchy itself. It would even be possible to maintain that since the fifteenth century, when an attempt was made to put together the nation of Spain, Spaniards have persistently expressed doubts about whether their country should have a monarchy. This seemingly visceral conviction survives into our own day. The monarchy, carefully restored together with democracy after the death of Franco in 1975, survives only because of immense efforts on all sides of the political spectrum, since it is the only aspect of modern political life to command respect. Underneath the surface, there is always doubt. Why have Spaniards held firm, over five hundred years, to the myth of a failed monarchy?

Not surprisingly, the rulers of Spain had a very hard time imposing their authority on a conglomerate of communities and realms that did not like working with each other. The kings sometimes encouraged publicists to put forward arguments in favour of their regime.[2] Monarchy as an institution, however, had to put up a hard fight in order to persuade possible supporters. Like some other countries, Spain was full of semi-independent nobles, cities and regions that had never been in the habit of recognizing superior authority. More often than not, they questioned any attempt to impose control from above. If a scholar were to write a history of the Spanish monarchy from the fifteenth century onwards, he would have to take into account the slanderous campaign against Henry IV, the father of La Beltraneja, and his shameful deposition in a public ceremony; the attempted assassination of Ferdinand the Catholic; the public scorn for Juana la Loca; the rebellion against Charles V; the indifference to Philip II; the contempt for Philip III; the disdain shown to Charles II; the open rejection of Philip V; and the shipwreck of all the monarchs of Spain from Ferdinand VII onwards. The dates and circumstances of all these rulers are not our immediate concern. Possibly only one monarch escaped from this universal obloquy. This was Isabella the Catholic (together with her husband Ferdinand). This long and dismal record of anti-monarchical attitudes was not, of course, peculiar to the Spaniards. The English executed more of their kings (the last victim was Charles I, in the seventeenth century) than any other European nation. But in time, the English achieved political stability. Spain, where opposition to monarchy was sometimes visceral, did not.

For a perspective on this deeply ingrained hostility to the institution of monarchy we have to delve deep into Spain's medieval roots. Unlike other western countries, where the person of the monarch was deliberately mythologized in order to give political stability to the state, in Spain kings had a restricted role. The country did not share the monarchical traditions commonly found in western Europe, and many parts of the peninsula had no kings at all. The Basques were always, effectively, a combination of republics, and continued to be so down to the nineteenth century. The medieval Aragonese had a 'king', but they treated him as an equal. Even in Castile, where rulers enjoyed more power than elsewhere in Spain, kings were in reality an exceptional case when compared with the monarchies of western Europe. They consciously rejected many of the symbols of power used by monarchies outside the peninsula.[3] They did not consider their office sacred; they did not claim any power to heal the sick (as the rulers of France and

England did); and they enjoyed no special rituals at the time of their birth, crowning[4] or death.[5] The imagery of magical royal power, common in other monarchies such as England and France, was notably absent in Spain. The rulers of Castile, from Isabella to Philip II and beyond, evolved no coronation ceremony and no cult of personality. Most of them even fought shy of the title 'Majesty': Isabella the Catholic was simply 'Her Highness' to her subjects, and the new form of address, 'Majesty', brought in by Charles V, was always felt by Spaniards to be alien. Time and again, the Cortes of Castile petitioned both Charles and Philip II to divest themselves of both the term and the ceremonies that went with it. Eventually, from 1586 on, in a measure that had been planned for nearly ten years, the latter cut out a great deal of courtly ceremony, avoided the title 'Majesty', and ordered that his ministers and officials address him only as 'Sir'.

Some historians feel that Philip II was a tyrant who lusted after personal power, and studies have been written comparing him to the French king Louis XIV.[6] It is difficult to discover the basis for such comparisons. A leading scholar has argued that, 'wherever the king [Philip] went on progress, triumphal arches and prints portrayed his "sacred majesty"'.[7] However, the king went on few progresses in his reign. An expert on the period confirms this: 'the king was little disposed to take part in this type of triumph after his return to Castile in 1559, apart perhaps from the entries into Seville and into Lisbon in 1581'.[8] This allows us to conclude that the notion of 'sacred majesty' was almost invisible. In any case, it is relevant to remember that the triumphal arches we know of (in Saragossa, Seville, Barcelona and Lisbon) were constructed to display municipal pride in the king's presence rather than expressly to exalt the king. The term 'sacred majesty' was, moreover, an integral part of the form of address used only for a period by Philip II (although always used by his father, the emperor), and normally abbreviated 'SCRM' in official documents (that is, *Sacra Católica Real Majestad*). City councils may have felt that such forms of address were a way of expressing their loyalty, but Philip eventually avoided the term 'Majesty' altogether and did not harbour dreams of being an emperor or a Bible-like king. Nor is there any documentary evidence to suggest that 'Philip saw himself as Moses',[9] a prophet–priest leading his people to the Promised Land. The king was extremely strict about his personal status but had a far more modest vision of his relation to his subjects, and he hated crowds. He never encouraged formal or extravagant terminology; he disliked the cult of personality and from the very beginning of his reign – to be precise, from the 1560s, as soon as he returned to Spain from a five-year absence abroad – he took steps to eliminate it.[10]

Given the absence of a cult of monarchy, writers in Spain followed a constant tradition (dating back to the Middle Ages) according to which the people had a right to resist tyranny.[11] In the crown of Aragon there was a perception among the elite that the crown had to govern with the approval of advisers, and laws could not be changed except through the consent of the Cortes. Similarly, in the crown of Castile the elites felt – as they clearly demonstrated in the 1520 revolt of the Comunero cities – that the king should secure their approval for changes. Monarchs were consequently quite conscious of the existence of restraints. In the later sixteenth century, the monarchies in France and England were encouraging officials to write books arguing that the crown had unlimited power. In Spain the reverse happened. Neither Charles V nor Philip II thought in terms of absolute power. The latter, frequently accused of being an absolutist (see below), never in his life laid claim to arbitrary power or made decisions by himself, and he always deferred to advisers.[12] He even tolerated anti-absolutist writings, since they were directed principally against foreign monarchs (such as Elizabeth of England) and not against him. One of his judges, Castillo de Bobadilla, specified that laws made by the king were not binding if they went against conscience, faith, natural law or established laws. The idea of *raison d'état*, he said, existed only in tyrannies and not in Spain.

The complex nature of political authority in Spain was ill suited to royal oppression. At the end of the sixteenth century, two prominent Jesuits, Mariana and Suárez, made themselves notorious by arguing that the power of the ruler comes from the people and is not valid without popular consent. It is interesting to note that their works were condemned in London and in Paris, but never in Spain. I recall that one of my tutors at Oxford, the distinguished scholar Hugh Trevor-Roper, demurred when I wrote in an essay that Mariana's most famous book, *On the King* (1599), had been publicly burnt in Paris but not in Madrid. How could that be, he asked, since the regime in Spain was more repressive? He eventually accepted my insistence that the facts were so.

Was the king the essential and crucial component of the emerging nation? The near absence of a cult of monarchy in the Spanish lands makes it difficult to follow the idea that the 'nation' of Spain grew up round the monarchy. 'The monarchy was, as in France and England, the core round which the future nation formed,' writes one historian (Álvarez Junco). If the statement is meant to apply to the early modern period, it needs to be substantially modified. There were ambitious approaches made in late medieval England and France to develop a cult of kingship, but in neither of these countries did the crown become the cornerstone on which the nation was constructed. Many other factors also went into the process of nation-formation in Europe. Spain, for its part, lagged a long way behind France and England. Since, as we have seen, it completely lacked a cult of kingship, the crown never became identified with aspirations to nationhood. In any case, with which territory would the crown have identified itself? Catalonia, for example, accepted the king of Castile as its ruler but did not consider itself part of the Spanish nation. Aragon and Valencia, to a lesser extent, shared that view. In Castile, which was the only territory to have a firm monarchical tradition, the idea of 'nation' continued to be very shaky. The Spanish lands had no experience of a national monarchy until as late as the eighteenth century, when Philip V abolished the autonomy of the crown of Aragon. Even after that date, the Basque provinces retained their autonomy, considered themselves to be free republics, and accepted the king but not the hegemony of 'Spain'. The monarchy, even in Castile, was always something that lacked form, theory and cohesion. It did not represent Spain, and a Spanish nation could not, as a consequence, develop around it. The conclusion that follows is inescapable. Spaniards, in the sense of citizens of the different states of the peninsula, did not feel firmly attached to the monarchy. This makes it easier for us to understand the strongly anti-monarchical opinions that prevailed among sections of both the elite and the people after the early decades of the nineteenth century.

The Golden Age of monarchy

There was one great exception to anti-monarchical sentiment, and it was so fundamental to later attitudes that we need to consider it before looking at anything else. The exception was something peculiar to Castilians alone; other Spaniards did not usually share it. After the conflicts and civil wars of the late fifteenth century, one ruler appeared to have achieved the impossible in bringing peace and stability to the kingdom of Castile. This was Queen Isabella. She married the ruler of Aragon, Ferdinand, and thereby sealed a permanent alliance between two of the three great kingdoms of the peninsula. Their marriage brought into existence a country called Spain. It also, in the view of many commentators of that period, brought civil peace, orderly government, good relations with the papacy, preservation of the faith through the Inquisition, conquest of the Muslim kingdom of Granada, the expulsion of the Jews, and the discovery of America. For all these achievements – which we shall not dwell upon here – the queen received the lasting appreciation of her contemporaries. Few rulers in history have ever received such eulogies. 'She was so excellent a ruler, that at no time since the city of Rome was founded nor at any time since Spain was populated, did any king, prince or emperor equal the superb merits of this queen,' a Castilian chronicler wrote shortly after her death.[13] If we can believe the chroniclers, she lived on in the memory of most Castilians as the sort of ruler they wanted: firm, impartial, honest, Christian. Her enemies, including the tens of thousands of expelled Jews, formed a quite different image of her. But for most of her countrymen she remained the ideal ruler.

Ferdinand, of course, shared in the glory, and attracted equally flattering eulogies. In 1640, the Aragonese writer Baltasar Gracián published a little eulogy titled *El Político Don Fernando el Católico*. It was a time of crisis for the Spanish monarchy, thanks to the threat of rebellion in Catalonia and later in Portugal. Aragonese writers were anxious to reassure themselves about their past and turned to the memory of their ruler, Ferdinand. 'This was a king who outdid all his predecessors,' wrote Gracián, 'a king who set an example to all future rulers.' His praises were for 'that great master in the art of governing'. According to Gracián, Philip II is said to have paused one day before a portrait of Ferdinand and remarked: 'We owe everything to him.' Later, in the mid-nineteenth century, Ferdinand's reputation suffered a setback, when Catalan historians who were trying to create a new historical memory for their region, as we have noted in Chapter 1, decided that the king had been too close a collaborator with what they called 'centralism'. As a result, they decided not to study him. When the distinguished historian Jaume Vicens Vives began producing a superb biography of Ferdinand in the 1950s – still the definitive life of the king, but unfinished after two volumes – he was criticized by nationalists, even though the study was written in the Catalan language.[14]

The impressive reputation of Ferdinand and Isabella rested on two pillars. First, they were by origin Spaniards, unlike all the subsequent rulers of the realm. 'They were monarchs of this realm alone,' one of the great nobles, the Admiral of Castile, wrote in 1522, 'of our speech, born and bred among us. . . . They knew everybody, always gave honours to those who merited them, travelled through their realms, were known by great and small alike, could be reached by all . . .'. Second, they ruled directly and in person, not from some far-distant capital city nor through bureaucrats, for they had neither. Above all, the person of Isabella had a lasting impact on the historical memory of the Castilians. Praised by every chronicler, both foreign and Spanish, she was not only 'the most feared and respected' (the testimony of the chronicler Bernáldez), but also the most universally loved, imposing her will with a unique mixture of 'love and fear' (the phrase used by Castiglione in his *Courtier*, published in 1528) that kept the nobles in their place until her death. The achievement of the monarchs was real enough, but, as the years distanced them, so did their legend grow. Every failure of subsequent years was contrasted with the presumed success of their reign. In the last years of the Franco regime, admirers of Isabella set in motion proceedings to have her canonised as a saint (see Chapter 3). The process ground to a halt, but is still active.

The myth of the Catholic Monarchs is not difficult to explain for, like all myths, it grew up in response to the needs of the time. At specific moments in the emergence of national feeling, as with Elizabeth of England and Henry IV of France in the crisis-ridden sixteenth century, there was a tendency to idealize the role of the monarch. It happened in the case of the Catholic Monarchs, even though their reign may have had fewer significant achievements than is often claimed. Since no rulers in history have ever enjoyed the unstinted adoration of their subjects, we would be right to suspect that all was not quite as perfect as appears. The praise lavished by official (government-paid) chroniclers of that time was meant to present just one side of the picture. The other side, made up of protests by political and religious opponents, was silenced. Quite apart from the Muslims and Jews, who suffered cruelly under the regime, many Spaniards had reason to criticize the government. It was the heyday of the Inquisition, which they founded. Satirical verses were composed against their regime.[15] Shortly after Isabella's death, the civil governor (*corregidor*) of Medina del Campo, one of Castile's principal commercial centres, was reported to the authorities for having declared publicly that 'she is in hell and he came only to rob this kingdom'.[16] The latter part of this outburst was an expression of rage by a Castilian against the Aragonese, but the attempt to assassinate the king in Barcelona several years before (in December 1492) reflected also a degree of discontent in Catalonia. Much more important than the possible merits of the king and queen, however, were the achievements perceived by subsequent generations. Those constituted the real myth, and they were powerful. 'As the situation in

Spain became more difficult [in the nineteenth century], eyes were directed to the Catholic Monarchs', a scholar of the twentieth century comments.[17] Writer after writer repeated the same theme, century after century. At the end of the eighteenth century José Cadalso, author of the *Moroccan Letters* (published in book form in 1793, some ten years after his death), had to go back three hundred years to find the only monarchs of whom Spain could be proud:

> The Spanish monarchy was never more contented within or more respected from outside than the time when Ferdinand the Catholic died. Consider, then, how the maxims on which that excellent state was founded have decayed from their old vigour. Bring this back, and the monarchy will be as it was when the House of Austria succeeded to it.[18]

Cadalso described Ferdinand and Isabella as 'princes who will remain immortal among all those who appreciate good government'. There was no looking back. When Diego Clemencín, the first Spanish scholar of note to study Queen Isabella, brought out a book on her (1821), aptly titled a *Eulogy*, there were protests from those who felt it was politically biased. But no biographer since, not even those who rejected the ideologically charged literature on her published during the Franco regime, has attempted to undermine the legend created around her and her husband. Every other reign, in comparison, was judged a failure by historians. It was one of the most successful, but also – because it called into question the evolution of the entire monarchy after her – most destructive myths of Spain's history. In the first half of the nineteenth century, the Liberals polished up the image. Anxious to denounce the despotism of the monarchy ruling over them, they fixed their gaze on the idealized reign of Ferdinand and Isabella. In 1813 Martínez Marina, in his *Theory of the Cortes*, argued that the Catholic Monarchs had respected the rule of law and representative government and thus 'took the nation to its highest level of glory'. Martínez de la Rosa (see below), in his *Historical Sketch* (1851), felt that the moment of greatest glory for Castile came at the end of the fifteenth century, 'with the most powerful empire in Europe and immense possessions everywhere'.[19]

Prescott, since he was read by Castilian scholars of the time (as we have had occasion to mention in the previous chapter), had an important share in stimulating the myth. Rounding off his great *History* of the reign, he concluded in 1838:

The modern Spaniard who surveys the tokens of his nation's present degeneracy, must turn for relief to the prouder and earlier period of her history. Such a period in Spain can only be found in the first half of the sixteenth century, in the reign of Ferdinand and Isabella, and that of their successor, Charles the Fifth; in which last, the state, under the strong impulse it had received, was carried onward in the career of prosperity, in spite of the ignorance and mismanagement of those who guided it. . . . There is no country which has been guilty of such wild experiments, or has showed, on the whole, such profound ignorance of the true principles of economical science, as Spain under the sceptre of the family of Austria. . . . From this sad picture, let us turn to that presented by the period of our History, when, the clouds and darkness having passed away, a new morn seemed to break upon the nation. Under the firm but temperate sway of Ferdinand and Isabella, the great changes we have noticed were effected without convulsion in the state. The splendors of foreign conquest in the boasted reign of Charles the Fifth were dearly purchased by the decline of industry at home, and the loss of liberty. The patriot will see little to cheer him in this 'Golden Age' of the national history, whose outward show of glory will seem to his penetrating eye only the hectic brilliancy of decay. He will turn to an earlier period, when the nation, emerging from the sloth and license of a barbarous age, seemed to renew its ancient energies, and to prepare like a giant to run its course; and glancing over the long interval since elapsed, during the first half of which the nation wasted itself on schemes of mad ambition, and in the latter has sunk into a state of paralytic torpor, he will fix his eye on the reign of Ferdinand and Isabella as the most glorious epoch in the annals of his country.

But it was Modesto Lafuente who summarized previous opinions and shaped the myth which both Liberals and conservatives were to share for the next hundred years. In the twenty-first century it is commonly believed that the myth was a traditionalist and reactionary one, but the truth is not so simple. The legend of Ferdinand and Isabella was needed by progressive intellectuals in order to expose the absolutist pretensions of their kings by setting a contrast with a reign that, in their view, achieved success without harming liberty. Lafuente was not sparing with his praise when he wrote of 'the reign of the Catholic Monarchs, wholly Spanish and the most glorious that Spain has had'.[20] Under these rulers, he wrote, Spain was the first nation in Europe (already in the fifteenth century!) to achieve political freedom:

Whereas in other nations of Europe the grim wall of despotism was raised, in Spain the people's rights were respected and the Cortes were summoned to make laws.

The consequence was:

The lofty spectacle of a people that regains its energy, organizes itself, grows, attains religion and learning, conquers and expands, spreads into immense territories, and dominates almost the entire world, all thanks to the powerful influence of a virtuous and prudent queen and a shrewd and experienced king.[21]

In order to back up this fantasy of past glory, Lafuente did not recoil from facing some difficult questions. What about the Inquisition, by no means a favourite of Liberals? Isabella, he answered, intended it to be more benign than it turned out to be after her death. And what about the expulsion of the Jews? Spain, he said, was only the last in a long list of nations – such as France and England – who had already expelled their Jews. What about the expulsions and persecution of Muslims after 1492? That, he retorted, was the fruit of fanaticism, prevailing at that time among both Muslims and Christians, and not peculiar to Spain. What about the extermination of the Indians of America? That occurred only after Isabella died, so she was not to blame.

The legend, espoused by all shades of opinion, from traditionalist to progressive, dominated the vision of the past for the next century and a half. When the army and Falange undertook their 'crusade' against the Second Republic in 1936, they adopted a specially tailored version of the Catholic Monarchs' story as their ideological inspiration. The nation would be remoulded in their image. In 1952 Franco's minister of education, the historian Joaquín Ruiz-Jiménez, claimed in a speech that 'it is once again possible to produce the Spaniard that existed under Ferdinand and Isabella'.[22] Another historian, Luis Suárez Fernández, who had made a special study of the reign, felt that the historical facts entitled him to make the following observations:[23]

I would now like you to allow me to call upon my profession as a historian (I can only offer what I have, for I have no other) to try and explain how I and other historians today see Spain. . . . [With Ferdinand and Isabella] arose the finest form of state that Europe had known, the Catholic monarchy, traditional and representative, to which the Caudillo has referred many times in order to mark the contrast with other, sadder, periods that Spain had to pass through at the end of the nineteenth and the beginning of the twentieth centuries. Spain was the first to create a state founded on law, a state that respected the liberty and dignity of man. Even the kings were subject to the law and not exempt from it. When one compares Isabella the Catholic with any other ruler of that time, the difference is abysmal: compared to her and her husband Ferdinand, Henry VIII is little more than a grotesque throwback tyrant. We must also have the courage to speak out for the things we are proud of. Against the whole world, Spain stood up for certain essential things which were not then in fashion. It stood up for the dignity of man. It stood up for the role of reason. It stood up for the relationship between truth and liberty. It maintained that honour and loyalty, keeping one's word and holding on to oaths are essential norms of conduct. We drew up the Laws of the Indies, which treated Red Indians like human beings,[24] we produced the International Law of Francisco de Vitoria and the role of reason in *Quixote*.

The dynasties that ruined Spain: the Habsburgs

In the two and a half centuries after Isabella's death in 1504, no monarch of Spain won full enthusiasm of the people. Indeed, according to the vision presented to the Cortes of Cadiz in 1810 by the progressive deputies, the country had been ruined by the foreign monarchs who took over the throne after her. First came the Habsburgs, who imposed foreign absolutism on Spain, abolished the Cortes, destroyed Spain's traditional democracy, curtailed the freedoms of the nobles and left the people without liberty. They condemned Spain to decline. The rights that the Constitution of 1812 aimed to restore, according to Agustín de Argüelles, were 'the fundamental laws of the Spanish monarchy before they were perverted from their nature by foreign dynasties'.[25] The key to the rejection of the rulers who followed Ferdinand and Isabella was the fact that they were foreigners, a viewpoint that coincided with the struggle being waged by the supporters of the Cortes against the French occupiers of Spain.

The Liberals, one should emphasize, did not snatch their anti-foreign interpretation out of the blue. There had been continuous criticism of the Habsburgs in early modern times,[26] with a constant insistence on the evil role of foreigners and foreign finance. In 1519, on the eve of the revolt of the

Comuneros, protests against the new dynasty and its foreign advisers began to spread through Castile:

> You, land of Castile, are most wretched and accursed, when a realm as noble as you is ruled over by foreigners who feel no love for you.[27]

The complaints continued sporadically for the next two centuries. Spokesmen for the Bourbon regime after 1700 were also quick to criticize the preceding dynasty. In the eighteenth century, the official Bourbon attitude to Habsburg rule within Spain was epitomized by a leading Catalan economist, Capmany: 'What was the whole of Spain before the august House of Bourbon came to the throne?', he asked rhetorically at the end of the eighteenth century, and offered his own answer: 'a corpse, without spirit or strength to feel its own debility'.[28] Around 1780, José Cadalso penned a *Defence of the Spanish Nation*, which remained unpublished until a French scholar brought it out in 1970, in Toulouse. Its thirty-seven folios include the judgement that 'the House of Austria frittered away the treasures, skills and blood of Spaniards on things alien to Spain' – a reference to the wars in Europe, and one that became standard among writers. Cadalso also viewed Philip II as a 'a king who damaged his people'. He did not spare the other Habsburgs either. Spain's decay, he concluded, was the logical consequence of Habsburg rule. Only the Bourbons had brought respite to Spain.[29]

According to these writers, the first great disaster had been Charles V, who crushed the liberties of Spain. It was a rather free interpretation of the revolt of the Comuneros (1520–1), when the chief cities of northern Castile protested against aspects of Charles's policy but were eventually defeated at the battle of Villalar. A key phrase used by Argüelles was: 'the liberties of the people perished on the fields of Villalar'. In his *Historical Survey* (1835), he laid out the broad lines of the Liberal interpretation. The higher nobility betrayed the people and helped the king to crush the popular rebellion. Charles took the opportunity to execute his opponents, and the kingdom was left 'to the mercies of the king', who was now absolutist. A reader of those times would have had little difficulty in identifying the direct object of these allusions, namely King Ferdinand VII. Charles made his triumph complete by turning on the nobles and excluding them from the Cortes in 1538. This oppression introduced 'a new era, in which the nation began to fall rapidly into decay'. The myth of 'decline' was thus set in motion. If there happened to be political and military successes for the emperor in Europe, they were merely a 'false glitter'.[30]

Modesto Lafuente set down the Liberal version in its definitive form. His presentation, which reigned supreme down to the early 1900s and is still to be found in some Spanish history-writing, began with the fundamental premise of a Spain ruined by foreign rulers and subjected to foreign absolutism. The solution lay, logically, in rejection of the foreign monarchy and support for Spain's essentially democratic traditions. 'The reign of Charles V', Lafuente stated firmly, 'attracts our admiration but not our enthusiasm.' His reasons were twofold. Politically, the Habsburg regime was one of tyranny, because it destroyed the representative institutions that Castile had inherited from the Middle Ages. 'The liberties of the people perished on the fields of Villalar. It was the last armed protest of liberty against oppression.' The fact that no liberties perished, that Charles did nothing to compromise the role either of the Cortes or of the Castilian cities and that there was no identifiable oppression was for the Liberals quite irrelevant. Lafuente's conclusion could not have been more uncompromising:

The liberties of Spain, won through such heroic sacrifice, and through centuries of such precious blood, were drowned in Spanish blood by two rulers of foreign origin. This is what Spain owed in political terms to the first two sovereigns of the House of Austria.[31]

Economically, the Habsburgs ruined a once prosperous nation. Spaniards under Charles V were sidetracked:

Blinded by the glitter of their territorial possessions and by their great deeds, bit by bit they forgot about the loss of their liberties and the exportation of their treasures and their sons, with whose blood those laurels were won. Industry inside the country came to a standstill, manpower dried up. Obsessed with dominating Europe, the Habsburg dynasty depopulated Spain, sacrificed its sons, spent its treasures and stifled its political liberties.[32]

In 1876, a historian and president of the First Republic (1873), Emilio Castelar, looked back without sympathy to 'that great corpse of an absolutist Spain' under the Habsburgs.[33] The unfavourable picture of Charles V was a wholly curious phenomenon, since this was an emperor who loved Spain, devoted immense attention to its affairs and decided finally to spend his last days there. Thanks to him, Spain rose to become a world power. Yet there were, of course, valid reasons – which lack of space does not allow us to touch upon here – for the hostility. The result was remarkable. In a nation such as Germany, where Charles was in constant conflict with both princes and people, historical memory at all levels took him to its bosom and valued him as a national hero.[34] By contrast, in Spain he was never appreciated as a national hero, and only in the twentieth century did historians begin to pay him due attention. Among the few dissenting voices in this hostile picture was the writer Angel Ganivet, who in his *Idearium* (1897) presented a somewhat different vision of Villalar. For him, the Comuneros represented the backward-looking, traditional and regional past, afraid of coming to terms with the new, progressive and open Europe represented by Charles V. This revised view of the emperor, which was supported by the new conservative revaluation of his 'imperial' role, began in the early twentieth century to replace the older Liberal vision.

The next disaster according to the Liberal picture – as we shall now see – was Charles V's son Philip II. Dithering between two imaginary monarchs, one – Isabella – who was the epitome of good and the other – Philip – who was the epitome of evil, the Liberals ended up being unsure about all the monarchs on offer. After that, the panorama they faced in terms of real-life politics did not simply get worse, it shattered.

The Liberal myth about Philip II

Two cases epitomise the unequal treatment accorded to their monarchy by Spaniards. On the one hand, the Spanish people created the indestructible myth of the greatness of Isabella and Ferdinand. On the other, they created an equally enduring image of the malefic Philip II. Both myths are extreme, but they continue to be held tenaciously. Why were they necessary?

Traditional hostility among Spaniards, towards the ruling monarchy of Spain reached its peak in the rejection of the most famous of Spain's rulers, Philip II. It is commonly assumed that Philip's malign reputation was a consequence of the political and religious antagonism of other European powers of his day. That was the picture presented by many writers, including Julián Juderías, who, as a solid conservative, was intent on blaming foreigners for any deficiency attributed to his people or to their rulers. The blackening of Philip's image was seen as a logical consequence of envy of Spain's dominant position in the European power conflict. The King of Spain was enemy to France, to England, to the rebels in the Netherlands, to Protestants in Germany and to nationalist-minded Italians, the pope among them. Everyone, therefore, contributed to the unfavourable image of the king, above all the English and Dutch.[35]

It is not always realized, however, that the Spaniards themselves were those who laboured most to undermine their own king. There were criticisms of aspects of royal policy even during his lifetime. Philip consulted extensively with his advisers, but that did not alter the fact that he stirred up opposition, in part because he ran his government like a dictator, in part because he ruled for a long time – over half a century.[36] There were always murmurs, and some of the murmurs at court were substantial, especially in the 1580s. To that decade belongs a much quoted letter written by the Jesuit Ribadeneira to the cardinal of Toledo, a royal councillor, which reflected the complaints of nobles who feared that the king might be moving his court to Lisbon, thereby ruining the circles of influence which they had built up in Madrid and Toledo. The letter did not reflect any significant social protest that we can identify. The first real criticism of the king during his reign emerged in the period of the Spanish Armada in 1588, when the scale of war casualties impinged on Spanish homes not as a constant haemorrhage, a consequence of the war in Flanders, but as a sweeping disaster that struck thousands of Spanish households. Echoes of the criticism filtered into the royal court through, for example, the prophecies of the young seer Lucrecia de León.

The next round of criticism after the 1580s occurred in a highly antagonistic situation that set Spaniard against Spaniard during the events at Saragossa in 1591, when a street satire in that city condemned Philip as a 'corrupt tyrant'.[37] The most damning criticism came only after the king died, when people felt they could criticize him safely. The best known tract, which circulated in manuscript in 1598, was by Iñigo Ibáñez de Santa Cruz, a friend of the king's disgraced secretary Antonio Pérez. It portrayed the former king as 'worse than Nero', and for his pains the author had to cool his heels in prison. The year of the king's death was also occasion for Cervantes to write a satirical sonnet, 'At the monument to King Philip II in Seville', which reflected on the vanities of life but contained no social criticism.[38] Hostility to the king did not surface at any significant level for a couple of centuries, but there seems to have been a lasting reaction to so many decades of fruitless war. References to him in the theatrical works of Lope de Vega and Calderón are formal and innocuous. The passage of time, however, allowed anti-Philip legends to mature and, eventually, in 1759, a century and a half after the king's death, we encounter the first vitriolic written attack. The distance in time and context is too enormous for us to consider the text (which was never printed or circulated, and was only recently discovered in the archives) to have been a genuine expression of discontent; but it certainly revealed total contempt for the monarch. The speaker, who personifies Spain, denounces Philip thus:[39]

> His lack of religion, his bad faith, the cruelties he wreaked on his son, on his women, his ministers and his vassals, his revenge comparable only to that of Nero, a mere suspicion being motive enough to sacrifice the life of even the most loyal subject. . . . Philip died after a painful illness, and the oppressed realm was relieved of his cruelties.

At the same period, José Cadalso in his *Moroccan Letters* felt that Philip II was certainly at the opposite pole to the greatness of the Catholic Monarchs. The king, he felt, 'died leaving his people exhausted by wars, weakened by the gold and silver of America, distressed by so many disasters, and longing for a rest'.

At this point we may consider what has happened to the king's reputation. Those early criticisms raised during the sixteenth century, when Italians, English and Dutch put their propaganda gifts to work against Spanish power, were nearly all justified. Into the seventeenth century, anti-Spanish publicists worked hard to create an unfavourable image of Philip.[40] Far from being a 'legend', as traditionalist writers who tend to be uncritical defenders of the king have always maintained, the criticisms were in large measure true. It was a fact that the Spaniards behaved badly in Italy (the country where the duke of Alba first earned his reputation for cruelty); it was a fact that the Spanish-controlled armies in the Netherlands acted mercilessly; it was a fact that the government had attempted, through bribery and then through coercion (through the Great Armada!), to overthrow the regime in England. Other nations, most notably England, were equally guilty of such faults. But they happened to have a better propaganda machine (the best printers were in northern Europe), and it was they who won the war of words. All imperial powers have to live with the fact that their misdeeds will be exaggerated and used to foment hatred. 'We are detested and hated,' a Spanish commentator wrote in the 1590s, 'and all because of the wars.'

In Spain the sources of the king's bad reputation among Spaniards have normally been identified as three in number: Antonio Pérez and his memoirs; González Montano and his work on the Inquisition (see Chapter 5); and Las

Casas' diatribe against Spaniards in America. In fact, if we are referring specifically to the formation of Spanish opinion, none of the three played any part in creating an opinion unfavourable to the king. Pérez's writings were prohibited in Spain and usually treated with contempt by Spaniards abroad. For all practical purposes, they were little known in the peninsula and never cited as reliable by other authors. Pérez remained a largely forgotten figure for two centuries after his death. An even more ignoble fate was suffered by Montano, whose work was, to my knowledge, totally unknown in the peninsula, and employed only for propaganda purposes outside it. Las Casas falls into a different category. He took no part in any campaign against the king of Spain, and is associated with the anti-Philip band only by those – usually polemicists writing in the nineteenth century – who have not read him. In reality, Las Casas was a close friend and collaborator of the king and always received his full support, since Philip shared his views.[41] Spaniards came to look on him with suspicion, not because of his campaign for the Indians, but because foreign nations used one of his tracts as propaganda against Spain. The friar's enemies were Spanish colonists in America, not the Spaniards or the king of Spain.

Two hundred years went by and the world continued to accept the unfavourable image of Spanish power, but nothing of substance was said by Spaniards inside the country against the reputation of the king. In Spain, two notable biographical studies were written in the seventeenth century, one by Luis Cabrera de Córdoba (published in full only in 1876, in Madrid), and one by Lorenzo van der Hammen (1625, Madrid). Quite naturally, both criticized aspects of royal policy, but they were not unfavourable to Philip himself. Later in the seventeenth century, the Italian Jesuit Famiano Strada wrote a remarkable study (1632, Rome) which attacked the king's policy in the Netherlands; yet not even he made personal attacks on the king. For Spaniards, his book had only one defect: it was clearly not pro-Spanish. Even so, a translation of the work was made in 1679, with the support of the king's official historian, Núñez de Castro. For some reason the translation was not published, and the printed work came out only in 1748, in Antwerp. For two centuries after the king's death no one thought of blackening his name, though they profoundly disagreed with his military effort in the Netherlands.

What happened, then, to create the myth of the wicked king? The answer lies principally with the Liberal movement that grew up in France and Spain in opposition to Napoleonic power. We must begin with a political event: the creation of the kingdom of Belgium (by way of secession from the United

Netherlands) in 1830, as a direct result of a struggle inspired by the Liberal revolution in Paris in July that year. Inevitably, historians of the new state reflected on the period when the Netherlands had fought to preserve its existence nearly three centuries before in the struggle against Spain. Among the pioneers of the new image of Philip was François-Auguste Mignet (1796–1884). He studied at Aix and moved to Paris in 1821, where he was joined by his close friend from his days at Aix, Adolphe Thiers, future president of the Third Republic. He worked first on the staff of the *Courrier Français*, a journal that opposed the restoration of the monarchy, and then founded, with Thiers, *Le National* in 1830. This newspaper was instrumental in precipitating the July Revolution, which brought about the accession of Louis-Philippe as king of France. Mignet was appointed director of the Diplomatic Archives (1830–48). He had made his name as a historian in 1824, when he published his two-volume *Histoire de la Révolution française*, in which he defended the legacy of the Revolution. It was translated into twenty languages. His work at the archives converted him into a specialist on the history of Spain, and in 1835 he published a semina collection of documents (unfinished, but still valuable) on the diplomacy of the War of the Spanish Succession (coincidentally, a work I had to consult when preparing my doctoral thesis many years ago). In subsequent years he wrote two books on Charles V, but perhaps his most successful work, after that on the Revolution, was his study of *Antonio Perez et Philippe II* (1845).

Mignet was fired by a great enthusiasm for Spanish history, and was given help on the documentation by colleagues in the archives of Brussels and Simancas. He relied for the rest on his own common sense and intuition, producing as a result an elegant volume, complete with footnotes and admirable scholarly apparatus. Mignet presents Philip as a man who was not only evil in himself but evil in his political intentions. The central event exposing Philip's maleficence was the murder of the secretary Juan de Escobedo. The Escobedo affair centres around the role of Don John of Austria as Spain's governor in the Netherlands and the struggle of that country for its freedom from Spain. Philip is seen as a tyrant (a 'vengeful master') who intended to crush the people of the Netherlands. 'To establish the Inquisition there, and build fortresses to keep the inhabitants in fear: that was his plan' – a plan which Mignet describes elsewhere as intended to 'make his rule as absolute and the Catholic religion as unquestioned in the Netherlands as in Spain'.[42] Every detail mentioned by Mignet is of course fantasy, but it must be said in his defence that he was echoing the view then prevalent among most good historians. His book was published in Paris the same year that Prescott's study of Ferdinand and Isabella became available in Spanish in the peninsula. Only ten years after Mignet, the American historian John Motley, in his immortal *Rise of the Dutch Republic*, similarly, described Philip, as a monster. Since that time it has been easier for the public to accept the image of monarchy as an enemy of freedom. To understand Mignet's unswerving support for this view, we need to recall that in French politics he was a leading opponent of the Restoration of the Bourbon monarchy. The fight for their liberties sustained by the Dutch against Philip II was, for him, a foreshadowing of the fight for their liberties by the French people, who were heirs to the Revolution.

The most important scholarly contribution to the image of Philip was produced in Belgium. Louis-Prosper Gachard (1800–85) was a French scholar, hired by the royal Belgian archives in 1826 as director-general, a post he held for fifty-five years. He was the author of several historical writings, among them *Don Carlos et Philippe II* (1867), the first study ever made of the theme, and still the definitive one. He also spent many weeks copying and cataloguing the correspondence of Philip II relating to the Netherlands. Gachard was one of the greatest European historians of all time, but he never freed himself from a profound dislike of the Philip II he claimed to find in the documents he studied. The attitudes of Mignet, Gachard and Motley, historians who ironically still remain largely unknown in Spain, determined the way that Spanish Liberals would interpret the person of Philip II. Because Liberals in France and Belgium saw the king as a tyrant, they did so too. Philip became, for the Liberals, the incarnation of absolutism, the enemy of freedom of thought and the tyrant opposed to regional liberties. And with him, the new Liberal historians castigated the entire record of his dynasty.

Many of the Liberals were politicians and men of letters who spent decades in exile as a result of civil conflict in Spain. They used their leisure years to create, through drama and verse, an image of Old Spain where the people had fought bravely against absolutism. A crucial component of this literary production was the systematic denigration of the person of Philip II, through whom they targeted the monarchy of their own day. In an early play, *Lanuza* (1823), a Liberal refugee from Spain, the duke of Rivas, sketched the main outlines of the thesis. Juan de Lanuza was the hero of the liberties of the kingdom of Aragon, who was cruelly and illegally executed by the tyrant Philip II in 1591. Similarly, in his preface to the duke's poetic drama *The Foundling Moor*, Alcalá Galiano condemned 'the barbaric state into which the

Spanish nation fell under the house of Austria'.[43] Philip II came to be viewed as the historic enemy of the 'progressives', not only in Spain but also in England, France and Belgium. The Spanish king now appeared in Liberal writings as the oppressor of all peoples, including his own.

Among the prominent Spanish constructors of the Liberal myth was Francisco Martínez de la Rosa (1787–1862), statesman and dramatist. A native of Granada, he went to the university there and then turned to writing. During the struggle against Napoleon he joined the patriotic side, entered the Cortes as deputy for Granada, and continued writing. His play *The Widow Padilla* (1812) depicted the widow of the sixteenth-century Comunero leader Juan de Padilla sacrificing her life in the struggle against the tyranny of a foreign monarch, Charles V. Martínez de la Rosa was drawn deeply into politics and, in 1814, when Ferdinand VII was restored to the throne, he was banished to the fortress of La Gomera on the North African coast, where he remained till 1820. In February 1822, at the age of only thirty-four, the king chose him to head the government. In April 1823, however, French troops under Angoulême entered the peninsula and put an end to Liberal rule. Martínez de la Rosa found himself once more in exile, this time in Paris. It was the beginning of a long and fruitful absence of eight years, during which he continued writing and publishing. The most prominent of the Paris Spanish émigrés thanks to his wealth and position, he lived comfortably and presided over soirées at which French and Spanish intellectuals mixed. A French diplomat noted that he was handsome and elegant, 'with the straight and proud bearing of a hidalgo from Granada'.[44] De la Rosa returned to Spain in 1831 and, when the Regent María Cristina took over after the death of Ferdinand VII, he became prime minister in January 1834. He proved incapable of coping with the insurrectionary movement which was tearing the country apart and resigned eighteen months later. He was not a great success in politics, but in literature was one of the chief promoters of the Romantic movement in Spain and the first to take themes from Spanish history and to serve them up to audiences as Romantic drama.

Among the works he wrote while in exile in Paris was the drama *Aben-Humeya, or the Revolt of the Moors under Philip II* (1830), which, once performed on the stage, achieved immediate success. The hero of the play was the romantic, tragic and noble figure of the Morisco rebel leader Aben Humeya. As in several other works produced in these years, Philip was presented as an arch-enemy of liberty, destroyer of the rights of the Aragonese, Portuguese and Dutch, patron of the tyrannical Inquisition and assassin of his own son, Don Carlos. One after another, the plays, poems, novels and operas attacking Philip II and the 'decline' he inflicted on Spain started to roll off the presses. It was one of the most successful achievements of the exiled Liberals, and it left a permanent mark on European perceptions of the king. The denigration of Philip II fitted perfectly into the political programme of Liberals struggling against the 'absolutism' of Napoleon, Ferdinand VII and Metternich, and was adopted also by American and British scholars of Protestant persuasion who followed the Romantic school.

Ironically, the new and hostile image of Philip II was not exclusively Spanish in origin but also based on French- and English-language sources. Moving at ease in the cosmopolitan world of Paris, Martínez de la Rosa drew on foreign scholars to give substance to his image of the Habsburgs, since Spanish historians had written nothing of note on the theme. The fruit of his studies can be seen in a work he wrote around 1850. His *Historical Sketch of Spanish Politics* made some reference to recent Spanish scholars such as Clemencín, but his chief source (as we have already noted in Chapter 1) was Prescott's *Ferdinand and Isabella* (which he cited in English as well as in Spanish), followed by Watson's life of Philip II (cited in French), the works of Ranke, and Coxe's *Memoirs of the House of Bourbon* (both read in French). On the Habsburgs, he was pitiless: 'The Spanish nation found itself ruled by monarchs whose first fruits were war at home and abroad, and who left us a legacy of war at home and abroad.' It was the bitter voice of a statesman who felt that his country had been betrayed. He identified in the sixteenth century the root cause of the problems of the nineteenth. When he came to discuss Philip II, his composure failed him:

> The character of this prince, his sly and stealthy policies, the hatred he professed for liberty under any of its forms, and his determination to interfere in the internal affairs of other nations in order to extend his power by any means were the reason why Spain's hopes of a more prosperous future came to nothing.

His summary of the achievement of the king was equally merciless:

> Within the realm we can see him working intently to destroy the rights and liberties of all the peoples, crushing all obstacles beneath his will, and his will was like iron, it sought to extend his unbending authority as far as the sacred inner reaches of the conscience.[45]

The classic Liberal formulation came from Lafuente, who was conscious of his own prejudices and attempted to be impartial, but in vain. 'We have found in Philip II', he wrote in his 1850 *History*, 'the gifts of a great statesman but also the qualities of a great despot. He refused to be dominated by anybody and had to dominate everybody, he had to be an absolute king. All his acts bore the seal of mystery and darkness.'[46] Not surprisingly, he confessed that 'we admired him, yes, but it was impossible for us to love him'. The charges he made against the king were similar to those levelled against Charles V: destruction of liberty and the ruin of the economy. He managed to rescue Philip from the oft-repeated accusation that at the 1559 *auto de fe* in Valladolid the king had made the outburst 'I would bring the wood to burn my own son', in case he were a heretic. Lafuente pointed out that the phrase was not unique, for Francis I of France had uttered it in the year 1535. (Whether an invention or not, the phrase was a commonplace. Almost exactly the same words had been used by the pope in an interview with the Venetian ambassador in Rome twelve months before!)[47] However, Lafuente did not absolve the king from complicity with the Inquisition. 'He enjoyed the flames of the pyres', he claimed.[48] The king, moreover, set up a system by which all his employees spied on each other out of fear: 'his officials had to be always on the lookout, for they knew neither the day nor the hour. They spied on and watched each other, each of them at the express command of the king.' Above all, the king delighted in the intellectual repression exercised by the Holy Office: 'He watched with delight how the Holy Office chained and crushed free thought, controlled and subdued thinkers, prohibited books and imprisoned and condemned their authors.'

The repression and misery caused by the king were implacable. Constitutional government was crushed:

The Cortes of Castile, mortally wounded at Villalar, finally expired, crushed under the iron arm of a powerful monarch who did not cease to trample on all that might serve to restrain his omnipotent power. The *fueros* of Aragon were shattered in pieces by the vengeance and the inexorable hand of despotism.

Lafuente's general verdict could not have been more damning. He pinpointed

the ruin in which Philip II left the Cortes, the oppressed state and poverty of the people, the depression into which trade, industry and agriculture had fallen as a result of so many wars, so many political and economic errors. . . .

As if this bleak picture were not enough, in 1858 a radical Liberal, Tomás Bertrán, found the picture of Philip painted by Lafuente to be too lenient, and claimed that it would be truer to explain that 'in the forty-four years of his rule, there was not a single day when he did not shed human blood'.[49]

Half a century after Lafuente, when more conservative historians were able to express their opinions, their views did not entirely coincide with the image of a diabolical Philip II. But, as we shall comment below (Chapter 7), they preferred to rescue the earlier monarchs of the Habsburg dynasty. The chief intellectual figure among them, Cánovas del Castillo, revised the prevailing theses in two main respects. Spain's greatness, he stated, rested both on the achievement of Ferdinand and Isabella and on that of Charles V and Philip II. By contrast, the negative aspects came to the fore with the later rulers of the dynasty, to whom Cánovas devoted no less than two solid works of interpretation: his *History of the Decline of Spain* (see Chapter 7) and his *Historical Sketch of the House of Austria in Spain* (1911). In the latter volume, which was in effect a re-writing of the previous one, he conceded that there were sombre aspects to the reign of Philip II: 'the expenses, the penury, the loss of men and money, long and expensive rebellions, schemes to free himself from his adversaries, terrible decisions that are difficult to justify'.[50] But, he suggested, nothing of that period was comparable with the horrors of his own day, considering the methods of those (i.e. the Liberals) 'who in our century have employed violence in order to defend their principles'. As for all the blood shed by Spain in the Netherlands in the sixteenth century, that was nothing compared to the bloodshed caused in the nineteenth century by Bonaparte and his supporters (again, of course, referring to the Liberals).

In general, it was the Liberal tradition, inherited almost wholesale by the intellectuals who led the Second Republic in 1931, that took up once more the tale of an evil Philip. In a book published in Barcelona in 1932, during the Second Republic, the author, in speaking of Antonio Pérez, commented that 'among the victims sacrificed to the passion and vengeful spirit of the tenebrous Philip II, an outstanding place is occupied by the secretary of state'. The same author described the impact of the Inquisition as follows: 'terror shut all mouths, though it could not silence the sound of protest, indignation and hate. That was the Spain of Philip II.' Hostility to the king was adopted without question by writers of all political persuasions, and continues today as fierce as ever.

Who were and are these writers? What had the king done to invite their opprobrium? To understand their reasons, we can try going back into the past, as Américo Castro did. In an appendix to the first edition of his *Spain in its History* (1948), this author commented on the theme 'Why the Spaniards did not love Philip II'. The appendix was a product of Don Américo's time, a little piece of polemic rather than a serious contribution, but it revealed that the author – living and working in Princeton at the time – was a true successor of the Liberal tradition which, one hundred years before, had put Spain's best-known ruler under the spotlight.

The Franco regime attempted to rehabilitate the monarch, not through research into the documents (for none was undertaken) but simply through acclamation. Foreign writers favourable to the regime and to its nationalist and traditionalist image of Philip II, such as the American W. H. Walsh or the German Ludwig Pfandl, were enthusiastically translated into Spanish. The only researched study of the king published in that generation was Braudel's masterpiece,[51] written in France; but the Spanish version was published in Mexico rather than in Spain. Inevitably, as a result of the Franco regime, the reaction against a proto-fascist vision of Philip ended after the 1970s in a return to the older, hostile, Liberal tradition. One way or another, the person of the 'Prudent King' was doomed to become a prey to ideologies, and nowhere more so than among professional historians. Attempts by foreign scholars to revise the old image through new research predictably failed to please either 'conservative' or 'progressive' opinion. New biographies in English, by Geoffrey Parker and by the present writer, have, inevitably, attracted ire for not falling into the clichéd categories dear to the heart of ideologues.[52] When the Spanish government decided to back the celebration of the fifth centenary of the death of Philip II in 1998, scholars reverted to their traditional ideological divisions. Some criticisms of the monarch were from the heart. A professor at the University of Valladolid suggested that Philip II deserved no celebration because he was in the same world class as tyrants such as Hitler and Stalin (and, of course, Franco). 'He inherited a realm that was growing in wealth and population, and left his successor a realm ruined, poor, depressed and without a future.'[53] The words were almost the same as those used by Cadalso two hundred years earlier.

The Liberal legend was also perpetuated by defenders of regional liberties in the peninsula, where Philip was remembered for having sent his armies into Portugal and Aragon. The case of Aragon is well known, but has received further political impetus from the resurgence of the regionalist cause in the aftermath of the Franco dictatorship. As revealed through the pen of a Saragossa history professor of today, the emotion aroused by events five hundred years ago is deeply and personally felt. According to him, the repression that Philip II ordered in 1591, when he sent his army into Saragossa to avert a possible rebellion, was merciless. The king was 'inhuman and pitiless', his officials descended 'on their victims like vultures on to carrion', and, 'when the constitutionalist option was wiped out, the triumph of absolutism silenced both tongues and pens'. 'For many years no one dared to talk.' Philip was a 'gravedigger'.[54] The conflict, the professor notes, was one between 'absolutism championed by the king and constitutionalism defended by the Aragonese' – a direct application of the categories employed by the Liberals in the 1800s. Elsewhere he notes Philip's 'profound political belief in absolutism', and concludes:

> Philip II had no credibility. His despotic government strained spirits until it made the situation unbearable and provoked an explosion of consciences. Dissent, even the slightest disagreement, was dangerous. Criticism of the monarchy, of the Inquisition, of official policy, could lead directly to prison, the galleys or the scaffold. The unlimited power of the monarch extended everywhere.

The writer of these dramatic phrases ends with an appeal for 'greater impartiality'. This quality of 'impartial' history has evidently served to keep alive, down to the twenty-first century, the reputation which the king earned among the Liberals of the 1820s.

At this point, it is worth pausing to consider whether Philip II was as much of an absolutist as his critics have felt he was. We have already noted that the word 'absolutist' and the concept of 'absolutism' did not exist in his day (Chapter 1), so in a sense it is futile to broach the issue. However, it is legitimate to ask whether Philip was in the habit of making arbitrary and illegal decisions without consultation, which is what the idea of being an absolute despot conveys. Top-level affairs of war, peace and rebellion were never, in practice, the sole preserve of the king. He referred everything, down to the smallest detail, to his councils and advisers, and never made decisions based only on his own opinion or preferences.[55] He always insisted on adequate information and consultation before proceeding to action. The

French ambassador stated that in 1559, when he raised a matter with the king, 'he asked me (acting wisely, for fear of being caught in matters of which he has no information or instructions) to refer to his council, so that they may decide'.[56] In the same way, Philip hesitated to make serious decisions until the force of events pointed in that direction. A subsequent French ambassador commented that 'he decides according to the way things turn out', but that he preferred to judge matters from a distance rather than be pushed into them. 'Very rarely does he depart from the advice of his ministers,' the Venetian ambassador Tiepolo noted. Important decisions always affected many people. The king never acted by himself; and never failed to consult before acting. A classic example is his intervention in the affairs of Aragon in 1591. From the outset, he consulted every relevant official throughout Spain, and did not move a finger without favourable advice.[57] The one point at which he did not shrink from decision-making was when he had to choose between conflicting opinions. In a private comment in his own hand, he explained his decision to intervene in Aragon as follows:

> There is no doubt that if this can be settled by benign means it will be better than having to use force. Besides this, there is the responsibility that I also have to the administration of justice in that kingdom, and the punishment of those who have put both Inquisition and justice in the condition in which they are. . . . I am determined to resolve this as necessary, even if it means involving my own person and whatever else is required. If for the sake of religion we have been through and done what you have seen in Flanders, and then in France, the responsibility is even greater to our own people, on our doorstep.[58]

Low-level decisions were not always easy to arrive at. Much government activity occurred in response to petitions from subjects. The task of sorting through petitions was a formidable one, carried out initially by officials in the different realms or by secretaries in Madrid. Petitions which passed this first hurdle had to be accompanied by reports and information before they could be allowed into the relevant council. The process could be lengthy. In nearly all cases, firm recommendations were made to the king. His decisions seldom reflected 'policy'. More precisely, they were responses to the opinions of his advisers. The councils were in theory advisory bodies only, in the sense that the king was not obliged to follow their views. In practice, they made very many firm decisions, usually on administrative matters. In 1567, a diplomat complained that the king 'never decides anything by himself but refers everything to his council; it is completely futile to go back to him over something the council has decided'.[59] Those were, however, early days. As time would tell, there were many issues on which the king could be both resolute and stubborn.

Whether decisions were big or small, the king of course had to accept ultimate responsibility. Like many executives, he disliked this. Inevitably, he would often try to shift the liability and blamed his advisers if things went wrong. This happened with finance, with Flanders, and with the Armada. Historians have consequently had the choice of adopting two differing approaches to Philip. For some, the blame for decisions and for their consequences was his alone. Philip, they felt, was directly and personally to blame for the revolts in his territories, for the policies of the duke of Alba, for the debts to bankers, for the wars abroad, for the problems of taxation and poverty, for the disaster of the Armada. Fifty years of failure, and all the fault of one man. This was the view taken by Lafuente and the Liberal historians and, in our own day, by a handful of Spanish and English-speaking scholars. For other historians, including the French scholar Fernand Braudel and the present writer, it is unrealistic to suppose that a single ruler in pre-industrial times, without any adequate communications, bureaucracy or military forces, could have controlled the development of half of the world and avoided the consequences of a lifetime of conflict. For that reason, my study of *Philip of Spain* concludes that

Philip was never at any time in adequate control of events, or of his kingdoms, or even of his own destiny. It follows that he cannot be held responsible for more than a small part of what eventually transpired during his reign. To many spectators, he was the most powerful monarch in the world. In the privacy of his office, he knew very well that this was an illusion. 'I don't think that human strength is capable of everything,' he mused in mid-reign, 'least of all mine which is very feeble'.[60]

The Braudel line of interpretation has been criticized by Parker as 'historical determinism'. The difference of approach may be explained as one between those who feel that great men control the tides of history, and those who feel that the tides are more likely to have controlled them. It is not a question of shifting blame, but of understanding how government worked in those days. We may recall the anecdote of Knut, the Danish King of England around the year 1030, who rebutted the views of his courtiers when they tried to flatter him and claimed that his powers were absolute. He disproved them by standing in the sea and demonstrating that the waves would not go back when he commanded them to. In practice, as any working historian might suspect, there is no significant divergence between the views of Braudel and Kamen and those of Parker. The latter concedes frankly that the personal role of the king 'cannot be the whole story, for structure too played an important role'. Indeed, he goes further than the present author in emphasizing the role of determinism, by stating that 'all the king's efforts to achieve his policy goals were doomed to failure'.[61] There can be few greater concessions to determinism than the introduction of 'doom' into the scenario of history.

The dynasties that ruined Spain: the Bourbons

Cánovas del Castillo, as we have seen, felt that the fortunes of the Habsburg dynasty were directly related to the past evolution and future hopes of the Spanish monarchy. The urge to look back in history became a constant of politics. Confident that the arrival of the Second Republic in 1931 would restore Spain to the success it had achieved under Ferdinand and Isabella, Prime Minister Manuel Azaña, in a speech given in 1932, denounced the Habsburg dynasty as 'a monstrous deviation in our history, which began in the sixteenth century, cut short the normal development of the Spanish soul, and placed all its energies and all its greatness at the service of a dynasty dedicated to an imperialist and Catholic ethic'. These sentiments are a good reflection of the ongoing obsession with the mythical past as in some sense a prefiguring of present reality. Both conservatives like Cánovas and liberals like Azaña agreed that the later Habsburg rulers had been a disaster. The myth of the failed monarchy cast its long shadow over political life from the seventeenth to the twentieth centuries.

There was, of course, substance to the negative picture of that period. After the death of Philip III in 1621, a pamphlet lamented:

> A king in power, a kingdom oppressed
> Or, more exactly, fleeced.[62]

And under Philip IV, his successor, the satirist Francisco de Quevedo permitted himself to comment:[63]

What the people most lament
Is that you do not have the will
To make use of your power.

The pamphlets and ironies continued under the last ruler of the house of Habsburg, Charles II. It would be misleading to take them all seriously, for they were ephemeral street propaganda that usually circulated only in the political centre at Madrid and were not reliable reflections of the country as a whole. A good argument in favour of this view is the contrast, during the reign of Charles II (1665–1700), between political disillusion in Madrid and a notable optimism in the regions, where elites in Aragon, Valencia and Catalonia expressed their satisfaction with the monarchy. When nineteenth-century historians came to consider these reigns, however, they quickly fell into a stereotyped narrative that produced the picture of a nation in decline (see Chapter 7).

The succession in 1700 of a new dynasty, the French Bourbons, apparently offered hopes of a revival of fortunes. Once again, however, the voices of doom were heard. The case becomes crystal clear with the history of Philip V. The change of dynasty should have improved matters, but it did not. During the War of Succession, a high proportion of the political class reneged on the oath of loyalty they had sworn to Philip V. It was an ill omen for the future of the dynasty in Spain. The most sinister turn of events happened much later, when Philip, following a brief abdication in favour of his young son Luis I, returned after his son's unexpected death for a second reign that began in 1724.[64]

The controversy over Philip's return to power brought into existence a serious division of opinion among the political class. Those who supported the king were viewed as supporters also of his Italian wife, Elizabeth Farnese, and of the Italian interest. They were reinstated under the new admin-istration, which took care to remove opponents from all key posts. Those who were against the king's return were largely traditionalists. They came from the aristocracy and clergy, and included all those who opposed further Italian influence. Firmly Castilian in outlook, they had supported Luis I as a truly Castilian king and now backed the rights of the next heir to the throne, Ferdinand, the young prince of Asturias. They came to be known as 'the Fernandine party', an alternative name for the group otherwise described by foreign ambassadors as 'the Spanish party'. In this way, the question of succession to the throne, fated to play a very long role in Spanish politics, emerged centre-stage. The regime's opponents did not cease to campaign, both through rumours and through pamphlets, against Philip's holding the throne. In August 1726 the king had to issue orders asking for an investigation of 'rumours circulating in Madrid and other parts of the realm, to the effect that His Majesty is going to retire from the government of the monarchy'.[65]

The most serious consequence for Philip was that the legitimacy of his rule began to be questioned for the first time. If, as some still felt, he had no right to resume the throne after having solemnly abdicated, then he had no right to rule. Until 1724, those who had questioned his right to the throne had done so principally for dynastic reasons, since an alternative king of Spain existed in the shape of the Austrian candidate during the War of Succession, Charles III. After 1724, however, it became possible to question Philip's right to rule simply on moral grounds. Above all, those who had looked to the succession of Luis I as the beginning of a new, truly Spanish reign, free from the influence of Italians and other foreigners, were now forced to see the return to power of precisely those influences they had long detested. It was the first serious split in sympathy between the Spanish crown and the ruling political class, and it had long-term implications which affected the Bourbon dynasty up to the beginning of the twentieth century.[66] A pamphlet of the year 1759 demonstrates that by mid-century the vision of collapse had returned:

> A mad king,
> A timid queen,
> A hunter prince,
> And all three equally ignorant.
> Poor leaderless kingdom!
> You will soon be finished![67]

For a good part of the eighteenth century, Spain's elite felt that it was out of touch with the ruling dynasty. Confidence was restored, in part, only during the reign of a king brought in from outside. This was Charles III, king of Naples and son of Philip V and Elizabeth Farnese. The momentous events of the French Revolution, however, shook the political establishment of all Europe and encouraged progressives everywhere to call into question the foundations of rule by monarchy.

The Restoration and the defence of monarchy

The Liberals in the Cortes of Cadiz were quite clear about what they understood by a good monarchy. Lacking any recent precedents, they went back to medieval times, just as the puritan revolutionaries in seventeenth-century England went back to Anglo-Saxon times in search of their ideal. 'According to the constitution of the Goths, and later according to the laws of Castile, our sovereigns have never been absolute', wrote one of the Cadiz deputies. The political elite was pulled in two directions by two wholly incompatible sentiments: a respect for traditional forms of government, personified in the monarch; and a desire for political changes of a type which the monarch (specifically, Ferdinand VII) tended to oppose. These sentiments had made themselves felt to a greater or lesser degree since the succession of the Habsburg dynasty in the shape of Charles V and continued to prevail under the first king of the House of Bourbon. It is no surprise to find an outstanding product of the nineteenth-century tradition, Salvador de Madariaga, claiming in his memoirs that one of the two great tragedies of Spain's history was the succession of the Habsburgs and Bourbons to the throne (the other tragedy was the discovery of America, which we shall touch upon in Chapter 4).

The Cortes of Cadiz gave permanent form to the doubts the Spaniards had always expressed about the monarchy. The 1812 Constitution laid down clear limits to royal power, so that it would not revert to 'absolutism'. That absolutism, we have seen, was attributed to the House of Austria. In the Cortes, Argüelles spoke up for 'the fundamental laws of the Spanish monarchy before they were perverted from their nature by foreign dynasties'.[68] The evil work of Spain's kings down to the nineteenth century passed in this way into the accepted vocabulary of the Liberals and their political heirs, the republicans. The breakdown of the Liberal scheme of politics in the later nineteenth century, however, brought Cánovas de Castillo to power, under King Alfonso XII, and made it possible to revise the older views on monarchy. For Cánovas, monarchy was the essential element required to give stability to a country plagued by revolutions and military coups. In terms of looking at the past, the Cánovas period made it possible to modify substantially the views propagated by the Liberals, and allowed greater scope for the emergence of strongly Catholic views such as those of Menéndez Pelayo.

Even supporters of the monarchy such as Cánovas did not defend it unconditionally. In a speech in the Cortes on 3 July 1886 he said: 'We conceive of a monarchy that can err, that can fall, but we cannot accept that this be provided against in the laws of the country' on the grounds that the king was supreme. 'There can never be any way to arrive legally at the suppression of the monarchy, because there is no legality without the monarchy.' Cánovas initiated a new approach to the question. Where Liberals damned both foreign dynasties that had ruled Spain since 1516, Cánovas and the conservatives corrected their interpretation (see Chapter 7). There had been ruin, certainly, brought about by both dynasties, but the worst of it was perpetrated mainly by the House of Bourbon, which had brought with it new ideas that went against the spirit of the people and led eventually to the glorious rising of 1808 against the French occupation. In contrast, the early monarchs of the House of Austria had done less harm and raised the nation to the heights of glory initiated by Ferdinand and Isabella.

The Catholic scholar Menéndez Pelayo (see Chapter 3) agreed with a good part of the conservative view. In his *Studies in Literary Criticism* (1884) he admitted the failures of the Habsburgs: 'A foreign dynasty, opposed in its traditions and family interests to the traditions and interests of the Spanish nation (and fatal to it in foreign policy), ended up being revered and defended with heroic enthusiasm, and with greater firmness and loyalty than any other royal house of Europe enjoyed, principally because it was the standard-bearer of the armies of the Church.' He also rescued Philip II:

> To claim that the polity in Spain in the Middle Ages was destroyed by the tyranny of the kings of the House of Austria is to fall into platitudes that scarcely merit rebutting. The spirit of the towns, the love for old and venerable liberties were kept as alive in Spain as anywhere else. Philip II did not substantially touch the *fueros* of Aragon, and the *fueros* of Catalonia and Valencia were preserved in full vigour until the House of Bourbon, which was the dynasty that really wiped out traditional liberties and initiated centralisation on the French model.

But Pelayo recognized that the Spaniards were not markedly pro-monarchic: 'as for monarchical feeling, often taken to be one of the characteristic aspects of the sixteenth century, it was low in intensity and very weak. Here kings were treated as great if they followed fashion and were more Spanish than anybody, not because they were kings.'

One of the cornerstones of the Liberal position was that the struggle for freedom was directed against foreigners. It was a position that had been, and would continue to be, basic to Spain's stance. School textbooks in the late nineteenth century expressly inculcated hatred of the foreigner.[69] The regime of Ferdinand and Isabella was viewed as acceptable because it was native; the regime of the Habsburgs and Bourbons was the enemy because it was foreign. In the same way, the visible enemy in 1808 was the French invader. Resistance to the invader became the cornerstone of patriotism, the nation, and the state. It was a position that survived unchanged into the Spanish Civil War, when the nationalist side was identified by its enemies with 'Moors, Germans and Italians' and the Popular Front government was seen as being made up of 'Reds, Jews and Freemasons', not to mention the foreign International Brigades.

Postscript: monarchy and republicanism

The ruling class in sixteenth-century Spain was, of course, never republican, though republican ideas could be identified at the time in several European countries. Contemporary critics of the 1520 revolt of the Comuneros – the revolt which became a cornerstone of Liberal myth in the nineteenth century and as late as the Spanish Civil War gave its name to republican militia units – alleged that some Comunero leaders admired Italian republican states and wished to overthrow Spain's monarchy and establish similar republics. Whatever the truth of the matter, the Comuneros remained in the memory of Spaniards as a movement which supported freedom and opposed tyranny. By extension, Spaniards never gave wholehearted support to the institution of monarchy. Even their political thought, as we have seen above, modified the power of kings.

They continued to accept the need for crown rule, but this attitude had changed by the nineteenth century. The stubborn contempt of many political leaders for the institution of monarchy and for the person who embodied it gave birth to a feeling that kings were by nature incompetent. Perhaps more than other Europeans, the Spaniards seemed to lack a firm commitment to the idea of a king. First, Spaniards, as we have noted above, had no feeling for the sacredness of monarchy and, although they concurred in a normal level of reverence, they did not treat the king as having a special political role in the way the English and other nations did. Secondly, they did not respect the principles of hereditary right, which was just as well since they had periodic discontinuities in the succession to the throne. The support of the rebel Comuneros, in 1520, for Isabella's daughter Juana la Loca as queen against the claims of the effective king, the foreigner Charles of Ghent, initiated centuries of dynastic problems, such as the unedifying spectacle of two kings in Spain during the War of the Succession (1702–13), or the dynastic conflicts and chaos of the nineteenth century, precipitated mainly by the Carlists. Attempts to make the monarchy respectable backfired. There were similar problems in the rest of Europe, notably during the nineteenth century. A recent scholar has cogently pointed out: 'In the same period in which royal legitimacy was made an ideological principle with a view to strengthening monarchy, it actually changed its meaning and gradually came to adopt plebiscitary connotations. Since the middle of the nineteenth century, kings have been deposed for the simple reason that they failed to meet expectations.'[70]

The way was well prepared for a rejection of the monarchy by the political elite in the nineteenth and twentieth centuries. From its birth as a nation in 1808, Spain did not cease to install and uninstall its kings. In 1808, Ferdinand VII forced his father to abdicate, and was himself forced to abdicate in favour of Joseph Bonaparte a few months later. Ferdinand was reinstalled in 1813, but he bequeathed an appalling legacy, since he had no male heir and the Carlists disputed the succession. His daughter Isabel II was eventually forced to abdicate in 1868, and the monarchy was not restored until 1874, in the person of Alfonso XII. The 'restoration', as it was called, failed to achieve political stability when the king died after a short ten-year reign, at the age of twenty-eight. By now the country was getting used to a semi-republican regime run by its privileged oligarchies. The long Regency that followed, in the name of the late king's widow, María Cristina, ended when Alfonso XIII assumed power in 1902, only to have to surrender it in 1931, when the municipal elections in Spain declared against the monarchy. It is common to suggest that Alfonso paved the way for his own fall by too close an association with the dictatorship of General Primo de Rivera, on the assumption that, had he been more democratic, he might have survived. One may add, however, that with or without Primo de Rivera the monarchy already had bitter opponents and for generations had made enemies on all sides and in all parts of Spain. Among the best-known opponents were the writers Unamuno and Blasco Ibáñez, neither of them Castilian by origin, whose efforts to bury the monarchy once and for all merely set the cap on a centuries-long tendency in Spanish history. In his 1903 novel *The Cathedral*, the Valencian novelist Vicente Blasco Ibáñez has the principal character observe:

71

About a century ago the monarchy ended in Spain. The last beloved and popular king was Ferdinand VII. A people deserves the king it gets. Afterwards the nation received the Enlightenment, it freed itself from tradition, but the kings did not improve, rather they got worse, and separated themselves more and more from the reforming and anticlerical tendency of the first Bourbons. The Habsburgs were reborn, like those parasitical plants that are uprooted but reappear after a time. If you want examples from the past with which to compare them, they bring to mind the Habsburg emperors. Jesuits, friars and clergy are in control and direct things, as in the best days of Charles II. Yes, Don Luis, you are right: the monarchy is dead. Between it and the country there is the same relation as between a corpse and a living person. The age-long sloth of Spaniards, their refusal to change attitudes, the fear of the unknown felt by all static peoples, are the reasons for the survival of this institution which cannot even boast, as in other nations, military success or territorial expansion as justification for its existence.

Rejection of the monarchy in the twentieth century involved a direct and conscious rejection of the myths associated with it. As we have seen (Chapter 1), the Catalan nationalists discarded the myth of Ferdinand and Isabella because it represented an idealization of the form of state imposed – so they felt – on Spain and on themselves. That rejection was shared also by the republicans in Madrid, who felt, in the last days of the monarchy of Alfonso XIII, that it was essential to jettison the entire view of the past inherited from the nineteenth century. In a speech in the bull-ring at Madrid in September 1930, Manuel Azaña, who was to become President of the Republic six years later, proclaimed that it was impossible to achieve anything 'useful or worthwhile if we do not emancipate ourselves before history' – a history that consisted of the 'doctrine invented four centuries ago in defence of and propaganda for a Catholic–imperialist monarchy'.[71] In those weeks in November 1930, Ortega y Gasset published a newspaper article that ended with the words, 'Delenda est monarchia!' ('The monarchy must be abolished!'). Literary figures greeted the end of the monarchy with enthusiasm. One of them was Azorín. When the Republic was born in 1931, he welcomed it by saying: 'Spain will recover its historic meaning, its true tradition, interrupted by the succession of the Habsburgs and Bourbons to the throne'.[72]

The new Republic collapsed, however, through the inability of its various successive governments to achieve political stability or to resolve adequately the profound problems facing Spanish society.[73] The result was the devastating Civil War of 1936–9. After much hesitation, the victors decided that their form of government (a military dictatorship) would in time evolve into a monarchy in order to assure political continuity and stability and also to renounce, once and for all, the experience of the Republic. However, they insisted that there was no intention of returning to the discredited monarchy of the nineteenth century, or even of the eighteenth century. The 'absolute' monarchy of that period was out of the question, for it was oligarchic. The 'liberal' monarchy that followed it was also ruled out, because it was a republic in disguise. There was only one option remaining: the traditional Catholic monarchy that Spain had allegedly enjoyed in the fifteenth century, 'the Spain that created our unity, the Spain of Isabella and Ferdinand, with the yoke and the arrows'.[74] Nearly five centuries after the event, Spain turned back wholeheartedly to its myths.

It took much painful reassessment for democrats to accept the return of the monarchy after the death of General Franco in 1975. Even today, in 2007, the monarchy in Spain has to be defended regularly in the press by historians who feel that it is one of the most valuable components of political life. In an article written in 2004, the historian Carlos Seco Serrano observed: 'Only the Monarchy – and it is immensely fortunate that we have this historical institution – can allow Spaniards to recover, half a century after the event, from the ferocious domestic hatreds which are still alive, in order to carry out what has been well termed a "model transition" towards democracy.'[75] A few weeks later another historian, Javier Tusell, made the same point: 'Ortega wrote in 1913 that it was necessary to give monarchy a chance. He was right when he said it, and the phrase continues to be valid over ninety years later.'[76] What Tusell did not mention was that Ortega changed his opinion afterwards and became a notable opponent of monarchy. In his 1930 article 'Delenda est monarchia' Ortega concluded that 'the Monarchy has been incapable of becoming a national institution, that is, a system of public power that gives priority to the profound demands of the nation and identifies itself with them. Rather, it has been an association of private groups that fed like parasites on the organism of Spain. That is why we believe that the Monarchy must be replaced by a Republic.'[77] He modified even this view in the light of subsequent experience, but by then the damage to the monarchical system had been done.

CHAPTER THREE

THE MYTH OF
A CHRISTIAN SPAIN

In the history of the world there is nothing comparable to what was achieved by Spain, because we incorporated into Western civilisation all the peoples who were under our influence. During its two great centuries the whole of Spain was on a mission.

Ramiro de Maeztu, *Defence of Spanishness* (1934)

Spain, the hammer of heretics

The tourist today who witnesses the intensely moving processions that wind their way during Holy Week through the streets of Seville, Valladolid and scores of other Spanish towns cannot fail to be impressed by the profoundly religious atmosphere. Statues of the grieving Virgin, illuminated candles, hooded cloaks, drums of lament that reverberate through the silence, plaintive hymns, take us back to an age of faith that seemed to have disappeared but somehow is still with us. The conviction that Spain was a country with a truly Christian faith is the cornerstone of classic culture. It is also central to the image constructed around the sixteenth and seventeenth centuries. Almost alone among European countries, Spain in the Middle Ages had no significant heresy. More than any other, it was in the front line defending the Faith against the Muslims. It expelled its non-Christian minority, the Jews; then, just over a century later, it expelled its population of Islamic descent, the Moriscos. Almost uniquely among European countries, it had no significant Protestant heretics during the Reformation. Unlike any other country, it had a coercive Inquisition that dedicated itself to uprooting error. The most militant order of the Counter-Reformation Church, the Jesuits, was initially created by Spaniards. Whichever way one turns, Spain's zeal for Catholicism shines forth. The triumphant words of the nineteenth-century scholar Menéndez Pelayo are well known to many Spaniards: 'One faith, one baptism, one flock, one shepherd, one Church, one crusade, a legion of saints. Spain, which preached the gospel to half the world, Spain, the hammer of heretics, the light of Trent, the sword of Rome, the cradle of St Ignatius, that is our greatness and our unity, we have no other.' The picture is a familiar one, easily recognizable by those who grew up during the thirty-five years of the Franco regime and were drilled into accepting it.

Much of that picture, however, may be viewed as a myth, created long before Franco. Like most of the myths presented in this book, it has an ideological agenda. From the sixteenth century on, the great political acts of the regime were presented by Spanish writers as acts worthy of a Christian people: the expulsion of the Jews, the expulsion of the Moors, the burning of Protestants, the wars in Europe. The printed literature of the time is full of Christian triumphalism. Reading those testimonies, subsequent writers felt they could interpret the evidence clearly. The nineteenth-century religious thinker Jaime Balmes referred to 'that religious unity which is part of our habits, our way of life, our customs, our laws, and which was there at the birth of our monarchy'. Half a century later, the writer Julián Marías claimed in his *Intelligible Spain*: 'the idea that gave birth to Spain was its identification with Christianity'. Writing in 1962, a leading public figure, Pedro Saínz Rodríguez, felt that 'there is abundant and easily accessible proof of our virtual unanimity in matters of religion and of the latter's influence on the life of Spain during the Golden Century'.[1] In the face of such testimony it is difficult not to conclude, as a contemporary scholar does, that Spanish identity was based on 'a seemingly indelible Catholic legacy'.[2]

The argument can be reinforced without difficulty by accumulating quotations from religious writers of early modern Spain on the essential Christianity of the nation. Since the overwhelming bulk of texts from that epoch is religious in nature, their conclusion could not be otherwise. Written texts dating back to the Middle Ages, for example, underline the essential Christianity of those who were locked in conflict with the Muslims of the south. The high points of Christian achievement in the sixteenth century, as seen through the eyes of a modern observer, are therefore unmistakable. They have led the cardinal archbishop of Madrid to affirm in 2005:

The renewed Christian vision of man and of the world that resulted from the profound renewal of the Church in Renaissance and Baroque Spain modelled and inspired a style of life and consequently of society that was eminently spiritual, open to generous dedication to missionary work. The evangelization of America, the school of Salamanca, the mysticism of St Teresa of Avila and of St John of the Cross, the educational work of St Ignatius of Loyola have remained as representative symbols of a period in the history of the Spanish Church which has transcendent and universal value. The historical Christian reality of Spain, from that time down to our own, remains unmistakably marked by the sign of 'Catholic'.[3]

It is significant that every name mentioned in this quotation comes from the sixteenth century. The technique of picking out specific and isolated highlights – a book by a university professor in Salamanca; the founding of a new religious order; a set of poems by a monk – as evidence that the country was profoundly Christian is clearly open to question. There was, it is possible to argue, another side of the coin. Did any of those events, such as the 'evangelization of America', ever happen? How profound was the belief and practice of the people, 'the historical Christian reality'? How long-lasting was it? In all countries from England to Russia, by the nineteenth century many commentators had admitted – as had the poet Matthew Arnold, meditating by the water's edge on Dover beach – that Christian belief no longer had a hold on the people. A parish priest in Russia in the 1850s bitterly criticized those who proclaimed 'that only in Russia has the faith been preserved undefiled', when, as he testified from his own experience, 'two-thirds of the people have not the slightest conception of the faith!'[4] This rough estimate was probably applicable to Spain in those same decades. What was the situation two centuries earlier, in early modern Spain, commonly regarded as the crucial period of faith?

Like other countries, Spain had profound flaws in its religious belief and practice during the Reformation. An absence of certainty in matters of dogma was accompanied by a widespread ignorance about religion, a common enough phenomenon in a society and era when illiteracy was high. In 1529 an influential book lamented that 'superstitions and witchcraft in these times are widespread in our Spain', and a bishop reported that people in his diocese 'know nothing about Christianity'. In many parts of the peninsula, preachers felt that 'superstition' (that is, unapproved beliefs) and witchcraft had a powerful hold on the people. Throughout Spain, among people of all racial and religious antecedents, it was possible to find expressions of disbelief in an after-life, like the statements made time and again by clergy and laity to the effect that 'nothing exists beyond being born and dying'.[5] In 1554 a prominent friar, Felipe de Meneses, claimed that everywhere in Spain there was ignorance of religion, 'not only among barbarous and uncivilized mountain people but also in those presumed to be civilized, not only in small villages but even in cities. If you ask what it is to be a Christian, they can no more give an answer than savages can.' Trying to find a parallel to the situation, Meneses could only compare the Spaniards to the savages of America: 'experience has shown that there are Indies in Castile and that in the very heart of Castile there are mountains, that is, mountains of ignorance'.[6] The description 'Indies' quickly caught on. In 1568, a dignitary of the city of Oviedo in northern Spain appealed to the new Jesuit order to come and preach to his people: 'these are veritable Indies that we have within Spain', he wrote. 'Nowhere in the Indies is there more need to hear the Word of God than here.'[7]

The apparently 'Christian' culture of the people of Spain between the sixteenth and nineteenth centuries left much to be desired, since both clergy and laity were equally ignorant of basic essentials. Religion ended up (as in many other countries) as an extension of social discourse rather than a system of faith; it was, in other words, what you did rather than what you believed. Religion was at the centre of village life, of community feeling and of armed conflict. Rather than being principally the list of practices laid down by the Church, it was the sum of inherited attitudes and rituals relating both to the invisible and to the visible world.[8] All sections of society, in both town and country, participated in the rituals, which on one hand determined the periods of leisure and work, and on the other assigned to people their roles and status within the community. There was no essential contradiction between Spaniards being nominally 'Christian' and yet at the same time having no real knowledge of Christianity. There was no formal separation between the sacred and the secular in early modern Europe; the sacred was always part of the profane world, on which it drew for its symbols and functioning.

It was a largely unlettered world, often isolated from the culture of the great cities.[9] The dominant realities were the precariousness of harvests and the insecurity of life. Food and survival, as in primitive rural communities today, dictated social, moral and religious attitudes. Poor diet, frequent crop failures, a high mortality rate were not mere hazards but part of the very fabric of existence. They were accepted as inevitable, but, then as now, men took out insurance against what they could not foresee or control. Religion was a major protective force and, where official religion seemed inadequate, other rites – such as witchcraft – were used. For all that, life was not a pessimistic attempt to ward off disaster. Given that some things were inevitable, there was every reason to abandon oneself to joy and celebration. In rural Spain the full-time labour of post-industrial society was unknown, and towns spent at least one third of the days of the year on holiday. Ritual festivities – plays, carnivals, processions – were a major, integral and regular aspect of life. They were essential to the community, which normally dictated their form and content; and they were pleasing to the Church, with whose great festivals (Christmas, pre-Lenten carnival) they coincided. The mixture of communal and religious elements in popular festivities had always caused problems and friction, but long use tended to hallow the ceremonies.

In a pre-industrial economy, virtually all rituals were related to the agrarian life of the community. The annual calendar began at Christmas, succeeded very quickly by an outburst of celebration for Carnival, which was the prelude to Lent, the season of waiting and reflection. After the spring solstice, the month of May arrived with its symbols of life and fertility. Work resumed in the fields, and the productive season was crowned by the midsummer fire rituals of St John's Eve. From July the harvest was gathered in, with further celebrations in the community.

Formal Catholic doctrine during the Golden Age of peninsular culture represented only one part of the essentially folkloric belief of Spaniards. Religious practice was traditional and sociable rather than theological. The practice of baptism, for example, was a social rite in which the whole community (the village, the neighbourhood) tended to take part. If what the Church offered seemed insufficient, people went outside it for folk remedies and practices, or for exotic knowledge, or for spiritual and mystical solutions to their anxieties. Within the heart of Spain, the members of the highest nobility at the court of Philip II became supporters of prophetic cranks.[10] Church dogma barely penetrated daily religion: for example, the doctrine of purgatory was being formally affirmed in Spain only as late as the 1600s,[11] and throughout that century there were bitter quarrels among the clergy over whether the Virgin Mary was born free of original sin. Matrimony tended to be a social rather than a religious rite, since the ceremony of a blessing in church was given secondary importance. Basic observance of the essentials of religion could be sporadic. In the town of Bilbao, wrote an inquisitor in 1547, 'the parish priests and vicars who live there report that one in twelve of the souls never goes to confession'.[12] In the north of Aragon, stated another colleague in 1549, there were many villages 'that have never had sight of, nor contact with, Church or Inquisition'. The profundity of Spain's Catholicism during and after the period of the Counter-Reformation is still open to doubt and debate.[13]

The problem was particularly serious in rural areas. In Galicia in 1585, for example, the inquisitors admitted that doubts about the presence of Christ in the sacrament were widespread, but 'more out of ignorance than malice', and that the virginity of Mary was questioned 'through sheer thick-headedness rather than out of a wish to offend'. They reported the case of the man in a tavern who, when a priest present claimed to be able to change bread into the body of Christ, exclaimed in unbelief, 'Go on! God's in heaven and not in that host which you eat at mass!' In Granada in 1595, a shepherd from the village of Alhama claimed not to believe in confession and said to his friends: 'What sort of confession is it that you make to a priest who is as much of a sinner as I? Perfect confession is made only to God.' The inquisitors concluded that 'he seemed very rustic and ignorant and with little or no capacity of understanding', and sent him to a monastery to be educated.[14] It was of course an age of illiteracy, but how widespread was ignorance of religion? If an improvement in elementary religious knowledge really happened, it was certainly not general. In parts of Spain that did not enjoy the density of clergy and schools to be found in Madrid and Toledo, ignorance was still the order of the day. So, too, was scepticism, which was born not out of hostility to official doctrine but simply out of giving priority to one's own common sense.[15]

The question to resolve was not whether Spain was Catholic, but whether it was Christian. None of the missionaries who went out into the villages and mountains in the sixteenth century doubted that Spain was formally Catholic. What they doubted, as their correspondence makes absolutely clear, is whether any of the tenets and practices of the faith were understood or observed by the people (or the clergy), and whether the day-to-day social life of communities was being guided by Christian precepts. It was not a peculiarly Spanish problem. Already in the early sixteenth century, well before the doctrines of the Reformation had taken root, competent observers in other parts of Europe were questioning not only the state of religion of the people, but even that of the elite. When they ventured outside the big towns, they found superstition and ignorance everywhere. In apparently Catholic France, 'near Bordeaux', reported an appalled Jesuit in 1553, 'stretch about thirty leagues of forest whose inhabitants live like rude beasts, without any concern for heavenly things. You can find persons fifty years old who have never heard a mass or learnt one word of religion.' In the half of Germany newly converted to Lutheranism, pastors complained in Wolfenbüttel in the 1570s that 'people do not go to church on Sundays. . . . Even if one finds a man or woman who remembers the words, ask him who Christ is, or what sin is, and he won't be able to give you an answer.' From Wiesbaden it was reported in 1594 that 'all the people hereabout engage in superstitious practices with familiar and unfamiliar words, names and rhymes . . . they also make strange signs, they do things with herbs, roots, branches . . .'.[16] Slowly, as new ideas began to filter in, the people probably began to understand what Christianity meant. Spain, it is possible to argue, was no exception to the process of change affecting other Europeans.

Confident claims by Spanish writers that the people were wholly Christian arose, quite simply, because nobody had examined their belief and practice. Traditional Church history, as it was written in Spain down to the 1960s, tended to limit itself to what happened among the clergy, and ignored completely the religion of the people. Half a century ago, historians in France and Italy first began to look at sources that would throw light on the real state of everyday religion. From the 1980s on, historians began to use diocesan papers, testaments and Inquisition documents to arrive at an understanding of peninsular Catholicism. There is now no doubt that a substantial period of reform – the Counter-Reformation – occurred in Spain,[17] but it did not occur until half a century after the death of Ferdinand and Isabella. In 1566 a royal official criticized previous efforts at reform and called for a new reform of the Church, 'not a three-day reform as we have had till now, but one that lasts'. In the 1570s, Philip II attempted to enforce the decrees of the Council of Trent, which he considered 'the one true remedy',[18] and supervised the holding of provincial councils of the clergy. The king, who insisted that all aspects of the programme should be under Spanish control, had two main objectives: to improve the quality of the clergy and to convert the people to true religion. To help him in his goal, he enlisted the Inquisition (which from this date began to look closely at the day-to-day religious and moral practice of Spaniards) and invited new religious orders from Italy (the Carmelites, Jesuits and Capuchins, among others) to enter the country and preach sermons. There were revolutionary innovations in everyday religion: the form of the mass was altered, thousands of new churches were built, pulpits and confessionals were set up for the first time, new devotions (such as the rosary) were introduced, the rules of marriage were changed, and lay associations (known as confraternities)[19] were set up in each parish. At the same time traditional community activities, such as processions and festivities, were put under clerical control. The reforms tried to give a unique role to male clergy, especially to the person of the parish priest; by contrast, women were allotted a secondary role in all Church activities.

The attempt to make the people Christian occurred precisely because there were no grounds for triumphalism over their religious practice. It remains open to debate whether the changes were effective and lasting, since much of the initial impetus for reform disappeared in little more than a generation. Outside the main towns, it is likely that old-time forms of religion continued without change. The Church played a relatively small part in the lives of country people, who occupied their time in a broad range of activities rooted in their traditions. The Counter-Reformation probably had little impact on this 'popular religion', which differed in content from one locality to the next, adopted its own local preferences in saints, and even insisted on having local versions of the Virgin Mary.[20] We may conclude that Spain in early modern times, like England and Germany, was undeniably Catholic in its public religion and social activity, but (as commentators of the time admitted) there were serious and profound anomalies in every aspect of belief and practice. There was certainly no evidence of exceptional devotion to the faith, or of a Spain that had renewed itself spiritually and was about to dedicate itself to converting Europe and America.

Political origins of the myth of a Catholic nation

However, what may or may not have been the true situation of belief in the sixteenth century was, for all practical purposes, irrelevant to the way in which the myth of a Catholic Spain evolved three hundred years later. Ironic as it may seem, the myth emerged as a result of the seemingly irresistible advance of anti-Catholic trends in the country. Towards the end of the eighteenth century, in 1767, the government expelled the entire Jesuit order from Spain and its colonies. It was not an overtly 'anti-Catholic' move, for it had the explicit support of important sectors of the clergy. The expulsion was backed, however, by a government made up of leading personages who were sympathetic to reformist ideas that came in from outside the country. The same class of politicians also backed the abolition of the Inquisition in 1813. It was the beginning of a period that seemed, both in Spain and in Italy, to be threatening both the clergy and the postulates of official religion. In the summer of 1834, street riots in Madrid led to the murder of seventy-eight clergymen. 'The events marked a turning point in the history of the Spanish Church.'[21] Many felt that the clergy had reaped its just deserts. 'The clergy, gentlemen, as a class, is fighting the principles of liberty in every nation, and is combating them in Spain!' The words were spoken in the Cortes at Madrid by the Liberal statesman Antonio Alcalá Galiano, who had just spent a decade of his life as an exile in England. Further anticlerical riots took place the year after, in the east of the peninsula, and particularly in Catalonia. A new and potent factor, mob anticlericalism, had entered into Spanish politics. In the autumn of 1835 the new prime minister, Mendizábal, introduced unprecedented legislation, which suppressed the religious orders and confiscated their property.

How could all this have happened in a profoundly Catholic nation? Much more was to come, and believing Catholics pointed their finger at ideas which, they claimed, had been brought in from outside the country and represented the forces of materialism, atheism and irreligion. Faced by the open religious scepticism of the Liberals, many of whom were strongly anticlerical, and by the secularist ideas of some progressive groups such as the Institución Libre de Enseñanza, Catholic publicists fell back on what they saw as the spiritual resources of the nation. They denounced the prevailing trends as foreign corruption, and emphasized instead the religious values that, in their eyes, had created Spain's historic greatness and formed the Hispanic character in past ages. Even if those resources had never really existed, they must be assumed to have existed. That was the ideal to which Spaniards had to aspire, or, more precisely, that was the ideal to which they had to return if they were to emerge from the confusion in which they now found themselves. The programme, as we might guess, combined a little bit of many other myths – about the united Christian nation, about the Christian monarchy, and about the decline into which the country was plunging. The most intense period of myth-creation about a Christian Spain took place, therefore, in the middle of the nineteenth century, when the advancing forces of materialism and unbelief seemed to be threatening the moral convictions of Spaniards. It was then that writers chose to remind their public that, despite everything, Spain was and always had been a truly Christian nation, indeed the only truly Christian nation in Europe.

A typical aspect of the myth was associated with the legend of Isabella the Catholic. Beginning with the pioneering study by Clemencín (1821),

Catholics were invited to look back to her as the ideal monarch of Catholic Spain. Even Liberal historians accepted her, not because she embodied a Catholic ideal but because (as we have seen in Chapter 2) she was visualized as the founder of a united Spain. In the 1950s, in the favourable atmosphere of the Franco regime, which was making an effort to establish its ideological continuity with the roots of Christian tradition, proposals were made to have Isabella declared a saint. This move came to a climax with the presentation in Rome in 1972 of an official document aiming to promote the beatification of Isabella.[22] According to this document, which seems to have reflected the thinking of Spanish bishops and of the official historians of the regime, Isabella carried out a 'profound reform' of the Church and, 'thanks to it, saved Spain from the religious wars that shed blood in Europe', set up an Inquisition 'to deal with the danger posed by the falsely converted Judaizers', and occupied Muslim Granada, with the result that 'by the beginning of the sixteenth century there were no more unbelievers in the realm'. The whole of Spain was thus saved as a completely Catholic country. Isabella and Ferdinand then put into effect a 'constitutional law' (this curious phrase refers to the decree of expulsion), and got rid of the Jews. 'The permission they had to stay in the realm was repealed' because they were causing 'great social and political disorder' and, by practising their religion, were openly breaking the 'pact of tolerance' that allowed them to be there. No other option remained but to expel them. 'The measure was the most humane and benevolent that could have been taken under the circumstances', so the Jews had good cause to be grateful, because the expulsion 'was carried out in the most just way that one could hope for'. Isabella next sent missionaries to America, because 'the Great Khan desired and awaited Christian missionaries'. In short, after so much Christian achievement and piety, 'under the Catholic Monarchs Spain experienced the springtime of its Golden Age'. The document, which patently reflected a profoundly rooted myth of Spain's essential Catholicity, has not been acted upon so far by the Church authorities in Rome. It is mentioned here because it represents a glaring example of the way in which a political ideology sought its justification in a manipulated version of the Christian past of the country.

The biggest single boost to the Catholic version of the past was given at the dawn of the twentieth century by a conservative scholar who was reacting against the anti-Catholic current in Liberal politics. Marcelino Menéndez Pelayo (1856–1912) was a polymath who almost single-handedly created the national image of a Catholic Spain. That myth was crying out for construction. By the middle of the nineteenth century, the country had undergone two generations of Liberal rule, the monarchy had fallen apart, civil war was rife because of the pretensions of Carlism, sections of the educated elite were looking to Germany for ideas and orientation, and the population had lost touch with the inspiration that religion had once offered. Menéndez Pelayo was born in Santander, studied at university in Barcelona and took his doctorate in Madrid, after which he travelled through southern Europe – Portugal, France and Italy. At the age of twenty-one he successfully earned himself a chair at the University of Madrid, entered politics in 1884, became a senator and afterwards a director of the National Library in 1898. By the time of his death he had published an impressive number of works on all areas of cultural creativity. His most memorable, his basic contribution to the Catholic and conservative myth, was his multi-volume *Heterodoxos* (1876), which he began writing at the age of twenty and published four years later.[23] His motive for writing it emerges clearly in his opening chapter. He was distressed by what Liberalism had done to Spain, by 'the impious and suicidal fury with which Spanish Liberalism has insisted on blotting out Old Spain'.

Like other Spaniards of inquiring mind, he was struck by the appalling fact that no one since Mariana (see Chapter 1) had given a historical account of Spain. 'Nobody', he wrote in the preface to *Heterodoxos*, 'has yet written the true history of Spain in the sixteenth and seventeenth centuries.' That was in part what he set out to do: to discover the truly Catholic Spain that others had neglected to identify. It was an impressive achievement of scholarship that won him an international reputation, though it tended also to turn the man and his work into a stereotype. A conservative in outlook, he was by no means the undiluted conservative in politics that his detractors have made him out to be. He differed from many prevailing attitudes and was free from many prejudices. His one constant feature was his unswerving conviction that the Catholic faith was the true essence of Spain. He viewed the sixteenth century as a 'key century in history', when the faith made Spain into the 'people chosen by God'. This view was sustained by rhetorical prose which had the power to convince and compel. Why, he asked, had Spain not become Protestant like the rest of western Europe?

> There was nothing more unpopular in Spain than heresy, and of all heresies Protestantism. The Latin spirit, given life by the Renaissance, protested with unusual vigour against the Reformation, progeny of Teutonic individualism. The single-minded genius of Rome rejected the

anarchic variety of free will, and Spain, which still had its arm dripping with Moorish blood and had just expelled the Jews, demonstrated, in its preservation of the unity it had achieved at great price, an incredible firmness and sturdiness, intolerance if you wish, but a noble and saving intolerance.

And why were there no heretical writings in Spain? 'The language of Castile was not made to utter heresies.' Starting with the undeniable fact that the Reformation never took root in the peninsula, he concluded that 'none of its doctrines succeeded in eluding the inevitable death that awaits in Spain any teaching repugnant to the principles of our culture'. In the epilogue to his remarkable book, pride in this achievement built up into a hymn to the glories of that past age:

The sentiment of *patria* is modern, there was no *patria* in those mediaeval centuries, nor strictly speaking until the Renaissance, but there was one faith, one shepherd, one Church, one liturgy, one eternal crusade and a legion of saints that fought for us. God gave us the victory, and rewarded our perseverance by granting us the highest among all the destinies in human history: that of discovering the whole globe and breaking down the ancient limits of the world. It was a happy age, one of signs and marvels, an age of youth and of vigorous life! Spain was or believed it was the country of God, and each Spaniard, like Joshua, felt within himself the faith and the valour to demolish walls to the sound of trumpets or to stop the sun on its course. Nothing seemed, or was, impossible, for the faith of those men, swathed, it seemed, in a triple coat of bronze, was a faith that moved mountains. In the secret places of God they were given the role of making the word of Christ resound among the most barbarous peoples; of sinking in the gulf of Corinth the proud vessels of the tyrant of Greece, and of saving, through the agency of the young prince of Austria, all western Europe from the latest and last threat of Islam; of shattering the Lutheran hosts in the swamps of Holland, with their swords in their mouths and the water up to their waists; and of winning, for the Church of Rome, one hundred towns in return for every town snatched away by heresy.

The passage ends with the peroration (quoted at the beginning of the chapter) that became familiar to more than a generation of Spaniards: 'Spain, which preached the gospel to a half of the world, Spain, the hammer of heretics . . .

that is our greatness and our unity, we have no other.' From that (wholly imaginary) high point of achievement in the past, Menéndez Pelayo turned his gaze to the depressing condition of late nineteenth-century Spain, from which glory had vanished and vision had perished:

> With continuous anti-religious propaganda, the Catholic spirit, which still survives among most of the people in the countryside, has begun to wane in the cities, and, although Spanish freethinkers are few, one may well say of them that they are the worst type of ungodly people that you can meet in the world, because the Spaniard who has ceased to be a Catholic is incapable of believing in anything, except in the omnipotence of a certain practical common sense, for the most part crude, selfish and vulgar.
>
> In default of great things to admire in the present, I have taken on my frail shoulders the unpretentious task of bearing witness to our former culture. In this book I have tried to remove the thorns, but it would not be surprising if contact with them has communicated to me some of their asperity. I have written amid criticism and struggle, not unlike the builders of Jerusalem in the time of Nehemiah, who raised the walls of the temple with a sword in one hand and a hammer in the other, defending themselves against the surrounding peoples who constantly attacked them. It is a hard situation, but in Spain it is inevitable.

The myth of Spain as the front line of the Catholic religion

Though anticlerical Spaniards may have questioned the views of Menéndez Pelayo at the time, none of them made any adequate attempt to rebut them through research, study or reflection. As a consequence, his presentation of the mythical Christian past enjoyed absolute triumph in the textbooks, and not a single line of informed dissent was written by any scholar for one hundred years afterwards. As may be expected, the absence of any alternative view was taken as confirmation of what the great conservative scholar had argued for. Throughout the early twentieth century, Church historians and ideologues repeated the affirmations of Menéndez Pelayo verbatim. He had claimed that Spain was the Hammer of Heretics, the vanguard of the Counter-Reformation. It was, consequently, perfectly normal for a distinguished Spanish historian of the last generation to write: 'All the history books speak of a reforming impulse that began in Spain and then spread throughout Europe.' Spain was, he stated, the origin of Catholic energy in

Europe. It did not receive missionaries from other countries; it was Spain itself that created and produced missionaries and sent them abroad.[24] Spain saved Europe for the faith. It is a picture that stands at the centre of any Spanish textbook of the history of religion. Yet the depiction is wholly at odds with what really happened; for, when this historian said 'all the history books', he meant, of course, 'all the Spanish history books'.

Contemplating the picture from outside Spain, one is forced to conclude that there is no evidence of a drive for reform originating principally in the peninsula. In cultural and religious matters, Spain was very much the recipient, not the donor. The magnificent study of spiritual literature in the peninsula undertaken by the French scholar Marcel Bataillon in 1937 is unequivocally entitled *Erasmus and Spain*, testimony to the impact of humanism on Spain rather than that of Spain on humanism. The greatest humanist of Spanish origin, Juan Luis Vives, was formed outside Spain, not within it. During the three centuries that stretched from the sixteenth, when Spain was host to the benign influence of Netherlands spirituality and Erasmian scholarship, to the nineteenth, when it became enthusiastic over Germanic Krausism, the missionary trends came from without. The most significant features of the Counter-Reformation (the sixteenth-century reform movement inspired from within the Catholic Church and directed in part against the Protestant Reformation) were brought from outside into Spain; they did not originate in the peninsula, where they were often hotly contested. Church historians in Spain usually sweep aside these facts, and many continue to write about a firmly Catholic country where nothing has changed over the centuries. In any case, they argue, there was little need for reform within Spain, because Ferdinand and Isabella had reformed the Church. The claim that the Catholic Monarchs reformed religion is, however, misplaced.[25] These rulers tried to reform a couple of religious orders in central Castile and appointed a handful of pious bishops; but they left untouched every aspect of the institutions, ritual, clergy and religious life of the Church throughout Spain. Religion remained as unreformed as anywhere else in Europe. As noted above, no effective moves for change were made until the 1570s (that is to say, for half a century after the beginning of the Protestant Reformation), when Philip II personally took an interest in the question and Spain became the first European country to impose the decrees of the Council of Trent.

Surely, however (it may be objected), the Jesuits were Spain's great contribution to the reform movement? This view results from the common misapprehension that the Jesuit order was essentially a Spanish one, and used Spain as a base for converting Europe. From its early days, the order was international rather than Spanish. It grew out of a decision taken by the Basque nobleman Ignatius Loyola and six young men (three of them Spaniards) who together took vows of poverty and chastity in a little church on the hill of Montmartre in Paris in 1534. After rejecting their initial intention to work for Christ in the Holy Land, the group decided to offer their services to the pope. The Jesuits thereafter were always based in Italy, which is where young Spaniards like Ribadeneira, Polanco and Nadal joined them. Ignatius himself spent all his active life in Italy. The first Jesuit to enter Spain was Araoz, who came over in 1540. Afterwards the Jesuits used their college at Coimbra in Portugal as the base from which they entered the country. The first Spanish college was founded at Valencia in 1544. The missionary work of the Jesuits in Spain was always directed from Italy, as is known to anyone who has studied the Jesuit archives in Rome. From the beginning, there was strong opposition to the order in Spain from the Spanish clergy, and at the court in Valladolid they were accused of being Lutherans. It took them about twenty years to become established and even then the hostility did not cease. Though many Spaniards came to play a prominent part in it, the order was always cosmopolitan and independent of Spanish control. Jesuits from the period of the Counter-Reformation played a very important role in defending Catholicism, but their contribution – which cannot be touched upon here in detail – is persistently misrepresented as an achievement of Spain. In reality, famous Jesuits such as Ignatius Loyola and Francis Xavier carried out their work without any reference to Spain.

The temptation among Castilian nationalists to exaggerate the historic role of the Spanish Church can also be detected in the case of the colonial territories. The missionary effort in America was both massive and heroic. Between 1493 and 1800, the crown financed the sending of at least fifteen thousand clergy, to America of whom a quarter went to Mexico (New Spain).[26] They laboured, worked, converted and also suffered. Did they succeed? This possibility has been passionately argued for, but also widely contested. Since the nineteenth century, the argument for success has formed an integral part of the 'Spanishness' myth; it will be touched on elsewhere in these pages. The official view was expressed by Cardinal Gomá, archbishop of Toledo, in a speech of 1934 (which will be quoted from elsewhere in this book):

One century after the beginning of the Conquest, America was virtually Christian. The Cross, together with the banner of Castile, lorded it over the vast expanses from Mexico to Patagonia, human sacrifice and horrifying superstitions vanished, magnificent churches sheltered under their domes a formerly barbarous people, and the virtues of the Gospel took root in new and distant lands. Jesus Christ tripled his kingdom on earth.[27]

The Christian faith, on this view, was the great legacy bequeathed by Spain to Latin America. Spain may have failed in everything else, but it succeeded in this. Success justified Spain before history and before God.

The spiritual endeavours of the Spanish clergy have often, with some justice, been viewed as the crowning glory of the imperial enterprise. Although other aspects of the colonial regime may have failed, it is claimed, the spiritual conquest succeeded and the Catholic identity was Spain's greatest colonial legacy. Bartolomé de las Casas had proclaimed that the principal purpose of the empire was not oppression but conversion. The missionary effort was certainly a very extensive one, which is thoroughly documented by those who took part in it. On all parts of the frontier, in old Granada, in Manila, in New Mexico, in the Andes, the old ways of life were substantially affected. Most of the clergy were professional optimists, always concerned to inflate the numbers of natives brought into the Christian fold, and always reporting on their own activities in the most glowing terms. Theirs is often the only evidence available; but it has to be handled with caution, because there is also substantial evidence of a massive failure. As I was writing these words (in January 2006), high up in the Andes an Aymara Indian was going through a ceremony in advance of his official investiture as the new president of Bolivia. During the day of 21 January 2006, at the site of the ancient pre-Christian shrine of Tiwanaku, he received homage from his people and accepted powers from the chieftains (*kurakas*) of the region. Not a Christian priest was in sight: they were present only at the subsequent official investiture. The scenario was such as to appal any Catholic missionary. Five hundred years after Columbus, the indigenous population in many areas of Central and South America is still actively engaged in its native religious traditions.

The myth of success, in other words, is open to serious doubts, although the value and valour of the religious enterprise cannot be questioned. The Franciscan missionary Bernardino de Sahagún commented from Mexico, in the sixteenth century, that 'as far as the Catholic faith is concerned, [America] is sterile ground and difficult to cultivate. It seems to me that the Catholic faith will persevere but little in these parts.'[28] It is possible that the Catholic faith survived with greater force than Sahagún perceived. Where it did so, however, the people chose what they wished and rejected the rest; hardly the result that the missionaries had hoped for. It will perhaps always be difficult to arrive at a balanced assessment of whether Spain succeeded in the religious aspect of its imperial venture. Nearly a century after the establishment of the Spaniards in Central America, the English Dominican Thomas Gage said of the Indians in his parish in Guatemala: 'as for their religion, they are outwardly like the Spaniards, but inwardly they are slow to believe that which is above sense, nature and the visible sight of the eye. Many of them, to this day, incline to worship idols of stocks and stones and are given to much superstition.'[29] The harsh campaigns against 'idolatry' among Andean Indians in the seventeenth century drew to an end in the 1660s and may have had some effect, but it was for the most part superficial. Although the clergy often used exaggerated language in their evaluations, there is little reason to reject the verdict of a priest in Peru in 1677 that 'the idolatry of the Indians is more solidly rooted today than it was at the beginning of the conversion of these realms'. In Peru, the programme of 'extirpation of idolatry' had to be renewed in 1725, and continued till the end of the eighteenth century. The struggle against the *huacas* (sacred symbols of the Andean Indians) was always an uphill one, doomed to frustration. A bemused Peruvian native of the eighteenth century asked a Jesuit: 'Father, are you tired of taking our idols from us? Take away that mountain if you can, since that is the God I worship!'[30]

The animistic beliefs and traditional rites were the central core of an indigenous identity, and persisted in one form or another all the way through the colonial epoch, even though modified. Natives who accepted Christianity did so at the same time as they continued with their old cultural practices. Those who refused to accept changes maintained a permanent, armed hostility. In 1700, in the peninsula of Darien, the Cuna people attempted to ally themselves with the Scots against the Spaniards. One of their chiefs was captured by the Spaniards and refused to reveal the location of a gold mine even when his captors cut off both his hands. He said: 'God sent devils down upon the earth like a fierce downpour of rain. Thanks to these demons you came to my country and your people occupied my land and ousted me from it.'[31] The Cuna people continued to attack the Spanish missions during the eighteenth century.

Two priests, both foreigners in the Spanish mission field, offer interesting though conflicting testimony to the impact of the new religion after a century and a half of Spanish rule. The early hero of the missionary effort in north-western New Spain was the Tyrolean Jesuit Eusebio Kino.[32] Born Eusebius Kühn near Trent in north-east Italy, he was educated at Ingolstadt, joined the Jesuit order in Bavaria, went to Mexico in 1681 and in 1683 became the first European to reach the Pacific by an overland route. He worked for a quarter of a century in Sonora, then in Arizona among the Pima people, and prepared the way for later missionary advances into lower California. His indefatigable travels and his revolutionary work as a geographer and explorer of the Colorado valley distinguish him as one of the great pioneers of the Spanish empire. In 1696, after ten years of labour, he remained wholly optimistic and could still write that he was 'received with all love by the many inhabitants'. On the other hand his contemporary, the Jesuit Josef Neumann, a Belgian of German origin who served for an incredible fifty years, from 1681 to 1732, in the Tarahumara country of the same Northwest, had a bleaker perspective. He wrote at the end of his career:[33]

With these people the result does not repay the hard labour. The seed of the gospel does not sprout. We find little eagerness among our new converts. Some only pretend to believe, showing no inclination for spiritual things such as prayers, divine services and Christian doctrine. They show no aversion to sin, no anxiety about their eternal happiness. They show rather a lazy indifference to everything good, unlimited sensual desire, an irresistible habit of getting drunk, and stubborn silence in regard to hidden paganism. And so we cannot bring them into the fold of Christ.

At almost exactly the same date, in 1730, a Capuchin missionary reported of the Guajiro tribes of New Granada: 'It is impossible to bring forth any fruit among these Indians; they have not given rise to even the slightest hope in all the time that work has been dedicated to their conversion.'[34] This view was expressed in a way that laid emphasis on the refusal of the natives to accept the Catholic religion. A quite different perspective, in that it laid the blame on the clergy, was expressed by the officials Juan and Ulloa shortly afterwards, in the 1740s, when they explained that the parish priests in Peru were guilty of 'total neglect and failure' to convert the Indians in their charge. 'Although the Indians have been Christianised', they wrote, 'their religious training has been so poor that it would be difficult to discern a difference in them from the time they were conquered to the present day.'[35] On balance, the testimony of the pessimists appears to be more convincing than that of the optimists.

Anticlericalism and a Christian people

The Catholic myth was born in the mid-nineteenth century in part because of the phenomenon of anticlericalism, which should not have happened because it could not have happened. How could an intensely Catholic Spain suddenly start assassinating its own clergy? Was anticlericalism the culprit? And where did it come from? Historians studying the French Revolution have faced the same problem, of explaining how a country apparently Catholic could suddenly turn against its Church and clergy. They suggested that, at some unknown moment in the preceding century, a thoroughly Catholic France had been somehow 'de-Christianized'. It was a promising thesis but it ultimately failed to convince, because historians perceived that there were weaknesses in the nature of the alleged Christianity of the people.[36] The same issue clearly arose in the case of Spain. Aware that there existed, among apparently Christian Spaniards, a very clear reaction against the beliefs and norms of the Church, some Catholic clergy in the nineteenth century – like Balmes – wrote original and valuable analyses of the situation. The present essay does not attempt to plunge into the question of how the Church in that period attempted to deal with evident religious problems. It is concerned more narrowly with the constant reiteration of the theme that the ideas and perceived triumphs of the sixteenth century should be seen by Catholics as the pole star of their aspirations.

The use of the concept of 'anticlericalism' has clouded the issue to some extent. By centring attention on the matter of attacks 'against the clergy', it has encouraged us to look for reasons – material, social, personal – as to why anyone should wish to do harm to the personnel of the Church. Scholars have produced many excellent studies of the question, all with legitimate explanations. Popular anticlericalism had existed since medieval times because the clergy made fiscal and moral demands on believers. Hostility to the clergy, both priests and nuns, took so many different forms that it is still impossible to reduce the matter to dimensions that are easy to understand. 'The poor', stated a man in Granada in the 1620s, 'pay tithes to the clergy so they can get fat and rich.' Another stated that 'there should be no more than four priests in the world, and even these should be hanged'.[37] There was, in addition, a politically motivated type of anticlericalism, fomented by those whose political views differed from those of the clergy. The Liberals in the early 1800s, and the Krausists half a century later, were vigorously opposed to the privileges and functions of the Church. Around 1900, it has been pointed out, 'bit by bit anticlericalism changed from being a formula of opposition to the social, moral, aesthetic and political universe of the Church, and became a specific principle of Republican Liberalism'.[38] Liberal and Republican politicians, as well as writers who supported them, encouraged attacks on the property and personnel of the Church. The progressive viewpoint was expressed in the following way by the left-wing newspaper *El Socialista* in 1899, just a year after the Disaster of 1898:

> The Church is responsible for Spain being a country incapable of adjusting to modern life. The Church is more responsible than any other institution or person for the disastrous state of affairs that we have endured for centuries, staggering along towards ruin and the most appalling collapse. Thanks to the Church we are hated throughout the world, thanks to it we do not have adequate intellectual conditions or the energy for recovery.[39]

Affirmations such as these were unmistakeable evidence of the existence of ideological groups bitterly opposed to the Church, its beliefs and its privileges. As a result, it was possible to maintain that such groups were the ones responsible for anti-religious excesses and that, despite them, Spain continued to be, as it had presumably always been, a truly Christian nation.

The myth of a wholly Catholic people remained and remains, therefore, profoundly ingrained in the minds of many Spaniards. There were indignant reactions when prime minister Azaña made his celebrated declaration in 1931 that Spain was no longer Catholic, but the most that Catholics would recognize was what cardinal Vidal i Barraquer admitted in that period to the pope: 'we have to admit that a Catholic Spain, such as we have conceived of it till now, does not accord with the true reality of the state of society'. The situation was widely known among the higher clergy, but they continued to cling to the idea that Spaniards were still Catholic at heart, and that the de-Christianization was the fault of corrupting foreign influences, 'anti-Christian principles and ideas brought in from outside', as one bishop put it in 1946.[40] Those alleged ideas, alien to the authentic Catholicism of the Spanish people, were variously listed as liberalism, materialism, scepticism, democracy, socialism, communism, freemasonry and a further unending list of corruptions brought in by the nineteenth and twentieth centuries. The drive against foreign viruses was justified in the light of history, for Spain had spent its energy fighting against corruptions such as 'the Erasmians, the Jews and the pro-French adepts of the Encyclopédie, who have cast their shadow over the history of Spain' (1933).[41] The very force and strength of the secularist and anticlerical movements in the 1930s and during the Civil War had the curious consequence of convincing a section of Catholics that Spain was truly Catholic, perhaps more Catholic than ever before. This surprising conclusion was asserted through the perspective of an idea that was already in circulation, but began then to take on greater force and is today well implanted in the polemics of public controversy: the idea of Two Spains. Their side alone represented the true Spain; the other side was not Spain, it was in effect an anti-Spain. That other Spain, proclaimed one of the intellectual luminaries of the Franco regime, the writer José María Pemán, 'was not authentic Spain, it was an invading army that occupied the institutions of our official life'. He called, therefore, for a new drive against this foreign intrusion, 'another War of Independence, another Reconquest, another Expulsion of Moriscos'.[42]

These sentiments bore fruit in the complete and official adoption of the myths so brilliantly laid out by Menéndez Pelayo. School and university syllabuses under the Franco dictatorship were altered in order to reveal once again the Catholic reality of the past. The official research body, the Higher Council for Scientific Research (CSIC), promised to bring about 'a restoration of the classical Christian unity of learning, which was destroyed in the eighteenth century'.[43] A crucifix was hung in every classroom. Eager young adepts of the official ideology dreamed of entering an adventure 'in a Spain just as it was when the Catholic Monarchs began to reign'.[44] The Catholic Church recovered its lost property and privileges, assumed a leading role in all social activities, and, to the amazement of the outside world, presented a nation that was 100 per cent Catholic, just a few years after the president of the Republic had declared that Spain was not Catholic. A spokesman for the regime, the writer Rafael Calvo Serer, announced (in 1953) that 'in Spain we are all Catholic'.[45] The leading institutions in Spain's society, and with them of course the Church itself, thus immersed themselves completely in a dream world which they had brought into being as a reaction against the persecution suffered by believers under the Popular Front government of the Second Republic. Recent Catholic commentators appear to accept the view that the massive participation of Spaniards in street religion in the 1950s (processions, pilgrimages, rosaries) was proof that the people had been won back to the faith.[46]

Looking back today at that situation, it is difficult to believe that this ever happened. For roughly forty years after the Civil War, the Spanish state took as its political ideal an imaginary fifteenth-century regime and gave official status to the religion practised by that regime. Spain became, on the outside at least, more Catholic than it had ever been in all its history. The older generation of present-day Spaniards grew up within the cultural context of those years, and many people inevitably continue to accept the religious principles of that time. The myth of a Catholic Spain consequently continues to exist too, albeit among a much reduced public. Indeed, the story of the splendour of sixteenth-century Catholicism is persistently repeated, not simply to invoke reasons for national pride, but also to sharpen yet further the contrast with the real state of religion in twenty-first-century Spain. The tourist industry, a fundamental component of the economy, has worked wonders in giving new life to cathedrals and monasteries, in stimulating celebrations of Holy Week and other traditional festivities, in commemorating the great religious figures of the past and the way they had made Spain a wellspring of faith. Yet that imagined glory of the past has to be set against the disappointment of the present. Only just over forty years ago, as I recall from my first visits when I was preparing my doctoral thesis at Oxford, it was impossible to get into church for mass if you did not arrive early. People jostled for places, and many simply waited outside. Today, those same churches are empty. 'The onetime spiritual powerhouse of the West, which supplied clergy to half the world and evangelized America and much of Africa, is now without resources', runs a news item in a prominent Madrid daily of March 2006. 'The Spanish Church has no priests. It lives only on the merits of the past. The facts speak for themselves. Spain still has 18,000 diocesan priests. But, for every two who die, only one is ordained. There is no assurance of filling the generational gap. The average age of the diocesan clergy is sixty-seven years, and 40 per cent are over seventy-five. In ten years, only half the parish priests will be left.' Religious orders import novices from Chile and India. In the village where I live in Catalonia, there has been no resident parish priest for four years. There is dust on the altars.

CHAPTER FOUR

THE MYTH OF
AN EMPIRE

Since God created the world, there has been no empire in it as extensive as that of Spain.

Francisco Ugarte de Hermosa (1655)

The empire as a tale for children

The Spanish empire has never ceased to inspire admiration. At its height, at the end of the sixteenth century, it incorporated within Europe the entire peninsula of Spain and Portugal, forts in North Africa, the territories of Belgium and the Netherlands, Sardinia, Sicily, and one third of the territory of Italy. Across the Atlantic it controlled a great part of the 'New World', from California and Florida to the southern tip of South America, and in the Pacific it held the Philippines and various other islands. When the ruler of the empire was Charles V, it was allied with Austria and the Holy Roman empire and dictated the destinies of Europe. Under its ruler Philip II, it was allied for a while to England. It was beyond any doubt the largest empire ever known in human history to that date.

But was it really an 'empire'? As many historians have repeatedly insisted, 'there never was a Spanish Empire'.[1] All the territories under Spanish control were 'a confederation of principalities held together in the person of a single king'. Apart from recognizing the ruler of Spain as their king, they shared no common laws or administration, they were (with the exception of the 'colonies') completely autonomous, and they did not construct any system of beliefs ('ideology') about empire. The French historian Pierre Chaunu, who in 1970 referred to the empire as a multiple monarchy or 'dynastic Grand

Alliance of the seventeen crowns', was perhaps the first to emphasize the unusual nature of an empire bound together only by dynastic right. British historians have recently recognized that this system of 'multiple kingdoms' could also be identified in other parts of Europe, such as the British Isles.[2] Some Spanish scholars use the term 'Catholic monarchy', which in practice they apply to the countries of the Mediterranean rather than to the totality of the Spanish territories in Europe. A recent study, which aims to underline the successes of Spanish power rather than its weaknesses and failures, opts for the term a 'monarchy of nations'.[3] The different phrases are merely the beginning of an attempt to understand the nature of Spain's power. However, for practical purposes, the link binding the states together has made the word 'empire' easier to use, and it has remained in the Castilian vocabulary, because it referred, and still does, to a real consciousness of power.

Because there was no formal empire, there could be very little theory about it, and the many Spaniards who were interested in political theory tended to debate two main issues: either the functions and powers of the king, or the place of the different communities (the status of provinces, for example, or simply the rights of peoples such as the Indians of America). One of the amazing – and even admirable – aspects of the Spanish imperial system was that its theorists spent most of their time arguing against the empire and in favour of the rights of the peoples who lived in it. In 1539, the Salamanca professor Francisco de Vitoria set out, in a lecture, the argument that peoples who are conquered (the reference was to America) do not necessarily lose their natural rights. His theories were followed by Spanish clergymen in the subsequent century, and were even taken up by foreigners. 'There is a strong sense', we are reminded, 'in which the members of the school of Salamanca and their heirs were anti-imperialist.'[4] This tendency to define and limit the authority of Spaniards in other lands was also pursued from a slightly different direction by Bartolomé de Las Casas, and effectively impeded the growth of any formal imperial theory. Las Casas is a bit of an exception to the statement that writers opposed the empire, because he in effect favoured greater centralized control (in other words, he was more of an imperialist than at first appears) for the sake of greater power over the colonists in America. His words were: 'The rulers of Castile and León are universal lords, and emperors ruling over many kings' – the 'kings' being a specific reference to the native rulers of America.

Normally, Spanish writers were not imperialist. It is significant that in the sixteenth century, when one of Philip II's advisers, Fadrique Furió Ceriol, examined the problem of policy in the Netherlands, he also expended some effort in defining and limiting Spain's authority. Spaniards – especially the soldiers among them – were proud of the world role they enjoyed, and expressed themselves in an aggressive way, but they seldom used the word 'empire' to refer to the entity they served. Indeed, some spent a great deal of time arguing that the notion of empire was 'a children's story',[5] a fantasy. Such arguments were, of course, really directed against other nations, such as the Germans and French, who might have had dreams of world power that the Spaniards did not want them to have. But they also demonstrate that, normally, neither Spain's monarchy nor its theorists were apologists of the empire. Indeed, the only writer of those times to come out firmly in favour of an 'empire' – and, even then, he meant empire in a moral rather than a military sense – was a seventeenth-century Italian, the friar Campanella.[6]

Although Spain did not, in the strict sense, have an 'empire' and few Spanish writers contributed to imperialist theory, both the word and the reality gradually took shape in the minds of Spaniards and became a recurrent myth that lodged itself yet more firmly in the imagination every time Spain faced a serious crisis. There were always writers who, inspired by premature enthusiasm (like the clergy who presented Nebrija's *Grammar* to Queen Isabella in 1492), saw an empire round the corner. In that same year, 1492, a poet dedicated to the queen a poem on her name, in which, he said, 'the *I* stands for *imperio*'. In most of those early contexts, the word meant what it did in Latin, authority or power, rather than what we now understand by it, namely a chain of conquered territories. From that point on, the references to empire become frequent. Empire gave to Spain a ranking among nations that it had not had previously. The undisguised pride was, of course, also mingled with fear that the other nations were simply exploiting a hitherto poor country. The royal official Luis Ortiz, remembered as one of the first intelligent *arbitristas* of the sixteenth century, expressed the fear in a (hitherto unpublished) letter of 1558 to Philip II: 'Your Majesty knows better than anybody that Spain is the source of money for the world, because of that which comes here from America', but this silver should not be allowed to leave the country; in this way, the many ills of Spain would be remedied, 'and Your Majesty will be the reason for the Spanish nation ceasing to be considered backward (*bárbaro*)'.[7]

At the very end of the reign of Philip II, a magistrate, Gregorio López Madera, was among the few who still clung to the idea that there had been no empire of conquest. 'All past empires have come into existence through violence and force of arms', he wrote, 'only that of Spain has had just beginnings, since it came together mostly through dynastic succession.'[8] It was a valid argument, though some at the time might have felt that, as in the case of Portugal, it was really force rather than succession that had the last word. Others had a different perspective, and were not concerned to make an excuse for Spanish power. López Madera's contemporary Pedro Salazar de Mendoza argued that the word 'monarchy' was no longer appropriate, because 'the empire of Spain is twenty times greater than that of the Romans'; and Juan de Salazar in 1619 (in his *Spanish Policy*) turned the argument round to say:

It is right to give the name of empire [*monarquía*] to the dominion and mastery that Spain now has over so many kingdoms, such diverse provinces and such extensive and rich states and lordships. Not only because the Catholic King is the only and sovereign prince not subject to or dependent on any other, but also because it is now the commonly accepted use, monarch meaning the greatest of kings, and monarchy the almost total empire and lordship of the world.

Forty years later, when Spain's supremacy was visibly on the wane, another writer, Francisco Ugarte de Hermosa, insisted on still seeing his country as a universal imperial power:

Since God created the world, there has been no empire in it as extensive as that of Spain; for, from the rising of the sun to its rising again, it illuminates the lands of this great monarchy and, throughout its course, not for one second do the lands of the monarch fail to receive its light.

In the course of time, the number grew of those who felt that Spain had an inalienable destiny to rule. As often happens, the notion of empire communicated the comfort of power at a time when power was slipping away, and it renewed confidence in the future of the nation. But, just as there had been no clearly enunciated Imperial Ideas in the early sixteenth century, so in the seventeenth there was an uncanny reticence. A distinguished diplomat of the mid-seventeenth century, Diego Saavedra y Fajardo (*d.*1648), even expressed doubts about whether the imperial enterprise had been worthwhile. He drew on his direct experience of European affairs to comment: 'it has cost a great deal to wage war in inhospitable and remote provinces, at the price of so much life and money, and with such great benefit to the enemy and so little to us that it may be asked whether we would not be better off conquered than conquering'. Faced, after 1635, with the onset of war against France, he set down in his *Political Enterprises* the striking opinions that 'I cannot persuade myself to suspect that the whole world should be Spanish'; and that war itself was 'a violence contrary to reason, to nature and to man's end'. Spain should, he thought, remain at peace with other nations, withdraw from Flanders and America, remain a strong Catholic state rooted in the Mediterranean (Saavedra's model king was Ferdinand the Catholic) and devote its genius to the arts.

The invention of Spain as an empire

A definite Imperial Idea took a long time to develop. It took on its firmest shape in the nineteenth century, when, in the absence of historical research, it was possible to read the facts of the distant past in a way that would support the political needs of the present. Imperial myths consequently came into existence, for example, in Turkey, Russia and Japan. And also in Spain. We can follow the evolution of the myth through the writings of the conservative element in Spanish politics.

At the beginning of the nineteenth century, the Liberals, who were opponents of absolutism and the Inquisition, also favoured a re-thinking of the colonial enterprise and declared themselves opponents of imperialism. However, their views were upstaged by those of the conservatives, who denounced the tragic state of the country under the Liberals and looked back with longing to that forgotten age, identified in their eyes with Ferdinand and Isabella, Charles V and Philip II, when Spain had conquered half the world. The crucial moment, for all shades of opinion, came in 1898 with the final loss of empire. Spain's political class looked round in desperation for some comfort in the midst of deprivation. Had the glory of the empire really perished? Did that not reduce Spain's role in the world to dust and ashes?

The intellectual elite was not slow to respond.[9] They elaborated a theory of empire that could meet the needs of a political class now bereft of ideas. In Catalonia there were thinkers who formulated a concept of 'empire' which fell in with the needs of a nascent nationalist movement.[10] In Castile, where nationalism also developed, the aim was to search back into the past for an explanation of the present. José Ortega y Gasset, for example, invented a notion of empire, seeing it as the necessary expression of Castile's identity. His words speak for themselves:[11]

'One Spain' was born in the mind of Castile, not as an idea of something real but as an ideal project of something possible. When the traditional policies of Castile managed to win over, to their own ends, the lucid and penetrating spirit of Ferdinand the Catholic, everything became possible. Spanish unity was achieved, but to what purpose? To live together, sitting round the home fire, looking at each other, like old women in winter? Quite the contrary. The union was achieved in order to hurl the energy of Spain to the four winds, to flood the planet, to create an even vaster empire. The unity of Spain was brought about for this and because of this. For the first time in history, a Weltpolitik was conceived. Spain's unity was created in order to attempt that.

But vague, fanciful ideas like these were not enough to create an effective myth. That could only be produced by professional scholars who offered a view of the past that would back up the politicians, soldiers and essayists. One of the most potent writings was a 1937 essay by a medievalist and leading philologist, Ramón Menéndez Pidal, on 'the Imperial Idea of Charles V'. Up until then, Spanish scholars had paid little attention to the career of Charles, who had been written off in Liberal history books (see Chapter 2) as the instigator of Spain's ruin. Now Pidal suddenly found a new role for the benighted Charles.

Born in La Coruña (Galicia), Menéndez Pidal (1869–1968) came from a prominent Asturian family. His parents moved in 1884 to Madrid, where he eventually completed a doctorate on medieval ballads and in 1899 secured the chair of philology at the university. His career thereafter was that of a wholly dedicated academic. In 1909 he gave lectures at Johns Hopkins and Columbia, and during the following year was instrumental in founding the Centre of Historical Studies in Madrid. His lasting claim to fame was to encourage the history of language as a scientific subject in Spain. He published a historical grammar of Spanish in 1904, and in 1914 established the *Revista de Filología Española*. In 1929 he brought out the book for which he became best known, *The Spain of the Cid* (it came out in English in 1934). Menéndez Pidal's brilliant scholarship in the fields of philology, literature and history laid the foundations for a conservative and Castilianist version of Spain's culture.

His contribution to the myth of empire was fundamental. Spain's loss of world status in 1898 changed matters drastically, as we have seen from the words of Ortega y Gasset. Somehow, intellectuals felt, their nation had been left out of the reckoning when people spoke of empire. After all, there had been no empire as great as that of Spain. The sharpest blow came when a German historian Peter Rassow published in 1932 a study on the Imperial Idea of Charles V.[12] Surely, Spaniards felt, Spain also played a part in that idea? In the following year, the German historian Karl Brandi published an article lending support to the view that Charles had relied on the theories of his chancellor, the Savoyard Mercurino Gattinara. The view was enshrined in his masterly biography of the emperor – still felt by many to be the best study on the subject[13] – published in 1937. That removed the Spaniards yet further from the possession of an imperial tradition. But they could not call into question the views of the Germans, because no Spanish scholar had ever studied Charles V (studies in Spanish, limited mainly to the peninsular context, all date from the 1960s).

At the time of the publication of Brandi's book, Menéndez Pidal was in exile from Spain, a refugee from the breakdown of the Second Republic. In 1937 he was in Cuba, where he was asked to give a lecture on Hispanic history. The lecture, published in a journal in Havana that year, was called 'The Imperial Idea of Charles V'.[14] Pidal argued that Gattinara played no part in the thinking of Charles, who had his own, very firm ideas on the matter. He never expressed them personally but ordered one of his spokesmen, the bishop of Badajoz, Pedro Ruiz de la Mota, to articulate them at a meeting of the Cortes of Castile in La Coruña in 1520. Mota's words were clear: 'this realm is the foundation, the support and the strength of all the others'.[15] 'This realm' referred to Castile and 'others' to the rest of Spain, but Pidal preferred to read 'this realm' as Spain, and 'others' as the future German realms of Charles. This reading, according to Pidal, was confirmed by subsequent phrases of Mota: 'the garden of his pleasures, the fortress of defence, the strength for attack, his treasure, his sword, must be Spain'. On the basis of these phrases[16] and of a few passages in two works written by two Castilians six years later,[17] Pidal felt that the twenty-year-old emperor (who, incidentally, did not even speak Spanish at that period) had absorbed Spanish ideas, become a Spaniard and was determined to convert his territories into a Spanish empire.

He thought up his empire by himself, using ideas inherited from Isabella the Catholic. Charles V became Spanish, and from that moment he sought to Hispanize Europe. I say 'Hispanize' because he wished to carry over into Europe the role of a crusading people that Spain had clung to faithfully for eight centuries, and which it had completed a few years before, through the war of Granada – whereas Europe, after a total failure centuries before, had forgotten the idea of a crusade.

In writing these words, he seems to have forgotten that in Austria, in the Czech lands and in Poland the princes did not need Spanish ideas because they were already actively trying to defend the Catholic states against the advancing Muslim Turks. Pursuing his vision of a Europe that had lost its religious vitality in contrast to Spain, Menéndez Pidal went on to maintain that the sack of the papal city of Rome by the emperor's troops in 1527 (Pidal dated the event to 1528) had taken place because of 'Spanish indignation at the conduct of the pope, who would not support the aspirations of Charles and of Spain in favour of European Catholicism'. Thus, by dint of an enthusiastic and erratic reading of the evidence, he managed to fit Spain neatly into the mainstream of imperial discourse. Even more, he saw the emperor as a personification of the great mythical idol of the 1898 generation, Don Quixote (see Chapter 6). Nearly three centuries after Cervantes, Menéndez Pidal followed the other intellectuals of his generation not only in restoring Quixote centre-stage but in actually making him the symbol of Spain as an empire:

> This stubborn sentiment of a crusade against infidels and heretics is what inspired the high Quixotism of Charles' policy, a Hispanic Quixotism that had not yet taken on the lineaments of eternity through the pen of Cervantes. The sentiment was Hispanic, and exclusively Hispanic, for it proposed that the principal duty of the emperor was, both personally and through his generals, to make war on infidels and heretics, to sustain the *universitas Christiana*, a medieval idea that was now revived and given life by Spain, with the desire to achieve the unity of Europe at a time when all Europe was breaking up and falling apart.

Pidal's exposition had little demonstrable basis and was conjured up in the lonely days of his exile in Cuba, when inspiration rather than evidence gave support to his ideas. That, however, was surely the purpose he intended: to invent an idea that would give back to Spain an honour it merited after the defeat of 1898. But it did far more than that. For the first time, it placed a ruler of Spain (it did not matter that Charles was not Spanish but a Netherlander) at the centre of the European picture, and argued that a concrete Spanish ideology was at the centre of his programme. Menéndez Pidal's efforts at creating a new Charles, who would be both imperialist and European, were replicated by subsequent Spanish writers. Pidal, let us note, was still careful to emphasize that Charles' Imperial Idea was not really Charles'; rather, it was borrowed from a Spaniard who preceded him as ruler: 'Charles was not the initiator of this new flowering and maturity, that was Isabella the Catholic.' The end result redounded to the glory of Spain: 'Charles V, by Hispanizing his empire, spread Spanishness throughout all Europe.'

The 'Hispanization' of Charles had interesting consequences, because, for Pidal, the European empire was now a mere projection of Spain's power, Charles' policies were essentially Spanish, and the victories of his armies were (we shall look at this below) Spanish victories. Suddenly, Pidal's thesis changed the entire vision of the past, and gave Spain an imperial ideology and drive that it had hitherto lacked. Many years before, Pidal had given medieval Spain dignity by resuscitating a legendary hero whose value few had appreciated: the Cid. To generations of teachers and pupils, but above all to politicians of the Franco dictatorship, the Cid offered a figure who made sense of a nation – medieval Spain – that, until then, had been seen as a mere composite of warring princes. In the same way, Menéndez Pidal's Charles V made it possible for subsequent Castilian writers and historians to place at centre-stage a nation that seemed to have been left out of the picture.

Pidal's achievement lay in being the first Spanish scholar to call attention to the crucial role of Spain in the emperor's policies. Subsequent historians, notably Ramón Carande and José Antonio Maravall, wrote definitive studies which underlined the importance of Spain's contribution to the work of Charles V,[18] although they gave no specific support to the 'Imperial Idea' outlined by Pidal. Since then, historians have argued through analysis of texts and of evidence such as public festive imagery that Spain and its outlook undeniably played a role in imperial ideology. One (non-Spanish) scholar points out that, by making use of classical and medieval imagery in the triumphal arches that cities erected for him at various stages of his career, 'Charles wished to emphasize the fact that he was the true heir and successor to his Spanish ancestors, Isabella of Castile and Ferdinand of Aragon, who had spearheaded the resolute and violent struggle against the infidels. Victory over the infidels was a motif greatly nurtured by imperial mythology.'[19] Spain has therefore with some justice come to be recognized as a factor in the evolution of the empire directed by Charles.

Where Pidal's exposition fell down, however, was in the claim that Spain had made a unique impact on the emperor's views. Pidal argued that the Spanish zeal for religion inspired Charles' policies, but it is clear, as non-Spanish scholars have pointed out, that 'Charles' idea of empire was rooted in the sacral aspects of the imperial office and in his role as the defender of the Christian commonwealth and preserver of tranquility and peace',[20] an attitude which drew on his experience of all the territories he governed, and not simply of Spain. His correspondence, laboriously catalogued by scholars, reveals the European, and not merely Spanish, scope of his political vision.[21] Pidal's claim that the struggle against the infidel was a uniquely Spanish programme which Charles adopted fails to take into account the fact that the biggest anti-infidel campaign of his reign actually took place in Germany, around the year 1532, when Charles supervised the defence of the city of Vienna against the besieging Turks.

During the Franco regime, the new role attributed to Spain under Charles V was greeted with acclaim and quickly found its way into textbooks and the writings of historians. 'Imperial Spain' was adopted as one of the myths favoured by the dictatorship. A reflection of it can be seen in a work, *The Empire of Spain* (*El Imperio de España*) (1941), by the respected philologist Antonio Tovar, who wrote appreciatively of the theories of Menéndez Pidal, and welcomed the opportunity for Spain to shed the 'profound inferiority complex' imposed on it by other European states at the Treaty of Westphalia. Tovar welcomed the possibility of the Spaniards becoming once again 'a people destined to command'.[22] They were lines written in a period when Spain 'commanded' nowhere, was in ruins after the Civil War, and the people queued up for food. The dream of once again 'commanding' did not go away when conditions improved. It is highly instructive to read history texts written in the 1960s, when an entire generation had absorbed the myth invented by Menéndez Pidal and accepted it as gospel. Unable to develop any adequate national or political ideology of its own, the dictatorship invested its money in propaganda, linking itself directly with the regime of the Catholic Monarchs and Charles V. The official cult of 'Spanishness' (*Hispanidad*), referred to below, had strong cultural features dedicated to promoting the Spanish language and historical links with the former colonies in America. But that cult was just a part of a general promotion of the historical empire and the reign of Ferdinand and Isabella. A recent comment on the part played by the 1951 Spanish film *The Dawn of America* (*Alba de América*) in this imperial propaganda about Spain in the New World, says:

> *Alba de América* reproduces the discourse of imperial Spain, recovering the providentialist, messianic and apocalyptic component of the Discovery and the Conquest. The interest of the State apparatus in this production was based on its potential for legitimization of the period during which it was conceived. The actual phenomenon of the Discovery is ultimately revealed as an excuse, useful only as a function of the ideological parallelisms that permit a connection to the political situation of Spain during the fifties. . . . What was indeed viable was the invention of an imperial myth aimed at internal consumption that would permit the creation of the deceptive self-perception that Spain was the 'chosen' nation, accepting the paradox that Spain was wealthy because Spain was poor. By means of films such as *Alba de América*, the spectators of a ruined country in which food stamps still existed could attend the spectacle of its own greatness. The global project of Hispanicity thus achieved great effectiveness in the internal politics of the country. In addition to promoting a conceited image of Spain, it allowed for a unification of the regime's political families. Falangists, Carlists, Catholics, and traditionalists could share the values and the projected hegemony that were inherent to this myth. Associated in addition with the ideology of National Catholicism and with the ideals of race, religion, nation, and empire, the myth ended up by converting itself into one of the legitimizing pillars of the dictatorship.[23]

That myth of 'Imperial Spain' did not vanish with the end of the Franco regime. On the contrary, it has continued to be alive in many sectors of the Spanish establishment, regardless of ideology of left or right.

The idea of an all-powerful Spain

Menéndez Pidal's arguments for a Spanish-orientated Imperial Idea reinforced the conviction that Spain was the centre of power. The principal component of the Spanish (or, more correctly, Castilian) myth was a belief in the sixteenth-century empire as an achievement of the nation's potency. For that achievement, it was necessary to place emphasis on the word 'conquest' until no other word seemed adequate to describe Spain's role in the world. The corollary was perhaps even more cogent. Spaniards had to be presented as uniquely capable of conquering, and the famous 'conquistadors' of America became historical idols. Understandable pride in Spain's leadership of the empire gave rise to the conviction that Spain alone had created it, through its own immense power and wealth. Ironically, that myth was given wholehearted support by English and American admirers of Hispanic civilization, who added substantially to it.[24] Non-Spanish scholars have, against all the available evidence, presented Spain as 'superior [in banking] to the north of Europe, first in Europe in war technology, the first modern state in Europe',[25] and, even more incredibly, as enjoying 'massive military capabilities and inexhaustible financial resources'.[26] A successful textbook of the 1960s presented a Spain that suddenly became dynamic, acquired energy and 'almost miraculously established' itself in America.[27] That miracle, so unequivocally asserted by those who were the experts in the study of Spain's past, has never ceased to give comfort to Spaniards. It is the basis of the myth (comparable in character to the now vanished British belief in empire) that still reigns supreme among many writers and politicians and in the popular mind. Spain was the great conqueror and the founder of worldwide Hispanic civilization.

Because the word empire usually involves an element of conquest, should we assume that Spain conquered its empire? Historians would, in general, say 'No'. Every textbook reminds us, quite correctly, that a combination of inheritances helped to join the territories of Castile and Aragon, and later brought in some Italian states and the Netherlands. Even the occupation of Portugal by Philip II in 1580 arose out of an inheritance claim. The dynastic basis of Spain's European empire is not therefore in doubt. Military force, it is true, often played a part in these developments, helping to acquire Naples, Navarre and eventually Portugal. In a real sense, however, these realms were never 'conquered', since they always retained their own institutions and autonomy, and never had occupying forces. At this point, removing the word 'conquer' from our vocabulary can irritate Spanish feelings. Allegations that the empire was not aggressive (an attitude we can date back to the mid-nineteenth century, when North Africa came to be considered, both by France and Spain and later by Fascist Italy, as territory ripe for occupation) will be seen by many as detracting from dignity. The very idea of a non-belligerent Spain made it – ironically – necessary to manufacture a myth of a belligerent Spain, the most powerful nation on earth.

The raw material for the myth was not promising. Early modern Spain was one of the poorest countries in Europe. In the peninsula it was not a united nation but a combination of separate states, it was so poor that it imported most of its food, it had no army and little naval experience, it did not even produce its own weapons, and its chief trading enterprises were mostly financed by foreigners, usually Italians. However, at the dawn of the sixteenth century it was catapulted into two momentous experiences: a projection into Europe through the succession of its king, Charles, to the imperial title; and a projection into the overseas world through the achievements of Cortés and Pizarro in Mexico and Peru. Spain suddenly attracted world attention. The American achievements, in particular, seemed so extraordinary that a legend was quickly created about the power of Spain. Spanish troops began to be seen on Europe's battlefields, for example in 1547 at Mühlberg, when Charles defeated the troops of the German Protestants. Very soon, the gold and silver of America, above all the silver that came from the mines at Potosí in Bolivia, began to finance the enterprises of the Spaniards and contributed to Spain's reputation.

Spain's undoubted successes in their turn helped to nurture an image of empire that attracted both admiration and hyperbole.[28] The image found its way easily into the schoolroom. A standard English textbook, published in the 1960s and widely used thereafter in Spain, recounted how 'the overthrow of the empires of the Aztecs and the Incas was achieved by no more than a handful of men. Cortés destroyed the empire of Montezuma with 600 soldiers and 16 horses.'[29] A current semi-official Spanish webpage follows the same approach (in the year 2006) when it explains:

> The great conquest of America, a continent eighty times bigger than Spain, was achieved in less than thirty years by a few thousand men from the peninsula, who traversed the continent in search of its centres of wealth in order to establish colonial settlements. They overcame the nerve-centres of the power and culture of pre-Columbian America, and conquered them militarily thanks to their armament and techniques of combat.[30]

These views were not exclusive to the twentieth century but were to be found already in the sixteenth. Castilians in the generation after the discovery of America were foremost in emphasizing their own successes. An enduring legend of the early Atlantic empire was created about the superhuman capacity of the conquerors. An early chronicler and witness of the great events in Peru, Cieza de León, commented: 'who can tell of the unheard-of exploits of so small a number of Spaniards in so vast a land?'[31] 'Hernando Cortés with less than a thousand soldiers conquered the great empire of New Spain', wrote a veteran of the American frontier, Vargas Machuca, 'Quesada with 160 soldiers conquered the Kingdom of New Granada.'[32] An official historian, Francisco López de Gómara, continued with the same extravagant story, written for the eyes of the emperor: 'Never has a king or people ventured so far or conquered so much . . . as our people have done, nor have any others achieved . . . what we have done in feats of arms, in navigations, in the preaching of the holy gospel.'

Confidence in the irresistible power of the Spaniards was boosted by chroniclers of the time and is still profoundly believed in. The empire continues to be the pride of nostalgic clergymen and of popular novelists, who find in it the theme and inspiration for re-creating in their pages a world of military glory that never existed.[33] A fictional image of the empire as an expression of Spain's capacity and might continues to militate in the minds of the public, which devours with enthusiasm novels about Spanish achievements in Flanders and in the Andes but remains indifferent to the real empire of the past. In the early nineteenth century, the exile Joseph Blanco White bore testimony to the way the myth controlled the popular perception of Spain's role in America:

> The hostility against me in the Cortes of Cádiz was due to my defence of the right of the Spanish colonies to equality with their mother country. Even as I write, when all hope of recovering the Hispanic American dominions has been lost, the spirit of the epoch of the conquest of Mexico and Peru still lives on, and in the very years that the colonies began to shake off their yoke the pride of conquest was as elevated in Spain as in the sixteenth century. Since that time [the sixteenth century], Spaniards had lived in the most profound ignorance of the course of human affairs in the rest of the world, and for that reason the prejudices they had inherited through the generations continued as strong as in the time of Cortés and Pizarro.[34]

In the later nineteenth century, when Spaniards first began to produce history textbooks, they limited their narrative to the epoch of blood and glory, with an emphasis principally on Cortés and Pizarro.[35] Nothing else was worth narrating, and they did not narrate it. Nineteenth-century Spanish critics of imperialism likewise concentrated their ire on the same persons and on the brutalities they were alleged to have committed. Politicians of Liberal persuasion advanced a vision of the all-powerful empire as an enemy of freedom because it suited their ideological premises. A professor of history and leading politician, Emilio Castelar, was following the same anti-imperialist line when he declared in the Cortes that 'there is nothing more frightful, more abominable, than that great Spanish empire, which extended like a shroud over the whole planet'.[36] Historians such as Lafuente gave due credit to the conquistadors for their heroism, but saw the empire as bringing about the ruin of Spain. Detailed study of aspects of the American empire did not form part of the research of Spanish scholars, and it was not until the mid-twentieth century, with the appearance of Francisco Morales Padrón and other historians based in Seville, that Spaniards began to look at their empire seriously. Meanwhile, in a supreme irony, the best studies on Cortés and Pizarro were written not by a Spaniard but by an American: precisely the Prescott who had pioneered peninsular history with his superb volume on the reign of Ferdinand and Isabella. His studies on the conquistadors were translated into Spanish and became standard works of reference for educated readers.

What was the Spanish empire?

There were undoubted military achievements in the creation of imperial power, but Castilians were not the only heroes nor could they have been so, for their lack of resources meant that they always needed outside help. The achievement of the fall of Granada, as explained by a Spanish historian, is a case in point.[37] Thousands of soldiers and volunteers came from other parts of the peninsula, and French, Swiss and English volunteers figured among the many foreigners. The naval forces which patrolled the sea and cut off any possibility of help from Africa consisted of Catalan and Italian vessels. The newly imported artillery was managed by Germans and Italians. Money to cover costs came not only from Castile but also from Aragon and from the pope, through Genoese bankers in Seville who handled the transactions. The fall of Granada in 1492 was a high point in Castile's military history, but it was also made possible through help from the rest of Spain and Western Europe.

Spain's military success, in short, was not achieved by Spaniards alone. As we have pointed out, the country did not have the manpower, the money, the armaments or the ships to embark on a career of conquest in Europe. The Spanish soldiers, of course, inevitably possessed and cultivated their military ethos in the same way that soldiers of other nations did. A Castilian poet in 1506 celebrated the deeds of his countrymen in Italy:

> Not only do we dominate
> The lands we have conquered,
> We also sail across
> Unnavigable seas.
> We are almost invincible !
> And even if as yet
> We do not control the whole world,
> The reason is not worth mentioning,
> For we have shown that we are able to do it ![38]

Despite this ethos and the participation of the famous *tercios* in numberless campaigns, conquest was not normally part of the Spanish soldier's job. After the Italian wars, Spanish soldiers participated in the unending Netherlands campaign, but were not used for conquest and annexation until Philip II's occupation of Portugal in 1580. The territories which the crown ruled in the sixteenth century came to it through inheritance rather than through invasion. Charles V in the 1540s gave the territory of Milan, extending over one half of northern Italy, to Spain. Belgium and the Netherlands were the dynastic property of the Habsburgs. So there was not much of an empire resulting from conquest in Europe, only (as we have already noted) a series of dynastic inheritances that Spain had to cling on to.

This has not impeded the growth of an image, which became current in the sixteenth century, of Charles V and Philip II bent on conquering the world. From the beginning of his reign Charles V insisted that his objective was peace, and historians have chosen to believe him.[39] In a very strange contrast, a few have chosen to believe the accusations made against Philip II. On the face of it, they may have good reason, for imperialism under Philip II was an undeniably potent force: Spanish troops under Philip II and his successors ended up fighting in Italy, in the Netherlands, in Greece, in Switzerland and the Rhineland, inside France and in central Europe. They attempted to invade England and Ireland. Spain was the only European power to maintain a continent-wide military presence. The issue in dispute, however, is not whether Spain had an imperial role (for it clearly had one), but whether Spain and, above all, Philip II had aggressive intentions. The image of Philip as expansionist was cultivated by his political enemies

(England, France) in the sixteenth century, and by Liberal historiography (powerfully influenced by French and Belgian scholars around the year 1830) in the nineteenth. The myth was a driving force behind the creation of English identity in the early modern period (it was, for example, a potent influence on Oliver Cromwell's conception of English patriotism[40]), and it influenced the emergence of Belgian and Dutch identity in the nineteenth century. The Dutch myth, in turn, found its way into the mainstream of Spanish historiography. Ironically, the myth remains the centrepiece of Castilian pride, because it sustains a macho image of Spain's power in the great age of empire, and any attempt to deny it is vigorously and angrily rejected.

As it happened, there were no macho men on the Spanish side during the reign of Philip II. Perhaps the most bellicose of his generals, the duke of Alba, was the very one who kept advising the king against foolish adventures.[41] Nor did the king ever give way, privately or publicly, to the sort of aggressiveness that political leaders habitually indulge in. If there were assertions that Spain was a warmonger, they formed part of the stock of accusations made by other nations, which (as Franz Bosbach shows clearly in his study on Universal Monarchy) tried to pin, on the king personally, accusations they were directing against the Spanish enterprise as a whole.[42] As happens with twenty-first-century American imperialism today, dissident nations accuse the imperial power of wishing to exercise world domination. In a well-documented study of 1998 (to which I have already referred), a distinguished scholar in the United States argued that Spain's mission of empire reached its apogee under Philip II. The king's policies, he suggested, were aimed actively at world domination. Since my own work on the king offered me completely different conclusions, this may be the place to comment on the issue. Philip II, says Geoffrey Parker, had an imperial 'Grand Strategy', and felt that God had given him a special ('millenarian') mission of conquest. Of the king's imperialist views in the year 1580, Parker holds that 'Philip and most of his courtiers saw the unification of the peninsula as a vital step on Spain's road to global mastery'.[43] On the religious aspect, Philip apparently asserted in the 1560s 'that religious principle should always prevail over political calculations', and basic to this assertion by the king 'lay a distinctive political philosophy which might be termed "messianic imperialism"'.[44] From that decade on, 'a unique aura of "messianic imperialism" came to pervade the court'.[45] The role of the king as Messiah was such, Parker argues, that Philip had a firm 'conception of his dual role as king and priest'. Both these tenets of imperialism and messianism were, according to him, always accompanied by 'a powerful propaganda exercise'.[46]

The plausibility of portraying Philip II as priest and Messiah depends on how one reads the documents. Philip II never showed any sympathy for theocratic or prophetic tendencies, as we know from his rejection of the prophetic persons who found favour with some of his courtiers.[47] It is relevant to emphasize that all national leaders with a deep personal faith, whether Oliver Cromwell or President George W. Bush, are likely to believe that they are tools in the hands of God and of Providence. Philip II was one such, though that did not make him a 'messianic imperialist'. Not a single word he ever said or wrote (in the hundreds of intimate and wholly frank letters that I and other historians have been able to examine) suggests that he saw himself as a Messiah, or that he had expansionist ambitions. Indeed, a recent summary by Parker of what is meant by 'messianic' reveals that he uses the word in a fairly innocuous sense. For him, it means simply that (like any believing Christian of that day or of ours) Philip felt that God would help him carry out the obligations of his role.[48] In this sense, many of us may feel that we, too, are 'messianic'.

More to the point is whether Philip II felt himself to be an aggressive imperialist. It is significant that not a single piece of manuscript evidence to show that the king sought 'global mastery' or a 'Universal Monarchy' has been produced by any historian – among them, Parker – since Bosbach published his study in 1988. Historians have sought diligently for plans or intentions of aggression, conquest and expansionism but found none. There were certainly Spanish writers who, as we have noted, claimed a universal role for the king of Spain. But without exception they were claiming a moral universality rather than political expansion. One of them was the Navarrese legist Miguel de Ulcurrun, who studied in Italy, became an official in Spain and in 1525 published his *Catholicum opus imperiale regiminis mundi*, in which he claimed a Catholic moral universality for the Emperor Charles V.[49] Another was Bartolomé de las Casas, whom we have already quoted. Some foreigners, especially in Germany, were aware of such claims and drew the conclusion that the rulers of Spain were aspiring to universal status.[50]

In the case of Philip, the issue is very simple: should he be judged by his words or by his deeds? His words do not supply an answer, since he made no imperialist utterances (Parker quotes none). From the beginning of his reign to its end, Philip's statements of pacific intent could fill a book. To demonstrate that the king was an aggressor, one needs to examine the evidence of his deeds. His troops were constantly at war in one part of Europe or another, making him easily appear as the most war-obsessed ruler of his time. But not a single Spanish expedition of the reign was bent on annexation or conquest (with one small exception, an expedition carried out in 1570 by the army of Milan, when, for strategic reasons, it occupied the port of Finale on the coast near Genoa). The botched Great Armada against England was never planned as an occupation exercise. The botched intervention in France, which went on for several years (and which Philip personally opposed until he saw no alternative), was an attempt to bring stability to a country torn apart by civil war and ripe to fall into the hands of Calvinism. There were, during this reign, no formal conquests in America (the king prohibited them in 1571). Spain, of course, periodically embarked on military expeditions (such as the famous campaign of Lepanto), but they were palpably aimed at security, not at global mastery. Even the most blatantly aggressive of his actions, the occupation of Portugal in 1580, was dynastic in purpose and was preceded by a careful propaganda campaign, in which he personally assured the Portuguese (who had in fact voted for him as king in their Cortes) that their autonomy would be guaranteed. Both during and after the occupation, he took pains to assure the Portuguese that it was not an invasion. The duke of Alba, who had to do the hard work, dissented vigorously from this position and insisted that the process of occupation was no mere tourist outing but a full-scale 'conquest'.[51]

Parker also suggests that the imperialistic attitude 'came to pervade the court'. Every bit of evidence demonstrates quite the opposite. From the 1570s Philip had already declared an end to further military expansion in the New World. A well-known private letter from a prominent Jesuit to the cardinal of Toledo in 1580 shows beyond doubt that there was deep suspicion at court as to where the Portuguese adventure might lead.[52] The Castilian nobility was never in favour of foreign adventures (and seldom served in them). Nor, indeed, was the chief minister, Cardinal Granvelle, a partisan of expansionism; he was convinced that the only military strategy should be directed against France. At court, there was strong criticism both of the occupation of Portugal and of Alba's part in it. If any ambitious publicists in Madrid or Lisbon wrote papers to the king encouraging imperialism, their words were neither read nor heeded by him. Indeed, what is most impressive about the atmosphere at Philip's two courts is the almost complete absence of military adventurism. There was aggressive pride, certainly, but no zeal for expansion. A recent scholar has reminded us that 'throughout much of the sixteenth and seventeenth centuries many of Spain's most powerful theorists were unhappy with the Castilian crown's claims to sovereignty even in those lands where it was de facto ruler, and nearly all vigorously denied that any prince could exercise universal sovereignty'.[53]

There were always chauvinists and expansionists in Spain, as in any country with a worldwide role. But universalism, or conquest, was a pipe dream, and the words of ambitious imperialists can be no guide to the policy and intentions of the king. The European territories under Spanish control were no adequate hunting ground for expansionism because they were autonomous states. The real 'empire', if we may call it such, was the overseas territory in America and the Pacific. And even there it is possible to call in question the idea of conquest. There were interminable armed operations. But a few hundred (as was the case with Cortés and Pizarro), or even a few thousand, Spaniards were unlikely to be able to defeat the civilizations of the vast continent of America. Thanks to painstaking research by scholars (mainly in the United States), we know that the famed conquistadors were not primarily soldiers. The group of men that seized the Inca emperor at Cajamarca in 1532 was made up of artisans, notaries, traders, seamen, gentry and peasants, a small cross-section of immigrants to America and in some measure a reflection of peninsular society itself. Similar groups were in action at other points in the New World. These few men, however, were incapable of making definitive conquests. Apart from the extraordinary events at Cajamarca, at every stage the newcomers relied on native help. The siege of Mexico city is the best known example. Eight months of planning, construction and recruiting were required before an attack became possible. When the attack was launched in May 1521, the situation had changed dramatically since Cortés' first landing on the coast, with four hundred men and the power of the entire Nahua people ranged against him. His band of Spaniards was now not much bigger, just over nine hundred men, thanks to recent arrivals. But he had on his side the majority of the cities that had been vassals and allies of the Mexica. The Indian historian of Texcoco, Alva Ixtlilxochitl, reported that just before the siege the ruler of Texcoco reviewed his men, and 'on the same day the Tlaxcalans, Huejotzingoans and Cholulans also reviewed their troops, each lord with his vassals, and in all there were more than three hundred thousand men'.[54] The Spaniards, whose weapons were of little use against the superiority of the enemy, would have achieved nothing without the help of the Indians.

That was the great secret of the Spanish empire.[55] At every stage it received the help of others. The Mexicans who helped Cortés were revolting against the tyranny of the Aztecs, and they continued to help the Spaniards to penetrate the other kingdoms of America. Every stage of the Spanish exploration of the New World was made possible by the aid of the native population, who in this way hoped to gain more power over their enemies, and also riches. It was the same in Europe, where the territories that made up the 'empire' willingly collaborated with the Spaniards in what became an authentic imperial adventure. There were profits to be made, and so Spain found many friends. Who paid for the ships that crossed the Atlantic to America? For the most part, Italian financiers. Who paid for the colonization of the Canary Islands? Again, Italian financiers. Spain emerged as the leader of a big multinational company, which functioned because it enjoyed the collaboration of everybody else.

We have seen that Spain did not normally have an army at its disposal (and there were no regular troops in America before the end of the eighteenth century). When the country had to go to war in Europe, it used American silver to recruit Italian and German troops in addition to its Castilian *tercios*, which were based in Italy. The Great Captain, the general who pioneered Spain's imperial hegemony in Italy, was Castilian, but could not have functioned without Italian troops and Italian money. Even the Swiss helped to support the Spanish empire, and Swiss troops fought in many Spanish armies. There was no religious problem, and both Protestant and Catholic troops served the Spaniards in fighting against the Dutch in the revolt of the Netherlands. Castilian soldiers were everywhere, but never constituted more than 20 per cent of the troops in a typical 'Spanish' army, and most of the commanders were usually foreigners. In the middle decades of the sixteenth century the Spaniards had few trained generals, so the nations of its empire helped. Spain's two greatest military commanders after the duke of Alba were Italians, Alessandro Farnese in the sixteenth century and Ambrogio Spinola in the seventeenth. Castilians were inevitably an essential component of all imperial enterprises, but the list of non-Spaniards who assisted at key points to maintain the empire is virtually endless: there were Portuguese naval pilots, German financiers and armament engineers, Italian bridge builders, Belgian technicians. Ambitious men in Europe who wished to earn a living served Spain. In the history textbooks used in Spain, all the achievement was (and still is) presented as uniquely Spanish. That promoted national pride, but it deprived non-Spanish colleagues of due recognition.

The warlike deeds of the Castilians came to be seen as superhuman and unique. Marcos de Isaba, who had served as a soldier throughout the Mediterranean, wrote proudly in the 1580s: 'I have seen with my own eyes what the valour of the Spanish nation has achieved, and the respect, fear and renown that Spaniards have gained both in the Old World and in the New in these last ninety years. The Germans and the Swiss have admitted that they are outclassed in strength and discipline.' The proof of such a claim, he said, could be found in the famous battle of Pavia (fought before Isaba was born), where 'it is both true and accepted that just eight hundred infantry, musketeers and pikemen, won the victory, shattering the fury of the French cavalry and the greater part of their army'.[56] This fantasy rewriting (and, inevitably, distortion) of history was extended to every major encounter in which Castilians participated. At the battle of Nördlingen in 1634 (see Chapter 9), where Spanish troops constituted one fifth of the imperial army, an account by a participating Castilian noble has the German troops after the victory cry out 'Viva España!' and 'Long live the valour of the Spaniards!', in recognition of the outstanding role of the peninsular troops. The same author, with pride, could not avoid the conclusion that 'all-powerful is the Monarchy of Spain, vast its Empire, and its glorious arms pulsate in splendour from the rising of the sun to its setting'.[57] The Germans, who had done most of the fighting at Nördlingen, no doubt had a different viewpoint.

Quite recently, historians have come to understand that empires do not function on the resources of only one nation. An enterprise has to be international if it is to succeed in obtaining the necessary expertise. The rule applies to the United States empire today, and it applied equally to the Spanish empire centuries ago. An example is the highly important slave trade, which helped to make the Spanish empire (and, later, the British and the French) function in the Caribbean. Spaniards had no access to African slaves and did not have the ships to transport them to America, so the Portuguese managed the whole enterprise for them. The same is true of the Spanish trading system. We often think that the Spanish controlled the riches of their own empire, but the reverse is true. Other nations helped the Spanish commercial system to work, so that they could reap the benefits. The result was that, by the seventeenth century, foreign nations (France, England, the Hanse, the Belgians and Dutch) controlled 90 per cent of the Atlantic trade, and consequently 90 per cent of the riches of that trade, including the silver.

Even the most famous aspect of the Spanish imperial enterprise, its dedication to spreading the Catholic religion, was not an exclusively Spanish effort. The first three missionaries of the Franciscan order to arrive in Mexico were not Spaniards but Belgians, and non-Spaniards continued to play a significant part in the missionary enterprise. The Jesuit who first established missions on the California frontier was an Austrian from South Tyrol, Eusebius Kühn. The most famous missionary in Asia was from Navarre and not from Spain: Francis Xavier.[58] There were never enough Spaniards to direct the world empire, and they needed the help of others. The empire, in other words, was a vast international enterprise in which everybody cooperated in order to achieve success. In places like the Philippines there were never enough Spaniards to run the colony, with the consequence that it was the thirty thousand or so Chinese residents in Manila who directed the economy. Spain's empire became a 'globalized' enterprise, in which different peoples and economies worked together. For the first time in history, an international empire integrated the markets of the world, as vessels from the St Lawrence, from the Río de la Plata, from Nagasaki, Macao, Manila, Acapulco, Callao, Vera Cruz, Havana, Antwerp, Genoa and Seville criss-crossed in an interminable commercial chain that exchanged commodities and profits, enriched merchants, and globalized civilization. African slaves went to Mexico, Mexican silver to China, Chinese silks to Madrid.

The great achievement of Spain, then, was not conquest but leadership. The myth of conquest gave satisfaction, both in the sixteenth century and in the nineteenth, to those who felt that violence was a necessary and desirable part of empire-building. In practice, this was completely irrelevant to the case of Spain, which had emerged to prominence because of dynastic inheritance and not through any great resources of its own. Within that context, Spaniards carried out their role with dexterity and efficiency. It was their audacity, courage and determination that helped the global empire survive. The empire of a few was sustained by the capital, cooperation and patience of many, whose contribution is too often forgotten by historians of the imperial nation.

The myth of a universal empire

The notion of an empire of conquest remains, in many imperial nations, a fundamental component of pride. In history textbooks and university courses, battles are used as criteria for explaining the past, and the capacity to shed blood is elevated to a position of supreme honour. For the British, their greatest military hero is the Duke of Marlborough, responsible for the death of thousands of soldiers at the battle of Blenheim. Visitors to the magnificent palace of the Marlborough family in Oxfordshire are unlikely to have their attention called to the famous poem on the battle, written in criticism over a century later by the poet Robert Southey. Spain, in this respect, is no different from other nations that attempt to create a myth about military achievements. Its most admired military hero, Cortés, is venerated because he directed the massacre of over a hundred thousand Aztec civilians. Another conquistador, Pizarro, is revered because he personally helped to slaughter around four thousand unarmed Peruvians in 1533. Above all, the country is seen by its teachers and politicians as a winner of battles. A very recent study claims for Spain the victories of 'Pavia, Mühlberg, St Quentin, Lepanto, Breda and Nördlingen'[59] in the early modern period. These military events are the greatest historical pride of the armed forces of the nation, because Spanish forces played an important role in each of them. The names recur in textbook after textbook. What the textbooks omit to mention is that not one of the victories was specifically 'Spanish'. In all of them, foreign soldiers, foreign generals and foreign money played the biggest part. The siege of Breda (1625) in Belgium, made famous by the masterly canvas of Velázquez, is a case in point. One may stand in front of it today, in the Prado art museum in Madrid, and admire the timeless courtesy of the victorious general as he accepts the surrender of the defeated army. Yet very little in that magnificent canvas is Spanish. It was a largely Belgian–Italian victory financed by an Italian banker, Spinola, who happened also to be the commanding general and the central figure of the painting.

Spanish leadership was always important, but constantly complemented by the contribution of allies. The victory of Lepanto (1571) is a clear example. Though repeatedly celebrated as Spain's most memorable military feat, more than any other victory of the age of empire Lepanto demonstrated clearly that, in war as in peace, the power of Spain depended on its allies. The fleet of the Holy League was in every sense an Italian and, above all, a Venetian fleet, with Spain relying heavily on Italian allies for support. Naples and Sicily alone contributed over half the galleys and more than a third of the costs. By contrast, Spain supplied the highest proportion of men. Of the 28,000 soldiers who accompanied the fleet, Spain contributed just under a third, around 8,500 men in four *tercios*. Spain could not pay its share of the costs, and Italians came to the rescue, supplying a part of the armaments, equipment and victuals for the expedition and paying out of their own resources for the ships and men they provided. The papacy made the most important contribution of all, by allowing Philip II to raise special

Church revenues that helped to defray the expense of the campaign. The total costs that fell on the Castilian exchequer have been calculated at five million ducats.[60] Of this sum, the government sent only sixty thousand ducats in silver. The rest was paid by Genoese bankers, who issued credit (in the form of credit notes known as 'bills of exchange') to cover the money, which they hoped to recoup later with adequate interest charges. Just as the military and financial contributions to Lepanto were shared between all the allies, so the victory belonged to all. In Rome, reported a cardinal, 'we are mad with delight, and above all the pope, who we really thought without exaggeration would die of joy, for the old saint has not slept these two nights'.[61]

In addition to the muscular image of a vast empire conquered militarily by an ever-victorious Spain, proponents of the conquest myth also put forward in the same breath an optimistic vision of the empire as a more or less benevolent institution. Menéndez Pidal, for example, contributed to fostering the image of Spain as a uniquely beneficent imperial power. When referring to America, he passed over in silence the demographic tragedy wreaked on the inhabitants of the continent, and reserved his praises exclusively for the New Laws, which friar Bartolomé de las Casas helped to promote. He spoke of them as 'those marvellous laws, fine enough to earn for Spain an amnesty before History for all the failings of its role in America'.[62] In the same vein, the Spanish Church in 2007 decided to press for the canonization of las Casas (after generations of vilifying him), hoping in this way to gain a moral amnesty for its record in colonial times. When literary scholars and historians, among them the American Lewis Hanke, interpreted the work of las Casas in a sense that seemed to be critical of Spain, Pidal took up his pen to attack las Casas as a madman and a Jew.[63] The viewpoint expressed by Pidal continues to be deeply rooted among some Castilians. In a recent magazine article, for example,[64] a journalist who enjoys a reputation among the public as a historian has presented a picture of 'peninsular unity' under the victorious Catholic Monarchs – who created an empire that had its roots in the middle ages, 'discovered' America because the empire generously wished to spread the gospel and 'had no hesitation in confirming the Indians as citizens with rights equal to those enjoyed in the Crowns of Castile and Aragon'. In America, 'the Spanish followed the Roman model of replacing the existing monarchies if they did not submit, imposed a common language, and developed an impressive work of infrastructures that included roads, aqueducts and educational centres'. In Europe, 'Spain was the only European power to respond to the pope's call to fight against Turkish expansion', though the policy of war was counter-productive, largely because of the foolish 'personal attitude of Philip II'. This bizarre perspective on the sixteenth century seems to be widely accepted by the public.

The beneficent face of empire, in which Spain is presented as doing good while everybody else is doing evil, also inspires the ideas of Gustavo Bueno, a writer unknown outside Castile but who is representative of a particular trend of opinion:

> For very exact and specific reasons, the Spanish empire, an empire that gave birth to kingdoms and nations, occupied (in the manner of the Romans) the lands in America that it discovered and established cities, universities, libraries, publishing houses, churches, and civil administration (all of which, out of a dialectical necessity coexisted with other, more selfish, interests that were based on the rapacity of private enterprises), whereas England and Holland created factories, colonies and even 'respected' the culture of the indigenous populations.[65]

A recent sympathetic reviewer of Bueno's *Spain against Europe* (*España frente a Europa*) (1999), in which the writer attacks Spanish participation in the European community because it subjects a morally superior Spain to morally inferior nations such as England and the United States, also contains a revealing summary of his views on empire, which derive directly from what Bueno perceives to have been Spain's role under Charles V:

> Spain was, in essence, inextricably bound up with the idea of an Empire that was universal, Catholic, and a creator of cities and of civilization. The idea of empire appeared already at the beginning of the early medieval Asturian kingdom. The Holy Roman empire of Germany was a fiction. The legitimate historical successor of the Roman empire, and particularly of the Roman empire in the West, was the Spanish empire. Spain's essence was its empire – which fell in 1898 – an empire that was Catholic and creative, not a robber empire like those of the British and the Dutch, and one that occupied a place in world history as a foe of Islam and of Protestantism, but also of Judaism. Judaism had no vocation for world empire, maybe that was why it never attempted to convert humanity.[66]

The idea that the empire 'fell in 1898' serves to maintain the confident image of a dominion that lasted for four hundred years, from 1492 to 1898. The image bolsters patriotic pride, but is true neither of the European nor of the trans-Oceanic territories. It is a question of definition and perspective. In the Philippines, for example, the Spaniards never controlled more than a small corner of one of their 7,000 islands. In mainland South America, the Spanish hold was no less precarious. There was a continuous Spanish presence, but it was rarely backed up by 'power'. It is doubtful whether the description 'empire' had any real meaning in the overseas territories, and the notion of a 'survival' of imperial control is consequently devoid of meaning if there was little control to begin with. In economic terms, as early as the seventeenth century the bulk of the economy of the New World was already under the control of non-Spaniards. By the end of that century most territories in the Caribbean were occupied by other Europeans. When the Americans took over Cuba in 1898, they already controlled 85 per cent of its foreign trade. What survived for four centuries was little more than an illusion of empire; the real empire had vanished long before.

Hispanidad, el Día de la Raza, and the new Spanish empire

The dream of recovering world status took shape, for governments of Spain, with a new concept, the celebration of the discovery of America.[67] In 1892 the conservative regime of Cánovas del Castillo heard that the United States was taking steps to celebrate the four hundredth anniversary of the date usually accepted as being that of the Discovery, the Twelfth of October. The Spaniards hurriedly put on their own celebrations, which fell in line with efforts they had been making to increase their influence among the now independent nations of Latin America. Cánovas put forward the idea that the date should be adopted by all the Hispanic nations as a common holiday. There was no response to this initiative. However, when the last bits and pieces of the Spanish empire disappeared in 1898, a change of heart took place among many of the Hispanic nations. They began to be aware of the threat to their interests represented by United States imperialism, and became more amenable to ideas emanating from Spain.

As Sebastian Balfour has pointed out,

the loss of the remnants of the empire after the disastrous encounter with the United States in 1898, destroyed the legitimising myth of empire. The empire had in the past provided the elites in Spain with an overarching purpose. For the economic elites it had offered the extraction of wealth and export of domestic products to colonies, for the Church a continued evangelical mission, and for the military an imperial status compensating its Third World pay. This purpose disappeared with the disappearance of the Empire.[68]

A new myth had to take its place. Quite naturally, the myth reverted to the glory of 1492. Latin American writers such as Rodó and Ruben Darío expressed their indignation at United States expansionism by embracing the cause and culture of the country they had once opposed: imperial Spain. In 1910, at a banquet in Montevideo, Rodó spoke in favour of 'the sacred sentiment of the *raza* uniting Spaniards and the Spanish Americans'. However, at that date the Twelfth of October had already become a widespread United States holiday, celebrated for instance by Italian residents to commemorate the Genoese discoverer Christopher Columbus. The role of Spain was being forgotten. In retaliation, a group of Spaniards in Cadiz in 1912, at the festivities held to mark the centenary of the Cortes of Cadiz, proposed that 12 October should be declared a national holiday. In the same weeks, the Dominican Republic adopted the United States' version of the holiday and began to uphold a Columbus Day (*Día de Colón*). From 1913, however, Mexico and other nations adopted a new form of the holiday, calling it *Día de la Raza*.

Each Latin American nation had specific reasons for marking *Día de la Raza*, but for Spain there could be no doubt what the day commemorated: the glory of the Hispanic race. From around 1919, the day was celebrated in Spain under this name. Within a decade, however, there were moves from conservative sectors to convert the name into *Día de la Hispanidad*, in specific celebration of the contribution made by Spain to western civilization. The chief promoter of this change was the writer Ramiro de Maeztu. His key book, *Defence of Spanishness* (*Defensa de la Hispanidad*), was published in 1934. It pronounced 'Spanishness' to be the hope of the world:

By discovering the maritime routes of East and West,[69] Spain completed the physical unity of the world; by securing the triumph, at Trent, of the dogma that secures to all men the possibility of salvation, and therefore of progress, Spain brought into being the necessary standard that enables us to speak of the moral unity of the human race. Consequently, Spanishness created universal history, and nothing else in the world, apart from Christianity, can be compared to what it achieved. For us, the spirit of Spanishness is a light from on high.

That same year, the primate of Spain, Archbishop Gomá of Toledo, gave a key pronouncement in Buenos Aires which deserves to be quoted, because it expressed fully the myth of Spain's empire and a vision – conservative but shared by very many both then and now – of how much America owed to Spain's sixteenth century:

America belongs to yesterday, but yesterday is, for history, the four and a half centuries that separate us from its discovery. The fact is there, the most transcendental in history, and history asks us for an interpretation and an explanation. America is, thanks to its discovery, a creation of Spain. Spain's achievement in America has risen above the exaggerations of Las Casas and the miserable envy of foreigners. It is impossible to fit into a speech and reduce to statistics what was done there in little more than a century. The arts flourished together with the sciences; architecture reproduced the form of our buildings in the south of Spain but also received the impact of the new race; the Mudejar, Plateresque and Baroque styles of Castile, León and Extremadura achieved an indigenous appearance on taking root in the flourishing cities of the New World. Painting and sculpture flourished in Mexico and Quito, and initiated a school; Spanish painters worked for the churches of America, and wealthy individuals left their collections of paintings to the cities of America. Spain did more than any mother would have done, she brought to life and fed, for civilization and for God, twenty nations which she did not abandon until they could lead a full life and she was left bloodless.

That is the essence of civilization, and that is what Spain did in these Indies. In conquering a vast empire she did more than Rome, for Rome enslaved its peoples whereas Spain gave them true liberty. And there is still the secret of race, or Spanishness, which is either a word without meaning or else it is the synthesis of all the spiritual values that, together with Catholicism, form the patrimony of the Hispanic American peoples. America is our work, a work that is essentially Catholic. The terms mean the same: race or Spanishness or Catholicism.

This day, the Twelfth of October, has been called the *Día de la Raza*. Of what race? What is race? Race, Spanishness, is something spiritual that transcends biological and psychological differences and concepts of nation and *patria*. It is something spiritual, divine and human at the same time. Expressed thus, Spanishness is the projection of the physiognomy of Spain outside of itself and among the peoples who form part of Spanishness. All the spiritual values of Latin America are Spanish in origin, because these values have been upheld for three centuries by the political and administrative activity of Spain.

Let us not be parasites or importers of foreign culture. Our soul and genius are without equal in any other people. We have a basis of traditional culture that the world envies. We have a language that very soon will be the most spoken on earth.[70]

The *Hispanidad* myth and the *Día de la Raza* both changed their names when, in the 1970s, Spain moved out of its authoritarian into its democratic phase. *Raza* was dropped because it recalled political ideologies associated with Nazi Germany. The imperial vision received a new facelift, and the emphasis on the sixteenth-century achievement was directed towards culture and language rather than at national chauvinism. In 1991, the Cervantes Institute was established as a series of centres for the spreading of Spanish culture. The symbol used by the institute, one that had been at the centre of the imperialist ideology of the 1900s, was the figure of Don Quixote, whose brave fight against the windmills represented in some degree the attempt of Spain to fight against the ghosts of its past and to emerge into a more tranquil post-imperial age.

CHAPTER FIVE

THE MYTH OF
THE INQUISITION

Cave of robbers, bastion of superstition and ignorance, insatiable devourer of human flesh, tyrant among despots, monument of barbarism. An invention without equal either in ancient or in modern times.

Antonio Puigblanch, *The Inquisition Unmasked* (London 1816)

Liberals against the Inquisition

When the British fleet under Nelson defeated the French and Spanish naval forces at Trafalgar in 1805, one of the mortal victims on the Spanish side was the naval commander Dionisio Alcalá Galiano. His infant son Antonio ended up as a leading Liberal politician, opponent of absolutism, and eventually (after eleven years as a political refugee, seven of them in London) prime minister of his country (see Chapter 1). A highly cultivated aristocrat, fluent in English and French, he was appointed to the first chair in Spanish language ever established in England, at University College London, in 1828. He devoted his inaugural lecture to attacking the Spanish Inquisition, which he accused of having repressed freedom of thought and of having crushed all intellectual initiative. He claimed that no history had been written in Spain since the middle of the seventeenth century, when, thanks to the Inquisition, his country had entered into 'absolute mental darkness'.[1] For Spaniards, this was to be a period when the Liberal myth of the Inquisition would be systematically presented to them for the first time; but the tone of Alcalá Galiano's message would not have surprised his Protestant audience. Sixteen years before, in the same city of London, another Liberal exile, the Catalan writer Antonio Puigblanch, had published a virulent attack on the celebrated tribunal.

Puigblanch (1775–1840) was born in the seaport of Mataró and educated in Church schools, after which he went to Madrid to complete his studies in law and classical languages. In 1807 he obtained a chair in Hebrew at the University of Alcalá. His remarkable scholarship was matched only by his profound concern for reform in Church and state. He was caught up in the politics of the Cortes which opened in the city of Cadiz in 1810, and in the following year published there, under the pseudonym Natanael Jomtob, his influential *The Inquisition Unmasked* (*La Inquisición sin Máscara*).[2] The pseudonym, he explained, came from Hebrew and meant 'God has set the day'. The preface stated his purpose clearly: 'My intention is to destroy the Inquisition from its foundations.' Without the advantage of access to the documents of the Holy Office that Llorente (see below) enjoyed during those same months, Puigblanch made use of a broad range of published sources to demonstrate that both the existence and the methods of the Inquisition (that is, its trial procedure, its rigour, its secrecy, its use of torture, its control of censorship) were against the rules of the Church and of civil society. His substantial volume of some five hundred pages, amply backed up by hundreds of footnotes and quotations in Latin, Greek, Hebrew and French, had an undeniable impact on readers in Spain. Political events dictated that he become a permanent exile in England, where in 1816 he published an English translation of his book.

Puigblanch's work was the first serious Spanish attack on the Inquisition since the sixteenth-century book by González Montano (see below). It still makes for interesting reading, although its value is somewhat limited because it habitually chooses to employ invective rather than solid evidence. Puigblanch wrote, for example: 'As befitted a tribunal created in the centuries of darkness, the laws on which it was founded are a stack of ravings of a sick mind. Perfidious in its words and villainous in its acts, it only felt happy when it had victims to condemn.'[3] Passion, clearly, was taking precedence over fact. At one point, Puigblanch accuses the tribunal of blighting all 'science' in Spain, but the only scientist he quotes is the Italian Galileo. Uninformed invective continued to be the main weapon employed by most opponents of the Inquisition in those years.

The ideas of men like Puigblanch and Alcalá Galiano served to place the Inquisition in a central position in the debate over Spain's identity. In the attempt to define Spain's past and its role in the present, the Inquisition took on a crucial role, both for the Liberals and for their later opponents. We are not concerned here with the mere fact of criticism or with its correctness or otherwise. There had always been Spaniards who criticized the Holy Office, notably in the period of the Reformation. The most effective of them was the first historian of the tribunal, who published a book at Heidelberg, in 1567, under the pseudonym 'Reinaldo González Montano'.[4] His work is often classified as being part of a Black Legend, a calumny invented by foreigners to blacken Spain's name. The volume certainly served as propaganda against Spain and helped other nations to form a hostile image of its religion, but it was largely factual (and therefore not a 'legend') rather than calumnious. On the whole, Spaniards of the sixteenth century were concerned to describe what they knew about the tribunal's actions, rather than to exaggerate – as European Protestants did – its supposed threats. There was no native Spanish myth of the Inquisition in early modern times. That was created only in the nineteenth century. The myth, when it arrived in Spain, owed little or nothing to the long tradition of anti-Inquisition polemic to be found in other countries,[5] since Spanish readers could not usually read foreign languages. The single exception was French, which many educated Spaniards could read and which served as their point of contact with foreign thought and the ideas of the French Enlightenment. In France, the eighteenth century had seen a remarkable spate of propaganda directed against the enemies of intellectual freedom, and the Inquisition inevitably occupied pride of place among these. Spanish admirers of the Enlightenment – including the Liberals – could not fail to consider themselves heirs to the French outlook.

The Liberal campaign against the Holy Office took form around 1810, in the period associated with the Cortes of Cadiz. The 'patriots' who took part in the debates about abolishing the Inquisition knew virtually nothing about the subject, but they were not put off by that. Some may have been guided by Puigblanch, but the most concrete source of information available was Juan Antonio Llorente. Llorente (1756–1823), from Aragon, was a priest who became an official of the Inquisition in Logroño, and in 1789 was promoted to being one of its secretaries in Madrid. In 1809, when the French king of Spain, Joseph, abolished the Inquisition, he asked Llorente to prepare a history of the tribunal. With all the archives of the Holy Office at his disposal, Llorente managed to publish in Madrid his *Annals of the Inquisition of Spain*, in two volumes, which came out in 1812, together with his *Historical Memoir on What Was the National Opinion in Spain about the Tribunal of the Inquisition*. The *Historical Memoir* served as the main source of historical information for the deputies in the Cortes of Cadiz when they carried out their own abolition of the tribunal.[6] When King Joseph's pro-French officials were forced to leave the country with him, Llorente accompanied them and published in French, in Paris, his great work in four volumes, *A Critical History of the Spanish Inquisition* (1817–18).

It is difficult to exaggerate the scale of Llorente's achievement. With a rare impartiality (not found, for example, in Puigblanch) and a deep commitment to the seriousness of the task he had undertaken, Llorente attempted to put together from his rich harvest of papers a solid account of what the mysterious tribunal had been busy doing. Subsequently, both his personal character and his historical accuracy were assailed, primarily by his own countrymen – but this was the normal fate of all historical research that dared to overturn old prejudices. There were inevitable weaknesses in a work so vast that would normally have taken several years and more than one scholar to produce, but Llorente's *Annals* and *History* were the first fully documented accounts of the Inquisition to have seen the light of day in over three hundred years. They revealed and exposed to public view corners of Spain's history hitherto kept in the dark; and, for those who doubted his account, the author published not only details of his sources but also *pièces justificatives* to confound criticism.

In the process, he and his contemporaries also laid some foundations for the myth that still dominates popular thinking. The preface to the abridged English translation of his work, published in London in 1827, has the following conclusion on the impact of the Inquisition:

> The horrid conduct of this Holy Office weakened the power and diminished the population of Spain, by arresting the progress of arts, sciences, industry and commerce, and by compelling multitudes of families to abandon the kingdom; by instigating the expulsion of the Jews and the Moors; and by immolating on its flaming piles more than three hundred thousand victims.[7]

Historians today would find Llorente's conclusion bizarre. We know that the Holy Office had no impact on population growth, played no perceptible role for or against industry and science, and executed little more than 1 per cent of the number of victims stated by Llorente. However, the Liberals were anxious to identify those responsible for the travails of their country, and who could be more conveniently blamed than the Inquisition?

The Liberal myth was given added force by the famous *Caprichos* of Francisco de Goya (1746–1828). As a solid, believing Catholic and an official court painter, Goya had no reason to fall foul of the Church. However, his friends (Jovellanos, Moratín) tended to be ministers who had little sympathy with the Inquisition and its political role. This is an indication of the personal opinions of the painter, who in the 1790s included occasional satirical references to the Inquisition and clergy in his work. Among his *Caprices* (*Caprichos*), for example, two (nos 23 and 24) are explicitly critical of the Inquisition. Goya's appointment as chief painter to the king (he painted his *Family of Charles IV* in 1800) presumably gave him protection from malicious critics, but some of his *Caprichos* were denounced to the Inquisition and, in self-protection, he donated the whole series to the king as a gift. Goya's pro-French friends took office in 1808 under the new king, Joseph I, in the hope of securing political reform. Goya, by contrast, refused to identify with any of the political groupings. His clearest ideological statement at this time, however, left little room for doubt about his opinions. The Liberals, as we have seen, were influential in the sessions of the Cortes that met in 1812 at Cadiz, where they led the parliamentary debate on the subject of abolishing the Inquisition. Goya's contribution to the proceedings was to paint two powerful satirical canvases depicting the Inquisition. Though the notorious tribunal was abolished by the Cortes, it refused to die and was restored to life by Ferdinand VII after the French, and with them Goya's pro-French colleagues, had left Spain.

Both as a pioneer and as one not specifically trained for the task he undertook, Llorente made many important slips, with the result that a powerful conservative and Catholic tradition in his home country dismissed his work as inconsequential, in the same way it would later dismiss the impressive work on the same theme (1906) of the American Henry Charles Lea. Llorente's *History* disappeared into the obscurity of libraries and was not republished in Spain until 1980, nearly two centuries later. This was an ironic twist, because many conservatives also agreed with the general drift of the Liberal interpretation. Their main point of disagreement was over the treatment of Philip II. The following statement by Cánovas del Castillo speaks for itself: 'The Inquisition pursued its career and bit by bit, like a serpent, wrapped itself round Spanish thought, until *under the successors of Philip II* [my emphasis] it tightened its grip and stifled and killed it.'[8] Conservatives, in short, might accept the Liberal view but refused to believe that it applied to the first two Habsburgs. (We should remember that, in the same way, the Liberals refused to admit that Queen Isabella had done anything wrong when she founded the Inquisition, so that both political tendencies had their own peculiar way of approaching the facts.) Other conservatives, of course, refused to recognize that the Inquisition had done anything worthy of criticism.

In a country where the Church dominated education, where historical research was scarce and there was no access to foreign scholarship, the conservative view prevailed and helped to marginalize politically the work of Llorente. The work of Lea, whose writings on the Inquisitions of Europe revolutionized historical science, remained unknown to, and unread by, Spanish historians until 1983.[9] The English language was evidently a barrier, but so too was ideology. In a book on the Inquisition published during the Franco period, a leading historian of the regime dismissed Lea's book (which of course he had not read) as 'historically useless'.[10] I remember reading this phrase one day in Madrid forty years ago, when I was preparing my own modest study on the tribunal, and it held me riveted. At moments like that, one comes face to face with impenetrable ideology. It was a remarkable example of the way in which one sole vision of the past could be imposed on a nation's reading public, and on its historians, for nearly two hundred years. Quite irrespective of what may or may not have been the truth about the Inquisition, two alternative myths, the Liberal and the conservative, dictated the way in which Spaniards would understand their historical past.

The sum total of the Liberal contribution to the image of the Inquisition, despite the constructive scholarship of Llorente, was to strengthen even further the idea that the tribunal had been an enemy of the human race. Drawing on their direct experience of the support given by Ferdinand VII to the tribunal, the Liberals logically denounced it as a tool of political oppression. They would have agreed with the conclusions of the German historian Ranke, who argued in 1827 that 'the Inquisition was the most effective instrument in completing the absolute power of the monarch'.[11] We can get an idea of the opinion widely held among educated and progressive Spaniards through the presentation given in his pioneering *Historical Studies on the Jews* by José Amador de los Ríos in 1848. As a good Liberal, Amador argued in this study that crown and tribunal shared the same objectives: 'the idea of the political unity of Spain and, enveloped within it, the idea of the religious unity of the country. To create the first, the second was a necessary condition.' He declared that, with the support of Philip II, the tribunal

> extended its terrible rule more and more. Till then it had punished
> dangerous tendencies, and persecuted crimes of sacrilege and belief with

the greatest severity and determination. Through its triumph, the Inquisition aspired to rule consciences, it wished to hold the key to human understanding, launched its anathemas against those who would not bow their neck to its projects, and welcomed into its prisons all those who dared to doubt the legitimacy of its law. So it was that, in a century of achievement for the name of Spaniard, when the Castilian flag flew from one end of Europe to another, while the arts and letters were cultivated by geniuses who rivalled the glories of Italy, there was hardly a single man of learning who was not thrust into the prisons of the Holy Office, victim of the envy and spite of the inquisitors.

Traditionalists to the rescue

The Liberal version of the Holy Office persisted unquestioned for over half a century before protagonists of traditional Spain appeared and attempted to dismantle it. The new defenders of the Inquisition included conservatives and Catholics who, while not partisans of the tribunal, had a completely different perspective on the role it had played in early modern Spain. Menéndez Pelayo, whose career we have outlined above (Chapter 3), was perhaps the only competent defender the Inquisition ever had. Apart from his master-piece *Historia de los Heterodoxos españoles* (1880), which we have cited more than once, he had also produced, at the age of twenty-two, a brilliant essay on *Spanish Science* (*Ciencia española*) (1876; see below), which aimed to prove that the Inquisition had not eliminated learning in Spain. He was not sparing of invective when it came to Llorente. He brushed him aside as 'lacking in erudition, puerile in criticism, insipid in style, without vigour or charm', and the *History of the Inquisition* as 'a pile of calumnies, dry and sterile, malicious, indigestible, vague and incoherent'.[12] Menéndez Pelayo had all the passion of a young zealot when he used these phrases, and Llorente is among the very few persons so passionately denounced in his great study. He directed his main attack against the Liberals, who had argued that the Inquisition had wiped out literature and learning in Spain:

It is a matter not just of love for one's country but also of historical justice to undo this progressivist legend, brutally imposed by the law-makers of the Cortes of Cadiz, which presents us as a nation of barbarians in whom neither learning nor art could arise because all was suffocated by the smoke of the Inquisition's pyres. Only crass ignorance of things Spanish, of the sort the brainless imitators of Voltaire lived happily in, could explain why, in an official document for the decree abolishing the Holy Office, they printed these words, a piece of evidence fit to condemn to eternal shame both its authors and the flock of Liberals who adopted these words and continue repeating them in chorus: 'Writing ceased in Spain when the Inquisition was established.' Did these small-minded orators, from whose wretched hands the new Spain was to emerge, not know that in the sixteenth century, the century par excellence of the Inquisition, Spain dominated Europe, even more through its thought than through its deeds, and there was no branch of science or learning on which it did not leave its mark?

'Writing ceased in Spain when the Inquisition was established'! Did it cease with the arrival at its peak of our classic literature, which possesses a theatre superior in fruitfulness and richness of invention to any in the world; a lyric poetry that nobody can equal in simplicity, sobriety and greatness of inspiration; among the poets, the only poet of the Renaissance to achieve a union of the old forms and the new spirit; a novelist who will remain an exemplary and eternal paragon of healthy and powerful naturalism; a school of mystics in whom the Castilian language appears to be a language of angels? What more can one add, if even the last followers of the giants from the age of decline, Góngora, Quevedo and Baltasar Gracián, are of more value than the whole of that eighteenth century which so foolishly despised them? The fact is that never in Spain was there more written, or better written, than in those two golden centuries of the Inquisition.[13]

Menéndez Pelayo was writing before anybody other than Llorente had made a close study of the original documents of the Holy Office. Quite apart from his critical analysis of the theme, however, he also indirectly helped to promote research. From 1887 he was in correspondence with Henry Charles Lea, who was then preparing his great studies on the medieval and Spanish Inquisitions, and helped obtain for him transcripts of documents from the Spanish archives. Maturity and courtesy mellowed the older man, and to make his views began to take their place in the arena of civilized scholarship. The tendency he represented, however, also continued to produce writings of a less scholarly nature. With very rare exceptions, such as the fundamental and pioneering studies by Fidel Fita, clergy who wrote about the Inquisition allowed their ideological views to influence their research. Studies by three of them were commented upon in 1962 by the American scholar John Longhurst. 'Nicolas López Martínez, Bernardino Llorca, and Miguel de la Pinta Llorente, who are understandably "reasonable" about the Inquisition, are all careful investigators whose historical methods of research are above reproach. They insist, however, that, because they work from documents, their viewpoints and conclusions are as "objective" and "unprejudiced" as their methodology. They likewise insist that all other historians who see things differently from themselves are "biased" and "prejudiced" and cannot be relied upon.'[14] Instead of advancing towards knowledge and impartiality, new research therefore fell into the trap of political partisanship that had always infected the Spanish academic world, where published work often tended to be judged by its service to ideology rather than on its intrinsic historical merits.

The two partisan approaches, which coincided with Liberal and conservative views of the Inquisition, continued to survive with surprising vigour well into contemporary Spain. This was because both views maintained that vital aspects of Spanish culture could not be understood or explained without bringing into play the responsibility of the Inquisition, for evil and for good. The nature and impact of the fifteenth-century tribunal consequently came to be seen as key to the way Spain developed four hundred years later. The myth of the Inquisition became both long-lasting and deep-rooted because it was essential to the maintenance of political ideology. Whenever it was necessary to explain a particularly contentious issue, there was nothing easier than to raise the cry of 'Inquisition!' in the same way that one might cry out 'Fire!' Since the Inquisition was perceived as a reactionary body, any attempt to modify its image in respect of the harm it may have done to the Jews, to liberty and to culture was likewise considered reactionary. As a consequence, the persistence of misconceptions was not significantly affected by the research undertaken in the later years of the twentieth century.

The high hopes that access to original documents would reveal the truth, in the same way that Llorente had managed to shed light on obscure corners of the tribunal's history, were rapidly dashed. The excitement of researchers was similar to that generated in recent years by the opening of secret state archives, notably of the Soviet Union and of the papacy. As has happened in the case of these archives, which at first promised to reveal forbidden secrets, the original documents did not supply the key to the whole story. I remember feeling disappointed when in the year 2000 the archivist of the Vatican took me and other scholars around the shelves where the 'secret' papers of the Roman Inquisition were at last brought out for researchers to consult. The same disappointment must arise when considering the documents of the Spanish Inquisition. Access to them has by no means dispelled the myths. Indeed, it has created more. The legend of the bloody Inquisition may have disappeared, but that has not impeded the survival of new approaches which use the Inquisition as a convenient tailor's dummy on which to pin new myths. One of the most widely disseminated ones, although it will not concern us here, puts forth the alleged Jewishness of Spanish *conversos*, a theme that draws its lifeblood from a very special way of reading inquisitorial documents. In their turn, the new approaches fortify mythical views about Spain's past.

The enduring myth of Spain's isolation

The most ineradicable of the judgements on the Inquisition was that it brought about the isolation of Spain, and consequently its ruin. The myth of isolation presents special difficulties because it is one strongly held by all shades of ideological opinion. Conservative writers have applauded the isolation, with the argument that it was the only way to preserve Spain's distinctive and superior culture. Liberal writers from the 1800s onwards asserted, by contrast, that Spain's isolation prejudiced it and cut it off from the mainstream of modern civilization. Lafuente wrote of 'the pressure exercised upon minds in various branches of learning by the harsh tribunal of the Holy Office, and the isolation from the intellectual movement in Europe that Spain suffered from the time of Philip II'. One way or another, the theory of isolation became a crucial weapon in the armoury of commentators because it offered a self-evident explanation or justification for different ideological views.

Down to the present day, writers lent support to the view that Philip II and the Inquisition sealed Spain off from contact with the outside world. An iron curtain, they maintain, came down separating the peninsula from the Western world. My own study on the Inquisition, first published in 1965, contributed (I regret to say) to this vision by arguing in its first chapter that Spain became a 'closed society' because of the tribunal. The idea has been of immense use in explaining the course of history. If Spain lacked philosophy, science, modernity, it was because it was deprived of the possibility of contact and interchange. The country, runs the argument, possessed immense potential, but thanks to Philip II it remained backward because Spaniards were not allowed contact with foreigners, could not study abroad and could not read foreign books. To back up these claims, commentators pointed to two specific laws: one of 1558, which regulated censorship of books; and one of November 1559, which apparently ordered the Spaniards who were studying at unapproved foreign universities to return home. Both seemed to be negative in their impact.

Let us first consider the law of 1559. Two centuries after 1559, the Valencian scholar Gregorio Mayans concluded that 'one of the reasons why the arts and sciences have declined so greatly has been the law promulgated by Philip II, prohibiting study in foreign universities'.[15] A century after Mayans, the view was stated with even greater force by Modesto Lafuente:

It is difficult to imagine that there would be a sovereign in the sixteenth century who would wish to cut his nation off intellectually from the rest of the world and to make it a crime for his subjects to teach other people or to learn from them. When Spain was deprived of literary contact with other nations, it was left in the rear of the intellectual advance of the world and way behind other peoples, as far behind as it had previously been in advance of all other nations.[16]

This claim was still being made four and a half centuries later, in 1998, when a Madrid professor of history argued that the king 'forbade young Spaniards to study in Europe', and another scholar affirmed that the king let his country grovel in ignorance: 'here, instead of publishing books we devoted ourselves to persecuting them'.[17] What consequence could this have had other than depriving Spain, previously the most advanced nation in the West, of intellectual contact with the civilized world? The 1998 statements – both utterly untrue – offer fascinating evidence of how some apparently informed scholars have explained Spain's history through myths and conjecture. In this case, the myth was always considered both desirable and essential, because it offered an immediate excuse for Spain's intellectual position. The writer Gustavo Bueno has affirmed: 'Many have pointed out that the specific cause of Spain's decline was not the Catholic Monarchs (on account of the expulsion of the Jews) but Philip II, because of the 1559 law forbidding Spaniards to study in Europe. This was the principal cause of the decline, the historic backwardness, of Spain.' Philip II remains confirmed beyond all doubt as the tyrant who deliberately condemned Spain to ignorance.

The problem is that the law of 1559 *never prohibited Spaniards from studying abroad.* It suffices simply to read the text (which seemingly none of the above commentators ever did) to see that it applied only to residents of the crown of Castile, not to all 'Spaniards'. The law decreed a 'ban on residents of these realms going to study in universities outside them'. The phrase 'these realms' was (we have seen) a traditional shorthand for the kingdoms of Castile and León. The law of 1559 did not apply outside Castile, namely to residents of the realms of Aragon, Catalonia, Valencia, the Basque country and Navarre, all of whom could continue to study abroad where they wished. For example, a resident of Aragon could still go to study, if he so desired, in France or Germany. For nearly ten years afterwards – a surprisingly long time for a king alleged to have been anxious to cut off access to the outside world – Philip did nothing more to control the movement of students. Non-Castilian Spaniards continued to study freely outside the peninsula. Only in 1568, when virtually the whole of the south of France was in the hands of Calvinists, did he step in with another law – this time for his subjects in the crown of Aragon. The opening words of the 1568 decree make plain what had been intended in that of 1559:[18]

> Some years ago we ordered the publication in these our realms of Castile of a law stating that no one should study outside them. Now we have decided to do the same for those realms of ours in the crown of Aragon.

It is relevant to point out that Castilians had seldom been in the habit of studying abroad. They appear, indeed, to be almost entirely absent from the available sixteenth-century matriculation lists of the leading European universities.[19] They had never gone to colleges in England or Germany, so the ban on 'studying in universities outside' was quite superfluous in their case. The main objectives of the king were to prevent Castilians from studying in the two places they had often frequented, the University of Paris in France and that of Louvain in the Netherlands, where Reformation heresies were growing alarmingly. There was no intention of stopping them studying abroad at the handful of colleges in Italy and Portugal which they had also always frequented, and those colleges were specifically mentioned in the law. The law affected resident Castilian clergy but not clergy in most religious orders, who came under a different (church) jurisdiction and retained the right to go to any European colleges approved by their superiors. In short, the law changed almost nothing in the studying habits of Spaniards, except for those few who were studying in Paris, which the king was anxious to put out of bounds because of the spread of the Reformation there. The 1568 law for the crown of Aragon seems, all the same, to have had some impact, for by the end of the century there was a rapid fall in the number of Catalans and Aragonese studying in France.

Did Spaniards stop going abroad to study? As often happens, they ignored the prohibitions and continued to study wherever they wished in Europe. The secretary of the Inquisition in Logroño, near the frontier with France, reported the case in 1584 of 'a Dr León, a medical doctor, who said he was a citizen of Valladolid, with two sons whom he said he was taking to study in Bordeaux. When asked why he was taking his sons to Bordeaux, where there was little security in matters of religion, and when there were so many good universities in Spain, he replied that if he did not find conditions suitable in Bordeaux he would take them to Paris.'[20] Nothing was done to impede the movements of the doctor, who left his sons in Bordeaux and returned peacefully to Valladolid. Several other scholars continued to study in France, but the Spanish government turned a blind eye. In 1616 an advocate in Barcelona informed the authorities that 'to avoid the expense of Spanish universities he went to Toulouse in France where he took the degree of doctor, then registered the degree in the city of Barcelona, and since then has been acting as a lawyer in the city'.[21] There is no historical basis for the picture of a Spain isolated from the outside world by king and Inquisition; that is wholly imaginary. If Spaniards ceased to go to foreign universities in the later sixteenth century, it was because cultural conditions had changed. Virtually all universities in the north of Europe had become Protestant, and the language of teaching was beginning to be the national tongue, which posed a problem of comprehension.

It is time to consider the fact that Spaniards, the centre of an inter-continental empire, were never cut off from the outside world. In an age when Spain was Europe's principal power, thousands of Spaniards of all ranks and conditions, including clergymen, nobles, students, soldiers and adventurers, left the peninsula and wandered everywhere on the continent or emigrated to America. The ban on study did not affect them. Even in Castile, people ignored the prohibition and kept sending their children abroad, to study at any place of their choice. If anything, Spain was the least isolated nation in early modern Europe. Within the peninsula, the population was also often in motion. In a superb study of the subject, a scholar reminds us: 'early modern Spain was a highly mobile society, its people constantly on the move'.[22] There were international centres where they also had contact with foreigners, such as the capital Madrid, the cosmopolitan port Seville, or the pilgrimage centres at Santiago and Montserrat. Italy had a generous share of Spaniards, whether soldiers, traders or clergy. It is possible that those who travelled abroad lacked a certain gift, that of curiosity, which might have expanded their horizons. This may explain why the seventeenth-century diplomat Saavedra y Fajardo commented that northern Europeans 'reconnoitre the world and learn languages, arts and sciences; Spaniards remain in tight seclusion in their country'.[23] It may also explain why a scholar such as Ramón Menéndez Pidal could affirm: 'the Spaniard is not interested in obtaining general cultural knowledge of foreign countries, hence he is not a lover of travel'.[24] That may have been true when he wrote in the 1920s, but it was not true four centuries earlier. Defects in the receptiveness of Spaniards did not affect the real fact that they could and did travel. The peninsula was never cut off, either for those leaving or for those coming in. It follows that, if Spaniards came to lack intellectual contact with foreign nations, a cause other than the pragmatic of 1559 must be found.

'Not thinking, not knowing, not reading': the prohibition of knowledge

We turn now to the censorship law of 1558. According to the isolation myth, Spain was not merely cut off from the outside, its citizens were also forbidden to read anything written in the outside world. This effectively destroyed its culture. The myth was accepted equally by Liberals and by conservatives. The conservative Cánovas del Castillo denounced the '1558 decree against books, which played so great a part in the intellectual decline of Spain'.[25] The famous *Indexes* of the Inquisition, which drew up lists of prohibited books, crushed (so runs the argument) all free thought within the country. At one and the same time, the Inquisition isolated Spain and strangled all freedom inside it. A Spanish scholar, Ignacio Sotelo, has affirmed recently (2003) in an authoritative journal:

> There is not the slightest doubt that in Spain during the sixteenth and seventeenth centuries fear of the Holy Office uprooted all intellectual activity. It provoked distrust of anyone who took up classical studies or profane learning, since these were deemed to be activities indulged in only by Jews, and even laymen or clergy too concerned with theological matters

might give the impression that they were influenced by Lutheran heresy, to the extent that the best way of freeing oneself from any suspicion was to continue being in the immense majority of illiterates.[26]

If this statement were accepted as true, we would have to conclude that no creative thinkers or speculative writers existed or produced work in the two hundred years referred to. As we have noted above, an adequate response to this type of sweeping affirmation had already been given by Menéndez Pelayo 125 years earlier. Sotelo concludes: 'in this social environment, one understands why neither the habit of reading nor the publishing industry flourished in the Hispanic world'. Startling as the claim may be that Spaniards neither read nor produced books, we should note that it forms part of a continuing reiteration of the old Liberal belief about the role of the Inquisition. These ideas have been voiced incessantly in the two centuries since the Liberals first formulated them. They appear, for example, in the views expressed in 1948 by the great historian Américo Castro:[27]

Not thinking, not knowing, not reading, was a protection against the sadism and predatory zeal of the personnel of the Holy Office, an effective remedy for the intellectual inertia of Spaniards in that period. What was serious was that the Spanish spirit was not prepared to battle openly in the field of intelligence. The most informed and free spirits say that the country suffered from a clerical tumour, which they sometimes identify as one of the causes of national decline.

The image of a Spain run by friars and monks and rendered illiterate by the tyranny of Philip II and the Inquisition formed part of an idea shared by other liberals of Castro's generation such as Ortega y Gasset, who in one of his essays presented the hypothesis of a 'Tibetization of Spain', that is, a Spain isolated and rendered backward by centuries of clerical dominance. The need for the myth is quite apparent. It explained perfectly why Spain, which by right should have been in the vanguard of intellectual and scientific life in Europe, was always condemned to be in the rear. It removed from Spaniards as a people, and from their elites and governments in particular, any responsibility for failing to come up to the standards of the modern world. In other words, if a Spaniard was not the inventor of the electric light bulb, it was because of the Inquisition. If Spaniards still do not read, two hundred years after the abolition of the Inquisition, it is because of the Inquisition.[28]

This is not the place to dwell in detail on the fact that the system of book control in Spain had no worse an impact than similar systems in other countries. Every country had firm controls: in England, the first list of prohibited books was issued in 1529, and in 1530 a licensing system was introduced. None of this crushed intellectual life in England, and there is no reason to think that Spain suffered either. Since the peninsula depended on book imports for much of its literature in both Spanish and Latin, and many Spanish authors preferred to publish abroad, there was a considerable and continuous flow of books both into and out of Spain. Nothing comparable occurred in any other European country. Since the early days of printing, the Spaniards had published outside the country. In the formative period up to 1501, some eight hundred titles had been published in Spain at thirty centres and, from 1501 to 1520, some nine hundred further titles were published.[29] Valencia and Barcelona, which have had presses at work since 1473, share the longest printing history of all Spanish cities. From the 1540s, however, a major change took place. Most Spanish books from that decade were published outside Spain.[30] The internationalization of the Spanish book was set in motion by the constantly moving court of Charles V. The Reformation controversies drew Spanish writers into the European book market. They wrote, of course, in Latin, the only international tongue. Alfonso de Castro, a chaplain to Philip II, issued his great treatises in Paris and Lyon; Pedro de Soto, confessor to Charles V, published the entirety of his works abroad, in Augsburg, Ingolstadt and Dillingen.

After the 1560s, when authors in all countries preferred to write in their own language if they wished to have a public, the tendency was for books in Spanish to be published in Spain. But that only affected a proportion of the books. Long after the decree of 1558, Spanish writers continued to publish abroad as much as they did at home. It was a freedom enjoyed, ironically, by authors in no other European country. The works published abroad were, of course, imported into Spain. No intention of heresy arose. In the late sixteenth century – that is to say, in the reign of Philip II – at least sixty leading Spanish writers published their works abroad, in Lyon in France, rather than in Spain. The fact was that the quality of presses outside Spain was much better, and controls less onerous.[31] Enjoying the ability to publish with impunity in the realms of Aragon, Italy, France or the Netherlands, Spaniards could boast that they had more freedom of literature than their neighbours. The flow of books into Spain continued without interruption. In Castile during the years 1557–64, the trader Andrés Ruiz brought in over nine hundred bales of books from Lyon and over one hundred from Paris. By the early seventeenth century there was a virtually free flow of books from French presses into Spain, most of it across the Pyrenees. The holdings in many Barcelona bookshops consisted almost exclusively of imported books, including works by Spanish authors who had been published abroad. Despite a great deal of bureaucratic interference, most of it from the Inquisition, and constant vigilance against heretical literature, no significant hindrance to imports took place.

Foreign presses continued to dominate the printing of religious works, not only of Bibles but also of mass books and works of devotion. The flow of literature never stopped, as the case of Barcelona shows. Ten years after the decrees of 1558–9, booksellers continued to rely for their income on the uninterrupted import of foreign books, many of which went to Castile. 'The books that enter through this frontier are very numerous,' the inquisitors reported from Catalonia in 1569, 'and even if there were many inquisitors we would not be enough to deal with so many volumes.' All the same, steps were taken to try and control books on religious themes. That same year 1569, a year after the crown had decreed that its subjects in the crown of Aragon should not be educated in unapproved centres, the government in Madrid passed a law stating that no religious books could be printed 'in these realms' (that is, in Castile) unless they were licensed by the royal council, and that none could be imported, 'even if printed in the realms of Aragon, Valencia, Catalonia and Navarre'.[32] When Spaniards wanted to read foreign books, they imported them for the purpose. The image of a Spain in which, for two hundred years, nobody thought, nobody wrote and nobody read, all because they lived in fear of the Inquisition, is so grotesque that the wonder is that anyone has seriously accepted it. Book control and censorship were systematically evaded in all countries where they were practised. In both Italy[33] and France,[34] the attempts at control were both 'futile' and 'inefficient'. The evidence for Spain is similar.[35] There are no convincing grounds for believing that the Spaniards were unique among Europeans in their efficiency at imposing control,[36] or that they were subjected to a regime of 'thought control' which 'fossilised academic culture' for three hundred years.[37] The view persists, however, not least among those who believe, rightly or wrongly, that all censorship is wrong and that their country has had too much of it.[38]

The Inquisition and race

Early modern Spain was a society in which Jews, both unconverted and converted, played a significant role. It was normal that anti-Semitism should play a part in politics and culture at that time, though perhaps surprising that it should continue to maintain its vigour throughout the five hundred years after the expulsion of 1492. Some commentators have suggested that Spain is today the most anti-Semitic society in Western Europe. The phenomenon of anti-Semitism is never easy to analyse or explain, but in this case its origins are usually, and quite reasonably, attributed to the activity of the Inquisition. The Inquisition acted in an unquestionably racialist way, since its activity was directed consistently against people from Spain's cultural minority groups. From the time of its foundation (1480), it pinpointed the Jew as the enemy of Spanish society. The people it arrested and brought to trial in its early years were, of course, Christians, for the Inquisition had no jurisdiction over non-Christians. But over 95 per cent of those Christians happened to be *conversos* of Jewish origin. The fact of Jewish ancestry was enough to invite suspicion and victimization. The anti-Semitism of the inquisitors was clearly not something they personally invented, but a result of prejudices and attitudes which were deeply rooted in Spanish society, born out of a long coexistence with probably the biggest Jewish community in Europe. Anti-Semitic prejudices were ingrained in Spanish society and survive to this day, both on the right and on the left of the political spectrum.

The persistence of prejudice against Jews, however, is something quite different from the myth that concerns us here. Within the past century, a view has circulated among professors of literature who, basing themselves apparently on literary evidence, argue that Spain during the sixteenth century was a society in the grip of an anti-Semitic obsession about blood purity, which they feel was the most crucial aspect of the Inquisition's role at that time. In a recent press interview, the writer Juan Goytisolo explained how he became aware of the relevance of the theme. It happened that, in the early 1800s, the exiled writer Joseph Blanco White referred in one of his English writings to the pain he had experienced in Spain after having had a brush with the statute of blood purity. When Juan Goytisolo read this passage in the 1970s, he became convinced that Spain had been permanently in the grip of anti-Semitism, and in his writings thereafter he repeatedly referred to the statutes of blood purity as being the bane of Spain. It is a tribute to the popularity of his work that the concept has caught on. He may have been right about anti-Semitism, but the real history of the statutes was (as the historian Antonio Domínguez Ortiz has rightly insisted)[39] connected more with social conflict than with racial prejudice.

The passage to which Goytisolo refers can be found in a series of essays which Blanco White wrote for a journal in England. From 1821, based in the quiet Berkshire rectory of Ufton Nervets, White wrote for the *New Monthly* a series of portraits of life and society in the Spain he had known as a boy and a young man. They were published the following year in book form, as *Letters from Spain*. In them, White makes the following observation:[40]

> There exists among us a distinction over blood that I believe to be peculiar to Spain. The great mass of our people accepts it so blindly that the most humble labourer considers its lack to be a fount of misery and degradation he is condemned to transmit to all his posterity. The slightest stain of African, Indian, Moorish or Jewish blood is a blot on the whole family up to the last generation, and not even the passage of years can remove the knowledge of this fact, nor can the obscurity and low origins of those who suffer this disgrace cause it to disappear. In this populous city [Cádiz] even the children are aware if the Inquisition punished one of the ancestors of a family as a relapsed Jewish heretic. Every person free of unclean blood is defined by the law as an 'Old Christian, free of the stain of unclean race'. The severity of this law, or rather of the public opinion that supports it, closes to stained persons access to any employment in Church or state.

Few legends have become so completely ingrained in scholarly inter-pretation of modern Spain as that of the alleged obsession with blood purity.[41] According to this legend, crown, state and Church combined to discriminate obsessively against anyone with Jewish blood. Some historians assure us that 'alongside the obsessive concern with purity of the faith there flourished a no less obsessive concern with purity of blood; both obsessions were at their most violent in the middle decades of the sixteenth century . . . and had the effect of narrowing the extraordinarily wide range of Spanish life, and of forcing a rich and vital society into a straitjacket of conformity. The movement gathered real momentum as a result of events in the later 1540s in the Cathedral of Toledo. The stamp of royal approval was firmly set.'[42] This bold statement has little basis in fact, but the fascinating idea of a society in the grip of racism continues to be repeated by writers, popular novelists and historians alike. The origins of the myth are many, though the most crucial is the elementary confusion between the matter of blood purity, on which we shall touch below, and the broader issue of anti-Semitism – a global prejudice that has always been powerful in Spain, no less so today.[43]

The central episode concerning blood purity, to which reference is always made, is the adoption at Toledo in the year 1547 of a special statute excluding clergy of *converso* origin from being appointed to posts in the cathedral. Some historians continue to cite the episode as a triumph of racial obsession. For some unexplained reason they fail to mention that there was immediate, highly placed, opposition to the statute: from the city council of Toledo, from Castile's highest tribunal, the council of Castile (which concluded that 'the statute is unjust and scandalous and putting it into effect would cause many problems'), and from a special session of the clergy of Castile, who declared that 'the statute in its present harsh form raises serious problems, and putting it into effect would cause even more'.[44] They also fail to mention that Philip II (governor of Spain, and not yet king) suspended the statute, which was only allowed to come into effect nine years later, when the pope gave it his approval. Substantial elite opinion always opposed the statute. Philip II's biographer Cabrera de Córdoba referred to it as 'detested by those who decide the principles of good government', and reported that the Cortes had an 'undying hatred' of the measure.[45] His statements are a reflection of the impressive opposition to ideas of blood purity – a far cry from the 'obsession' that is often imputed.

The policy of discrimination through tests for blood purity (one had to prove that one's grandparents were not of Jewish origin) continued for a long time, but with very limited impact. We can offer four reasons for this. First, the small number of institutions with statutes (less than a sixth of Spain's bishoprics, for example) refutes any idea of an obsession sweeping the country. The statutes, moreover, were unknown in most of Spain during the sixteenth century, and existed almost exclusively in Castile. Second, they were always controversial and were never widely accepted. The same pope who had reluctantly approved the Toledo statute criticized it as being contrary to canon law and ecclesiastical order. In Spain, a continuous debate, directed largely *against* the statutes, was unleashed. Third, where statutes existed, those who wished to avoid them did so through recourse to bribes or fraudulent proofs.

Finally, even where statutes existed, Spaniards found it possible to impose them with a typical laxity, which in many cases undermined their existence. In Toledo in 1557, one year after Philip II finally permitted the famous statute of 1547 to come into force, a *converso* was appointed as canon of the cathedral.[46] The king regularly ignored statutes where they existed, and sometimes even broke the rules. It was usually very difficult for people of Jewish origin to get into the exclusive military orders of Castile. Philip, however, conferred a knighthood of Santiago on a famous Flanders war veteran while ordering that no enquiry be made into his purity of blood.[47] Most notoriously of all, city councils and cathedrals which had statutes of blood purity systematically ignored them when it suited their purpose. The Cathedral of Murcia adopted a statute in 1517, but immediately ignored it and did not make use of it until eighty years later. Toledo city council had had a statute since the year 1566, but throughout the period leading *converso* families continued freely to occupy posts.[48] In Cuenca, which had a long history of anti-Semitism, *converso* families during the late sixteenth century in fact occupied 50 per cent of the posts on the city council.[49] The gap was vast between adoption of statutes and their implementation.

Throughout these years, then, there was a profound ambivalence about the implementation of exclusion. *Conversos*, whether or not punished by the Inquisition, might in principle be excluded from many important bodies; in practice – as the leading constitutional authorities of the time testified – they were capable of acceding to most public offices in Castile and the rest of Spain. Throughout the period, *conversos* can be found both as students and as professors in the major universities. When in 1562 the rector of Salamanca University proposed introducing a purity statute, the university assembly voted that 'before introducing it we should consider carefully the many types of problems that might arise'. Finally, 'it was resolved that for the time being it should not be introduced'. When another attempt was made to introduce a statute in 1566, Philip II himself stepped in to prohibit it.[50] As Domínguez Ortiz has concluded, in the universities 'no legal barrier was ever raised against descendants of *conversos*'.[51]

In brief, the idea of a society and Inquisition gripped by concern for purity has little basis in fact. Some persons and groups of anti-Semitic inclination may have been obsessed, but there was no generalized 'violent' support for it, nor any resulting straitjacket of conformity, and the voices in its favour were losing momentum by the mid-sixteenth century. Above all, there was no stamp of royal approval, and in his last years Philip II attempted to get rid of the existing statutes. The rules about blood purity continued in force in several parts of Spain down to the nineteenth century, and affected many individuals to a varying and by no means negligible degree, though by then they were in the nature of a tool to exclude competitors for posts rather than a weapon of racialism.[52] The real worry that drove institutions to maintain the statutes was a concern for 'honour', to uphold social standards, which were deemed to be compromised by newcomers, especially if they were of Jewish origin.[53] The Inquisition played little part in the process of racial discrimination, a practice which rightly earned the loathing of Blanco White.

Despite the overwhelming evidence about the limited context of blood purity statutes, the myth about their role will possibly continue to survive because it offers a beautifully easy explanation for the complex nature of social relationships in Golden Age Spain. We choose myths because they confirm conclusions at which we have already arrived, regardless of whether they are true. In this case, the conclusion arises from a regrettable confusion between the question of blood purity and the rather different, and certainly more profound, problem of anti-Semitism, for which the Inquisition had a certain responsibility that it shared with the rest of the people of Spain.

The Inquisition against science

Popular writers and novelists have quite reasonably used the Inquisition as an element in their imaginative creativity. Without them, the Holy Office would cease to excite the curiosity of the general public. Yet the wish to perpetuate legends instead of attempting a historical analysis is still powerful, and another of the enduring and fiercely defended myths about the Inquisition – related, as we have seen, to the notion of Spain's isolation from the outside world – is that its history explains Spain's deficiencies in culture, science and philosophy. When Menéndez Pelayo turned his attention to this question, he published seven of his articles on the subject as *Spanish Science* (1876). His essays were attacked by Liberal writers, one of whom claimed (1876) that in the sixteenth century the Inquisition and the Habsburgs, between them, had destroyed freedom and thought:

> Never did the fury of intolerance and despotism reach further extremes than during the reigns of the first kings of the House of Habsburg. It was then that royal power destroyed the last vestiges of our liberties, and the Inquisition persecuted thought with the greatest cruelty.[54]

The ensuing debate in the press was reprinted in the final edition of the work, in three volumes (1887–8). Menéndez Pelayo was indignant at the way the Liberals had presented the story. He denied that the tribunal had repressed knowledge, and declared that it was the Enlightenment that had hurt science, mainly through the expulsion of the Jesuits (1767), an act he described as 'a death-blow for Spanish culture, which has not recovered since then'.[55] The debate, for someone who reads it today, is impressive for the almost complete indifference shown by the participants to what really happened in the past. In effect, Menéndez Pelayo's critics were concerned only to uphold the Liberal view of the sixteenth century, regardless of what the real facts might be; while Menéndez Pelayo, who was rather more concerned about the facts, did not let slip opportunities to attack the blatantly a priori arguments of his opponents.

Menéndez Pelayo's analysis was the first serious look at what may have happened to creative and scientific literature under a system of censorship, but his arguments were ignored by those wedded to the view that the backwardness of Spanish learning was due solely to the Inquisition. When we examine the statements offered by his opponents, it is clear that, for them, factual evidence was irrelevant. Their main contention, one fundamental to the Liberal version of history, was that Spain had been intolerant in the sixteenth century, and that this had destroyed the nation's cultural potential. The fact that other nations had also been intolerant but had not suffered similarly was inadmissible evidence. The Inquisition must not get off scot-free. When the controversy over science took off again in the twentieth century, those who blamed the Inquisition also had the luxury of pinning further blame on the dictatorships of that period. In general terms, the Liberal myth – as still upheld in the year 2003 by the author mentioned above (Sotelo) – runs as follows:

The debate over Spanish science broke out with greater fury than ever when the history of the home country was called into doubt by the Liberals in Spain in the last third of the nineteenth century. It was not just outside Spain that doubts were raised, as happened in the eighteenth century, when Spanish books had disappeared completely from European libraries.[56] A revealing detail is a letter from the young Lessing to his father, saying that he is going to learn Spanish because it is a language that nobody knows. In 1876, Gumersindo de Azcárate dared to state the obvious, that the Inquisition, which had completely annihilated liberty, was the reason why for three centuries Spain turned its back on the development of philosophy and modern science. Marcelino Menéndez Pelayo, a twenty-two-year-old boy steeped in an unbending Catholicism, replied with a book, *Spanish Science*, in which he identified himself wholly with the Inquisition and attempted to demonstrate with a long list of names and books in all the branches of learning that not only had it not impeded the development of science but it had actually strengthened it by protecting the faith. A decisive[57] reply from Ortega, the very person who is said to have 'made the Castilian language suitable for philosophizing', stated: 'Before he published his book one had the suspicion that there had been no science in Spain, after he published it became totally clear that there had never been any science.'

The debate over Spanish science surfaced once again during the Franco regime. On the one hand, Menéndez Pelayo was declared patron saint of the imperial and Catholic Spain that they hoped to establish, on the other, they persecuted with bitter fury any sign of liberal thinking even if it was right-wing, and of course the brunt of the hatred was directed against the most illustrious figure of Spanish liberal thought, José Ortega y Gasset.[58]

These lines demonstrate clearly that the real division of opinion over the question of science had little or nothing to do with an analysis of possible explanations, and everything to do with differences in ideology. Each opinion was categorized carefully into its own little box, with a political label prominently attached. The true issue, as to why Spain had produced no prominent scientists or philosophers, was never approached seriously. Nor did participants in the debate consider why Spaniards in the early modern period had possibly the least dedication to science, measured by the standard of the university affiliation of scientists,[59] compared to any nation in western Europe. Looking at the debate today, it is puzzling why the Inquisition was ever dragged into it, since the tribunal was never, at any stage of its evolution, involved in the prohibition of scientific thought.

CHAPTER SIX

THE MYTH OF
A UNIVERSAL LANGUAGE

One of the things that a nation should take particular care to achieve is that its language becomes universal.

Gregorio Mayans (1734)

The triumph of the Castilian language

Looking back in time, Spaniards were proud of the way in which the language of a small corner of Europe became converted into the common speech of thousands in America and Asia. That pride gave rise to a myth which, in the twenty-first century, remains stronger than ever. The use of the Spanish tongue seemed to be a vindication of Spain's power, culture and worldwide success. The myth therefore became an integral part of other myths, notably that of decline. If Spain's imperial achievement has collapsed, writers said, at least one great gain has been reaped: the world has been taught to speak Castilian. Language was therefore seen as the most universal, most profound and most enduring of Spain's successes in the early modern period. A Castilian writer boasted forcefully in 1580 that 'we have seen the majesty of the Spanish language extended to the furthest provinces, wherever the victorious flags of our armies have gone'.[1] Seventy years later, Baltasar Gracián claimed that there were two universal languages, Latin and Spanish, 'which today are the keys of the world'.[2] The claim was not true then, and became even less true as the years advanced.

An undoubted primary consequence of Spain's imperial identity was the diffusion of the Castilian language. The basic reference for this claim is, of course, the presentation of the humanist Antonio de Nebrija's *Grammar* to

Queen Isabella in 1492. When she wanted to know what purpose it served, her confessor, Fray Hernando de Talavera, bishop of Avila, broke in and spoke on Nebrija's behalf: 'After Your Highness has subjected barbarous peoples and nations of varied tongues', he explained, 'with conquest will come the need for them to accept the laws that the conqueror imposes on the conquered, and among them will be our language.' In the preface that he wrote for the *Grammar*, Nebrija followed Talavera's line of thought and claimed: 'I have found one conclusion to be very true, that language always accompanies empire; both have always commenced, grown and flourished together.' The sentiment was by then a commonplace; Nebrija copied the phrase from the Italian humanist Lorenzo Valla. The meaning of the reference was no novelty either, and reflected in good measure Nebrija's concern to advance his career by keeping on good terms with the government of the day. 'Language' in this context was not limited to vocabulary and grammar. It implied, rather, the imposition of culture, customs and, above all, religion on subjected peoples. Language was power. Was that power real?

Generations of scholars have learnt to accept that the age of empire was also that of the flowering of Castilian language and culture, a visible fulfilment of the intuitions of Talavera and Nebrija. The fact that Castilian is, in the twenty-first century, the principal language of up to a fifth of the human race is a source of continuing pride to Spaniards. Castilian was a crucial locus of identity because it became in some measure the language of empire. It was the first European language to be used on an extensive scale not only within the homeland but also in many other distant territories. Spaniards used it everywhere in order to communicate with other Spaniards. It became the medium of writers, clergymen, diplomats, and officers in the international armies of the crown. Latin was never a competitor as an effective imperial language, for few Spaniards understood it or read it. It was taught in Church and village schools, but for most people, and even for the clergy, it was a virtually dead tongue. In 1587, the author of a Castilian–Latin dictionary published at Salamanca confessed: 'the lack of the Latin language among Spaniards is noticeable to other nations'. Many other contemporaries said the same thing.[3] The rise of imperial power, by contrast, favoured the use of Spain's main language. A Navarrese professor at the Portuguese University of Coimbra published a book in 1544 in Castilian, with the comment that 'it is understood now in most Christian nations, whereas few people read Latin because they have not studied it'.[4]

Moreover, thanks to the existence of the empire, the Castilian tongue enjoyed advantages available to none other in Europe. Printing presses in the two most developed European nations, Italy and the Netherlands, made their resources available to Castilian authors, in part because the principal printing houses were there, but also because their territories had direct political links with Spain.[5] Unlike the English, who could expect to publish a book in their native tongue only in their own country, Castilians had the choice of publishing in any of the realms of the peninsula, as well as in the other states of the monarchy and in France and Portugal. By the 1540s, as we have already noted, more books by Spaniards were being published outside than inside the peninsula. They appeared mainly in Antwerp, Venice, Lyon, Toulouse, Paris, Louvain, Cologne, Lisbon and Coimbra.[6] When Philip II wished to print quality books in the 1560s, he published by preference in Antwerp and Venice. Because of the higher quality of foreign printing, there were good reasons for Spaniards wishing to publish outside the country.

The literary achievement, of which later generations were justifiably proud, was indubitable. Castilian works became known to Europeans and foreign presses published translations of Spanish works. The peak period for English interest was in the reign of Elizabeth I, when the two nations were in continuous conflict, covert or open, and Richard Hakluyt published in 1589 his great compendium of western (including Spanish) travel literature, *The Principall Navigations*. Until the mid-seventeenth century at least, Englishmen took an interest in Spain and its literature, which they translated and imitated.[7]

The Dutch shared an interest in the same literature: exploration, navigation, histories of America and of the Orient, as well as occasional works of literature[8] such as the drama *Celestina*. In the early modern period, private and public libraries in the Dutch Netherlands stocked over one thousand editions by Castilian authors, and 130 editions in translation from Castilian. In total, they stocked nearly six thousand editions of works in all languages dealing with Spain.[9] Even in Switzerland, which was not part of the empire, the printers of Basel published 114 editions of works by Spaniards between 1527 and 1564, and a further 70 between 1565 and 1610.[10] At no time, save for reasons of heresy or political crisis, did the Spanish Inquisition obstruct or interfere with this impressive literary output.

Was Spanish the language of Spain?

The undoubted success of the Castilian language in the peninsula, as well as abroad, prompts us to ask whether it was an expression of Spain as a nation. The term 'national tongue' for Castilian seems not to have appeared until the year 1884, when it was used by the official Castilian dictionary, issued by the Royal Academy of Language. The Academy distinguished it from other tongues spoken in the country, which were termed dialects. The emphasis on the role of language in the nineteenth century was, apparently, part of Spain's self-discovery as a 'nation'. Some experts in political thought tend to accept that language is a basic feature of a nation's identity, that a nation cannot exist without a common language, and that each nation should have one language which is its own. From the eighteenth century, when the German writer Herder emphasized that language gives a basic identity to a nation, there has been a fundamental stress on the priority of a common tongue among promoters of nationalist movements. This emphasis, however, has little support in what really happened historically. Language, we may say categorically, does not create a nation. In nearly all cases, the nation came before the language. Renan argued, with good reason, that 'language may invite us to unite, but it does not compel us to do so'. In all European countries, the adoption of a common language occurred long after the basic lineaments of the nation and state had fallen into place. In the unified Italy of 1860, only a tiny minority – less than 3 per cent – spoke the (Tuscan) dialect that would soon become the national language. In pre-revolutionary France, half the population either did not or could not speak French.[11]

The same situation held good for Spain. Nebrija may have had foresight in drawing up a Castilian grammar in 1492, but at that date possibly only half of Spain's population spoke the language and, almost certainly, more than 95 per cent could not write it. Nobody else, either in Europe or overseas, spoke Castilian. Exponents of the view that Spain was a nation in 1492 would have to accept the sad reality that a national language was not one of its basic constituents.[12] Nor is it possible to be too optimistic about the evolution of majority languages. It has been suggested that 'one of the secrets of Castilian domination was to be found in the triumph of its language and culture over that of other parts of the peninsula and empire. Castile's cultural predominance derived from the innate vitality of its literature and language at the end of the fifteenth century.'[13] The notion of a 'triumph over' other languages and cultures seems, when in perspective, inappropriate, but it formed – and still forms – an integral part of the conservative, imperial myth. Languages extended their cultural areas very slowly, and Spain formed no exception to the rest of the continent. It has rightly been pointed out that, 'between the fifteenth and seventeenth centuries, politically motivated programs of language promotion were pursued assiduously in most parts of western Europe. As a result of this process, the major vernacular languages of the region, including English, French, Spanish, German, Italian, Swedish, Portuguese and Dutch, were transformed from mainly spoken, highly localized dialects, with small and unstable vocabularies, into the richly abundant, uniform and standardized written languages of state administration and literary production with which we are familiar today.'[14]

As a rule, language was not transmitted through books. The success of printed literature obviously had a very limited impact in a world where very few people read books, where illiteracy was overwhelming, and where all significant cultural contact was oral rather than written. The situation in the Iberian Peninsula was typical. Spanish works might be best sellers in Barcelona bookshops, but in the streets nearly everyone spoke Catalan. 'In Catalonia', claimed a priest from that principality in 1636, over one hundred years after the beginning of the Habsburg dynasty, 'the common people do not understand Castilian.'[15] The situation could be found elsewhere in the coastal provinces of Spain. As late as 1686, regulations for shipping in Guipúzcoa had to stipulate that vessels carry a Basque-speaking priest, since among the seamen 'most do not understand the Castilian tongue'. The absence of a common national tongue, a fairly normal phenomenon in most European states, was particularly striking. Castilian was not understood at all by a good part of the natives of Andalusia and Valencia (if they were of Islamic origin), Catalonia, the Basque country, Navarre and Galicia.[16] The problem was brought home forcibly to missionaries who tried to communicate with congregations in these parts of the country. In the formerly Muslim areas, where Arabic still survived as a spoken tongue, the missionaries tried in vain to learn Arabic and to get their message across to the people. In Catalonia, all the non-Catalan clergy made efforts to learn the local tongue, and the Jesuits for example took care to appoint only Catalans to work in the province. Throughout the Habsburg epoch, the plurality of languages within the peninsula was of necessity recognized and accepted. Castilian, however, was readily accepted as the lingua franca of Spaniards. It was acknowledged as such without any pretensions to its being the *only* language of Spain. As Gregorio Mayans explained in his *Origins of the Spanish Language* (1737): 'By "Spanish language" I mean the language that all Spaniards usually speak when we wish to understand each other perfectly.' A similar view was expressed in 1811 by the Catalan Antonio Puigblanch, though he went further and suggested, as Unamuno was to do later, that non-Castilian languages should be suppressed: 'It is essential to abandon the language of the province. He will always be a stranger in his own country who does not adopt the national language as his own.'[17]

The Castilian tongue in a wider world

In the early sixteenth century, Castilian had barely begun to make an impact on Europe judging by the unpublished sixteenth-century *Dialogue of Language* (*c*.1536) of the exiled Juan de Valdés, resident in Italy at the time. At the beginning of his work, he admitted that his native Castilian had less standing as a literary language than Tuscan (the dialect that later became known as 'Italian'), because Tuscan 'was given form and richness by Boccaccio, by Petrarch . . . whereas as you know the Castilian language has never had anyone writing in it with the care and consideration that would be necessary for someone to use it with confidence'.[18] Valdés preferred to speak and write in Castilian, but did not read it much, 'because since I understand Latin and Italian I do not bother about Castilian'. However, Castilian soon became a necessary part of the baggage of educated people, thanks to the international role of Charles V and Philip II. But it never equalled the status of Italian, which remained, for Europeans, the universal language of culture.

It is relevant to quote the example of Johann Ulrich von Eggenberg (*d*.1634), a Bohemian noble whose love for Spain began during a visit in 1600–1 and who collected the works of Cervantes and Lope de Vega. He also supported the Habsburgs during the Battle of the White Mountain. Today his rich collection of books is preserved in the beautiful castle library of Český Krumlov, in the mountains outside Prague. In the years when he bought foreign works, he collected twenty-eight items in Spanish, but also twenty-four in French, and the overwhelming bulk of his purchases was in Italian, 126 books.[19] The Latin culture that penetrated central Europe was, despite Spain's power and influence, predominantly Italian. When the Austrian nobility of this period wished to broaden their cultural horizons, they went to study at Padua, Bologna and Siena rather than in Spain. When they bought foreign books, they preferred works by Italians.[20] The same happened in France, where the marriage in 1614 of King Louis XIII to a Spanish princess, Anne of Austria, stimulated a short-lived vogue for things Spanish at court. Cervantes in Spain seems to have been under the erroneous impression that, as a result of the marriage, everyone in France began to learn

Castilian.[21] It was in reality a fashion limited strictly to the court, which lasted little more than a decade and was opposed by most of the French elite.[22] From mid-century the vogue returned for Italian culture, which had always been the major influence in France and never lost its predominant position.[23]

In the same way, Spanish had an ambiguous role in America. In Mexico, for example, the missionary friars used the Nahuatl language in their religious work but otherwise always gave preference to Spanish, both because it was easier and because it became a lingua franca in areas where other native dialects were used. The fusion of cultures through written Spanish was, however, always more apparent than real. Beyond the written word, the real world for the natives of America consisted of sounds, colours and presences that remained beyond the reach of the perceptions of Spaniards.[24] It was a universe quite alien to the Europeans, who failed to understand it and rejected it as pagan. As was to be expected of a European tongue in a complex alien environment (the English and Dutch faced similar problems in their colonies), Spanish spread very slowly. The Castilian language was spoken by Spaniards wherever they went, and was even used by Basques in northern Mexico as a lingua franca, although many of course continued to speak their own native tongue. On the New Mexico frontier, pidgin Spanish was employed as a lingua franca among the indigenous peoples, and European words entered their daily vocabulary. But in colonial times the language of the Spaniards never attained universal status, except in administrative matters, when it was the only practical one to use. At the level of culture, Nebrija's prediction that Castilian would become the 'language of empire', that is, that Castilian culture would predominate, was never fulfilled.

It was little more than a delusion to imagine that the Castilian tongue could become the universal language of the empire, for few natives of America in the colonial period managed to write it.[25] When Guaman Poma wrote his *Chronicle*, he depicted a confrontation between Indian and Spaniard where the inability to communicate was total. Poma saw the Spaniards as being interested neither in the country nor in the people of America but only in their gold: 'driven by greed, many priests and Spaniards and ladies and merchants took ship for Peru, all was Peru and more Peru, and more and more gold and silver, gold, silver from this land'. In one of the most telling of the drawings in Poma's *Chronicle*, the Inca Huayna Capac addresses a conquistador and asks: *Cay coritacho micunqui?* ('Do you eat this gold?') To this the Spaniard replies, not in Quechua, which he does not understand, but in Spanish: *Este oro comemos* ('We eat this gold').[26] The irony is that the communication barrier was overcome by a commodity, gold, that made all communication superfluous. Garcilaso de la Vega, who wrote his monumental *Commentaries* in Spain, observed the lamentable inadequacy of many Spaniards in matters of language and the consequent gap of comprehension between cultures. The Indians, he wrote, 'do not dare to give an account of things with the proper meaning and explanation, seeing that Christian Spaniards abominate everything they see'. Even the learned Spanish missionaries confused basic terms in Quechua.

In Asia, Spanish failed to take root at all. During the age of early European commerce, the accepted lingua franca was Portuguese, spoken even by Asian traders to each other and adopted perforce by Spaniards if they wished to communicate with Asians. Hindu rulers in Ceylon and Muslim rulers in Macassar spoke and wrote Portuguese.[27] To communicate with other Europeans the non-Portuguese missionaries habitually spoke Portuguese, with the consequence that some began to lose fluency in their own language.[28] The Navarrese Jesuit Francisco Xavier (whom we have mentioned) used Portuguese rather than Spanish as his main medium of communication in Asia. As late as the eighteenth century, officials of the British East India Company in India had to learn to communicate with their employees.

In a colony such as Manila, where Spaniards were a tiny minority, Castilian had a slim chance of survival. The earliest Spanish missionaries came face to face with the phenomenon of Chinese preponderance. The first books to be turned out in the islands were printed by the resident Chinese (known as 'Sangleys'), who used their experience from the Chinese continent to introduce block printing and to pioneer the necessary typography. Books on the Christian religion were written by Dominicans. But they were printed in the native tongues at a time when the government in Spain was officially trying to discourage these in favour of Castilian. The first known printed work in the Philippines, in 1593, was in Chinese and written by a Dominican. The second, a *Christian Doctrine* or catechism published that same year, had facing pages in Castilian and Tagalog. In a *Memorial on the Life of a Christian* published in 1606 in Chinese, Fray Domingo de Nieva explained (in Chinese) that 'when religion does not use language it is obstructed, when faith is explained in an unknown script it will not be recognized'.[29] Like many of his fellow missionaries on the American mainland, he had come to the conclusion that Castilian was, in reality, an obstacle to empire. Unless and until Castilian could compete successfully with other tongues, no proper communication was possible. He and his colleagues patiently devoted themselves to Chinese studies, not so much because of the Sangleys, who were awaiting the gospel in the Philippines, as because of the mighty Chinese empire that lay beyond them and awaited conversion.

The achievement of the clergy in language studies was of fundamental value, since in many cases they rescued dialects from probable oblivion and opened bridges to communication. In 1612, the Franciscan Francisco de Pareja produced the first word-book, designed for the confessional, of the Timucuan dialects used in northern Florida. It was the first time that the language appeared in printed form. But it was also, to all practical purposes, the last, since both the Timucuan Indians and their language very soon became extinct. The efforts at ethnology were admirable, but usually achieved little. In practice, the clergy found themselves obliged to stick to Spanish. Many religious orders, the Franciscans among them, very soon gave up the attempt to teach Indians in local dialects and limited themselves to Castilian. In the peninsula, clergy ministering to the Moriscos gave up the attempt to learn Arabic. The result was an exclusive reliance on Castilian, with all the attendant consequences. In 1642 a Portuguese writer commented that, during the years of their presence in his country, 'the Castilians permitted use of their language alone, and treated the Portuguese language worse than if it were Greek'.[30] Chauvinism in matters of language was common to all empires, and it would be unjust to criticize the Spaniards for following a path that was quite normal. The truth is that the clergy made extensive efforts to keep up a dialogue between their own tongue and that of their parishioners. But the policy seldom worked. By always falling back on the use of Spanish, they effectively cut off contact with non-Castilian cultures, which continued to use their own languages. Well into the eighteenth century, parish priests in the Andes would preach their sermons in Castilian, while uncomprehending natives would listen in polite silence.

Some clergy in Manila, like the Dominican Domingo de Navarrete in the mid-seventeenth century, assiduously learnt Tagalog, Mandarin and Fukien. The first grammar of Tagalog was the achievement of Francisco Blancas, who produced an *Art and Rules of the Tagalog Language* in 1610.[31] All these pioneering works had a single purpose: to enable the European to understand, speak and write the native languages. They therefore adopted an exclusively one-way approach to the process of transfer of meaning. The Castilian language was translated into native terms; by contrast, little attempt was made to translate native concepts into Spanish. By grasping a set of perceived words and actions and freezing them within a recognizable vocabulary, the colonial missionaries brought into existence something that was defined according to Castilian concepts alone. The result was an often neglected aspect of the impact of empire: its failure to understand the way subjected peoples really thought.[32] Missionaries lived with native Americans and Asians for decades and claimed to be able to speak their language and even to write it, but at certain moments of conflict they suddenly realized that they had no real comprehension of the way people thought. The conquerors and the conquered appeared to be speaking the same language, but they were really living in two different worlds of meaning.[33]

Charles V and the Castilian tongue

The purpose of the preceding paragraphs has been to give some historical context to the frequent claim that at the height of its Golden Age Spain's language dominated the western world. During the period covered by this book, the most notable world empire was indeed that of Spain, with settlements and fortresses in every continent of the globe. Yet, as we have noted, in Europe the only language with any pretensions to cultural universality was Italian, soon to be succeeded, from the seventeenth century on, by French. Italian was, after Latin, the most common language used by diplomats in Renaissance Europe.[34] It was used, read, studied and spoken by all elites, from London and Brussels to Vienna and Warsaw. Spanish also came to be used widely, but its role is usually mythologized because of an incident in 1536. In that year, Emperor Charles V delivered a speech in Spanish in Rome, in the presence of the pope and of the diplomatic representatives of the city. His discourse was seen by all sides, particularly those within the Italian context, as innovative and aggressive. Writers who appear not to have read the speech or not to be aware of the circumstances in which it was made have gone as far as to say that the emperor vindicated the Spanish language before the whole of Europe. The context was somewhat different.

The previous year, 1535, had been one of military glory, when the emperor and his Italian allies managed to capture the city of Tunis on the North African coast. No sooner had he completed the mission than a new military threat emerged, this time from France. The emperor sailed directly from Tunis to Sicily and Naples, where he spent the winter and dedicated himself to the administration of his kingdoms in southern Italy. In March 1536 he accepted an invitation from the pope to discuss common problems, and on

5 April 1536 was in Rome. Two days earlier, French troops crossed the frontier into Italy; there was now a state of war between France and the emperor.

Charles had a lot of business to discuss with Pope Paul III, who consequently organized a triumphal entry for him. On 17 April, Charles addressed an assembly of cardinals and diplomats, in the presence of the pope. The speech is the only public discourse in Europe ever delivered in Spanish by the emperor. It is also the basis for the claim, made repeatedly in the twentieth century, that the emperor declared Spanish to be the universal and official language. For instance, Menéndez Pidal stated in his *Imperial Idea* that the Spanish language

> began to be used everywhere, above all after Charles V made it resound under the domes of the Vatican,[35] in a speech before pope Paul III, on 17 April 1536. In this way the emperor, who spoke not a word of Spanish when he was eighteen, now at the age of thirty-six proclaimed the Spanish tongue to be the common tongue of Christendom and the official language of diplomacy, a fundamental fact to help us understand his Imperial Idea.[36]

This reasoning was echoed by Manuel Alvar, in a brilliant article on Charles V's command of languages.[37] Inevitably, Alvar followed Pidal's argument, stating that, 'from within the history of the Spanish language, the words of Charles V arouse feelings that we still experience. The emperor declared the Spanish language to be the universal means of communication, extending well beyond the frontiers of Spain.'

What really happened in Rome that spring day of 1536 was far removed from what Pidal claimed when he gave his stimulating lecture on the Imperial Idea in Havana four hundred years later, in 1936. Charles V was very angry with France for having broken the peace, and startled the assembly by refusing to speak in his own tongue, French. Instead, he spoke in Castilian. He angrily denounced the threats to peace posed by France, and France's unacceptable alliance with the infidel Barbarossa. Holding up in his hand a sheaf of secret correspondence between Francis I and Barbarossa, he said: 'I myself, with my own hands, seized at La Goletta these letters I am holding'.[38] He challenged Francis I to resolve their differences by a personal duel rather than endanger the lives of so many Christians. At the end of his long peroration, delivered without any notes, he insisted repeatedly, 'I wish for peace, I wish for peace, I wish for peace!' His audience was stunned, many of them because they had not expected to be addressed in a language little used among diplomats. The bishop of Mâcon, one of France's envoys to the papacy, spoke up and asked the emperor for a text of the discourse, since he did not understand Castilian. Charles replied tersely: 'My lord bishop, let me be clear: do not expect to hear me speak in any language other than Spanish, which is so noble that it deserves to be known and understood by all Christian men.' His intention, evidently, was not to vindicate Spanish, but to speak it precisely in order to irritate the good bishop, who could not understand what he was saying. Charles' own advisers were perplexed by the unexpected vigour of his 'sermon', as they termed it, and by the use of Spanish. The next day, when his ire had cooled, the emperor summoned the two French ambassadors in private but he still refused to speak French and gave them a verbal summary '*in italiano buonissimo*', of what he had said in Castilian. Charles, in short, had a very specific reason for refusing to speak French. He always gave precedence to that language both in private and in public life. By contrast, his use of Spanish in the presence of the cardinals implied no intention whatever of declaring it a universal tongue.

And indeed, afterwards Charles did not – to my knowledge – make any more speeches in Spanish outside of Spain. Spanish never became the official language of international diplomacy. One and a half centuries later, a French writer claimed that the emperor used to say that 'if he wished to speak to ladies he would speak Italian, if he wished to speak to men he would speak French, if he wished to speak to his horse, he would speak German, but if he wished to speak to God he would speak Spanish'.[39] Even if the anecdote were true, it would not affect the interpretation of what really happened when Charles moved about his dominions. He simply limited himself to speaking the appropriate language within the appropriate context. His rule was always to speak French, whether in Germany or the Netherlands. It was the language he spoke in private to his family, and in public to his advisers and courtiers. It was the language in which he wrote his memoirs. He also used Castilian, of course, in correspondence related to the peninsula, and also in official meetings where Castilians happened to be present.

At this early period, there were in reality few serious objections to using the language, for Castilians had not yet become an unloved imperial power. There was opposition to them both in Germany and the Netherlands, but out of xenophobia, it seems, rather than because of anything they had done. It was not until the revolt of the Netherlands, thirty years later, that the situation changed considerably, thanks in good measure to the duke of Alba's harsh policies. When the duke of Parma, Alessandro Farnese, became governor of the Netherlands a few years later, he encountered in that country a great tide of hostility to things Spanish. As a consequence, he took care to present himself as an Italian rather than a Spaniard,[40] and his public discourse was always in Italian or in bad French, never in Spanish, a language he spoke perfectly but preferred not to use.

The language of Cervantes

Spanish, therefore, became widely used and appreciated, but could not compete with Italian in the sixteenth century or with French in the eighteenth. This cultural failure gave birth to the need for a myth about Spain's language. The principal weapon which would be used in the formation of this myth lay hidden way back in early modern times. The weapon was Cervantes' novel *Don Quixote*, the first part of which was published in 1605. From the 1800s, but above all around the year 1900, the novel embodied, for many Spanish intellectuals, the hope of a resurrection of greatness for their country. It is difficult for other Europeans to grasp the scope of the myth that came to be created around it. It was as though (to take an English parallel) Shakespeare's play *Hamlet* were suddenly and insistently cited, three hundred years later, by the statesman Benjamin Disraeli, the novelist Charles Dickens and the poet Rudyard Kipling, as the cultural work with which they hoped to advance British civilization throughout the globe. The key slogan among some Spaniards was 'the language of Cervantes' – an appeal to, or rather invocation of, that language as a sort of magical talisman that promised a solution to the world's ills. Behind that invocation, however, there also lurked an imperialist assertiveness (based on Charles V's speech in Rome in 1536), which was the foundation of the claim to Castilian being a 'universal language'.

The context of this resurrection of Quixote was complex, and has been well studied by scholars. My reference here is merely to its part in the myth of linguistic imperialism and in the myth's connection with the sixteenth century. After the drama of the Disaster of 1898, Cervantes' novel came to be viewed as a last and final hope for Spanish civilization precisely because it was seen as a product of the Golden Age of success in the sixteenth century (in the same way that the Portuguese political elite in the nineteenth century invented a national day around the presumed date of death – 10 June 1580 – of their most famous poet, Camões).[41] Commentators around the year 1900 were reading into the work a vision of Spain's moral status in a world threatened by the materialism and technology of the United States. In a letter of 1898 to Angel Ganivet, Unamuno claimed that the novel was 'the eternal symbol of humanity in general and of our Spanish nation in particular'.[42] Probably the first literary commentary came from the exiled Nicaraguan poet Ruben Darío, who was in Spain when the crisis occurred and expressed his rage through an essay, *D.Q.* (the initials of Cervantes' hero), which he published the following year in Buenos Aires. Darío saw in Quixote a personification of those high ideals which had made Spain great and would eventually rescue Hispanic culture from the monster (the United States) now threatening it. The Uruguayan writer Rodó, whose essay *Ariel* (1900) was a feverish response to the invasion of Cuba, subsequently went on record with the opinion that 'the philosophy of *Quixote* is the philosophy of the conquest of America', in the sense that Quixote represented spiritual values that had dignified the Spanish conquest, whereas the American aggression represented vulgar materialism. The Quixote cult received its most powerful boost with the celebration in 1905 of the third centenary of the novel's publication.[43] Less than a decade had passed since the Disaster, and commentators used the novel in its historic past as a means of analysing what had gone wrong with Spain's present. In a subsequent essay Unamuno wrote: 'It may be that we have to seek the hero of our way of thought not in some philosopher of flesh and bone, but in a being of fiction and action, more real than all the philosophers, namely Don Quixote.'

From being a work of literature, *Quixote* was converted into a political weapon, to be used by every commentator on the spiritual and social situation of Spain. A whole new world of public discourse was opened up. Every significant intellectual made his contribution, so that *Don Quixote* became *par excellence* the surgical tool which writers used to prise open and analyse the inert corpse of their native country. The new interest in Cervantes had little to do with culture and a lot to do with national pride and mysticism. The president of the Second Republic summed it up nicely in the 1930s: 'We claim to see in the defeat and disappointment of Don Quixote the failure of Spain itself.' Writers like Unamuno and Ortega paid attention to the morally uplifting principles of the novel, while would-be reformers (the 'regenerationists') found in it modernizing values. Among the sceptics who thought that the cult was irrational was an engineer from Huesca named Lucas Mallada (*d.*1921), one of the early promoters of Darwinism in Spain and a sharp critic of writers who (like Unamuno) preferred dreams to the possibility of scientific progress. In a penetrating study, Mallada wrote:

'Among us there exists in all social classes a defect that I shall express in one sole word: fantasy. The land of Don Quixote is a land of dreamers.'[44]

The accumulation of names writing on the Don Quixote theme, over a span of two decades shows that the fascination – unparalleled in any other European country – with a two-centuries-old work of fiction was a serious cultural phenomenon. Through the generations, the fascination has developed into an almost religious veneration, in which the novel is revered – even more than the Holy Bible – as a sacred book, read aloud solemnly every year in Madrid on Cervantes' birthday by public figures, paragraph by paragraph, by day and by night and from beginning to end. Unamuno defended the trend: 'my worship of *quijotismo* as the national religion'. The Valencian novelist Vicente Blasco Ibáñez perhaps expressed more than anybody the celestial significance of the mad knight of La Mancha. He affirmed the role of Cervantes' novel as 'the Bible of our people' and as 'the representative of the spirit of Spain and of all humanity'.[45]

'Spanishness' and the myth of an imperial language

In 1734, the Valencian scholar Gregorio Mayans, a fervent admirer of Italian culture, admitted to Spain's chief minister, the Italian José Patiño, that Spain had failed to extend the influence of its language. 'One of the things that a nation should take particular care to achieve', he wrote, 'is that its language becomes universal.' That had only happened, according to him, in the great days of Philip II, when Spanish had reached the furthest corners of the earth. Now, by contrast, it had been superseded by English and French, whose literature, science and languages were supreme in the world. 'The fault', he said, 'is ours, due to our inadequacy.'[46] Mayans' words show the continuing power, even at that time, of the myth of imperial language. All imperial nations need to extend their language, because without it they are unable to communicate in, and govern, other territories. It was normal for European colonists in the overseas territories to impose their own tongue, but also to study indigenous tongues in order to open up channels of contact. In certain circumstances – as happened in the sixteenth century, when the Spanish crown tried to restrict the use of native tongues in order to help colonial administrators – the promotion of Castilian became a practical and desired option.

The unquestionable success of the Spanish language, in virtually every continent of the world and, above all, in Spain itself, gave enormous scope for comfort when the achievements of the empire began to turn sour. Confronted by a collapse of imperial power, increase of economic tribulations and lack of popularity in the world, Spaniards could take comfort in the idea that, even if they failed in every other respect, at least they had once dominated the globe through their language. It was at that stage that myth took over from reality. In Latin America the official mythology, upheld by Spanish missionaries but also by the state, was that the greater part of the population had been Hispanicized and spoke Spanish. In reality, it is doubtful whether Castilian was spoken as a principal language by more than a tenth of the visible population in the colonial New World, where the vast majority of the people continued to maintain their own society, culture and language, and for the most part had no regular contact with Spaniards. Even the black slaves tended to preserve their own African languages rather than speak the alien tongue of the slave masters. At independence, in the early nineteenth century, the national leaders had difficulty finding enough educated administrators with a knowledge of Spanish. Promotion of the language, therefore, became a priority for Latin American politicians simply because the Spaniards had failed to do the job.

One hundred years after independence, the cultural leaders of the Latin nations were still attempting to impose Castilian, in the hope that its generalized use would contribute to a sense of national identity. Intellectuals in Peru, for example, recognized that, four centuries after Columbus, Quechua was still the first language of the majority, and they proposed that Castilian be imposed in order to modernize culture.[47] A telling case is that of the Philippines, where, after three and a half centuries, in a territory covering seven thousand islands and with a population speaking over three hundred dialects, the Spaniards never managed to teach their own language to more than 5 per cent of the inhabitants.[48] The missionaries themselves tended to use native tongues in their work, since Spanish was not understood in the islands. In the period of American rule after 1898, an active educational programme was put into effect, with the result that, by 1939 (that is, within forty years), over 26 per cent of Filipinos spoke English. Ironically, the anti-American native resistance began to propose that Spanish should be cultivated as a lingua franca in order to give the Filipinos a common sense of identity.[49] The language, curiously enough, continued to be most in use among the huge Chinese population, who are still today the last bastion, in the islands, of the language of Cervantes. In both Peru and the Philippines, then, it was, ironically, the pro-indigenous movement that attempted to give a boost to a language that had not been universal during the old imperial regime.

The attempt to use the old imperialist language to further cultural nationalism had a certain logic for some leaders in Latin America and could not fail to delight Castilian nationalists in Spain, where the patriotic ideology of *Hispanismo* began to develop. 'Spanishness', or *Hispanismo*, especially after 1898, was directed principally against the United States and the English language. But it also fuelled the fires of Castilian nationalism and was used against the minority languages of the peninsula, which were in danger of becoming active vehicles for provincial separatism within Spain. Unamuno, a Basque by origin and a conservative in politics, showed himself an intractable enemy to all threats to the language of Cervantes. He recommended that the Catalan language be eliminated and predicted the 'inevitable death' of Basque as a language. 'Every day,' he announced, 'I am more of a fanatic for the language in which I speak, write, think and feel.'[50] Unamuno's chauvinism over language is illustrated by his furious reaction to foreign criticism of the terrible events in the Tragic Week in Barcelona in 1909. Foreign writers, including Ernst Haeckel, Anatole France and Maurice Maeterlinck, had criticized the harsh repression. Irritated by their attitude, in September 1909, Unamuno wrote an outraged letter to the Madrid newspaper *ABC*, in which he stated that Spain was being systematically defamed, partly because of the envy that Europeans felt at the fact that Spanish was the world's principal language, something which they could not forgive. We are superior to Europeans, he proclaimed; the spirit of San Juan de la Cruz is superior to that of Descartes. If they claim to have achieved scientific inventions, well, 'let them invent, later we shall apply their inventions'. In the same period he advocated the suppression, in the former Hispanic lands of the New World, of all languages apart from Spanish. These sentiments were echoed by Ortega y Gasset, who believed no less firmly in the unique virtues of Castile. 'Only Castilian heads', he maintained in *Invertebrate Spain*, 'have adequate capacity to perceive the great problem of a united Spain.' Castile alone had created Spain, and Castile's language alone was the true language of Spain.

Shortly after the loss of the colonies in 1898, Spanish writers took part, with the politicians, in a movement to affirm the benefits that their culture had brought to the New World. The movement was continued a generation later, during the dictatorship of Franco, by granting state funding for the establishment of institutes for the promotion of the Castilian language in key foreign cities. The broad lines of this attempt to recover status in the world may be summarized as follows. The doctrine of *Hispanismo* included, among many other postulates, 'the existence of a unique Spanish culture, lifestyle, traditions and values, all of them embodied in its language; the idea that Spanish American culture is nothing but Spanish culture transplanted to the New World; and the notion that Hispanic culture has a hierarchy in which Spain occupies a hegemonic position'.[51] The New World, in this post-imperial view, was perceived as a virtual *tabula rasa* with little coherence of its own before it received the decisive imprint of Castilian. That language immediately created the Hispanic *raza*, the highest form of civilization. This attitude to the Spanish tongue was carried to the New World by cultured exiles from the peninsula, and was also promoted by Latin Americans at international gatherings in which writers (such as the Mexican novelist Carlos Fuentes) were invited to back up the Castilians in eulogies of the culture that Spain had conferred on America. In a typical pro-*Hispanismo* speech in Rosario (Argentina) in 2004, Fuentes put forward the idea that 'in the beginning, America was a vast unpopulated territory', waiting only for cultural input, which it received when 'indigenous America was injected with the immense Hispanic legacy, from the most multicultural land of Europe: Celtic and Iberian, Phoenician, Greek, Roman, Jewish, Arab and Christian Spain'[52] – a highly imaginative vision of the impact that Spanish emigrants really had on the New World.

The theme of *Hispanismo*, however, affects us here only to the extent that it drew on a mythological version of early modern Spanish culture on which it could base itself. The myth was constructed in great measure by the same prolific intellect that would in 1936 construct the theory of Spain's imperial leadership under Charles V (see chapter 4). This gifted artificer was Menéndez Pidal, the philologist who dedicated his whole life to the Castilian language. In the wake of the 1898 Disaster, Pidal was deeply convinced that Castilian had a mission in world history. 'The ultimate objectives of his linguistic work,' it has been pointed out, 'were to counter anti-Spanish sentiment and secure the loyalty of the Spanish and Latin American elite to the project of constructing a modern Hispanic community in which Spain's leadership would be recognized.'[53] The apparently neutral issue of language became converted into an animated political battleground in which the main issue was Spain's claim to cultural hegemony. Pidal argued that Castilian had intrinsically superior qualities, and that it had proved itself historically as a unified and a unifying language, both in the peninsula and in the former colonies of the New World. The corollaries of this position were evident. Other languages must give way to Castilian, notably in the peninsula, where regional languages must be downgraded. With this objective before their eyes, partisans of his point of view had little difficulty imagining that the Castilian (that is, 'Spanish') language had been the regenerator of the western world. The clearest exposition of this doctrine was made (as we have seen) by Maeztu:

> In the whole of world history there is no achievement comparable to that of Spain, for we have incorporated into Christian civilization all the races that were under our influence.[54]

This was the period when, for the first time in 1918, Spain began to celebrate the Twelfth of October as a national holiday. In a 1934 speech in Buenos Aires to celebrate that date, the cardinal primate of Spain, Isidro Gomá, defined the concept of 'Spanishness':

> I would say that it is the projection of the physiognomy of Spain beyond itself and on to the peoples who constitute the Hispanic community. It is the Spanish temperament, not the physiological temperament but the moral and historical, which has been transmitted to other races and nations and lands and has marked them with the seal of the Spanish soul, Spanish life and deeds. It is the genius of Spain which has hatched the genius of other lands and races and without altering their nature has elevated and purified it and made it like itself. That is what I understand by race and Spanishness.

The core of Spanishness was language. There are various reasons for enthusiasm about a language. It may be one's only tongue, and therefore highly prized. It may be a language in which one has invested money for technological purposes. It may be associated with one's country, and therefore stir patriotic feelings. The unusual aspect of concern for Spanish as a universal tongue was perhaps without parallel. The zeal for its universalism derived from the conviction that it had achieved greatness for Castile in the sixteenth century, and that this historic greatness would rise to even greater heights in the future. It was this concern that converted the issue into a myth, though of course not all Spaniards agreed with it to the same extent. Some years ago, the director of the Cervantes Institute, a body set up precisely in order to sspread the merits of the language of Cervantes throughout the world, commented with remarkable impartiality that obsession with the status of their language had caused among some Spaniards a mixture of 'historical frustration (that is, "we should be the first"), a persecution mania ("there is an international conspiracy to prevent us from being the first"), and sporadic juvenile bragging ("we are in second place but soon we shall be in first")'.[55] He summed up perfectly the essential reasons why the myth continues to excite polemics.

Almost uniquely among languages, Castilian excites claims to universalism that are seldom made by speakers of, for example, English or Russian. A recent (2004) discourse by a Mexican writer, Enrique Krauze, offers a perspective on the political motives behind what may appear to be merely a cultural ambition:

There is a benevolent empire on which the sun never sets. It is the empire of the Spanish language, a realm that is both ancient and modern, cultural and spiritual, a virtual nation without frontiers, multiple, complex, varied, changing and full of promise. Spanish spreads with pride, it no longer belongs only to Spain nor is it principally of Spain.

Castilian, Spanish, is one of the most living and vibrant languages of the world, and one of those that advance with most energy. To narrate the astonishing history of our language may be, or appear to be, an absurdity, but it is never out of place, because its evolution is one of the undisputed glories of Western civilization.

The language became so rooted that the descendants of the Jews expelled from Spain in 1492 continued using it and yearning for it across the centuries. Even today, that old Spanish survives miraculously. For language is a territory of religious peace, above questions of faith.

We come to the age of Charles V and Philip II. A flood of captains, soldiers, adventurers, missionaries, artisans and traders from Castile, Extremadura, Andalusia carried Spanish – and they rooted it more or less profoundly – to the limits of the empire, to the remote Philippines. In the royal courts of Europe, there were translators of the language of the emperor. In the capital cities there were readers of Lope de Vega, Calderón, Quevedo and the other excellent writers our language enjoyed in the Golden Century.

The Hispanoamerican nations renewed contacts, both between themselves and with Spain, after 1898, and out of this convergence a new miracle was born: a reconciliation of the trunk with its branches, in the areas of thought and literature. When in 1900, in his *Ariel*, the Uruguayan José Enrique Rodó called on the Hispano-American countries to deepen their spiritual heritage by spurning the crude materialism of the Anglo-Americans, he was expressing a disquieting prophecy. So we arrive in the twentieth century. And at this uncertain beginning of the twenty-first, Spanish is the protagonist of a new, thrilling but also dangerous episode. I refer, of course, to the presence of thirty-five million Spanish speakers of the first, second or third generation inside 'the entrails of the monster', as Martí expressed it, of the United States of America. Given the foreseeable demographic trends, it could be a powerful weapon, a weapon that, besides, in a not-too-distant future, could influence in a decisive manner the political life of the United States and, as a natural consequence, of the entire world. That is our natural frontier.[56]

The specifically political dimension of these sentiments emerged clearly in comments Krauze made to the press. The agency Notimex reported that 'the Mexican writer Enrique Krauze proposed a spiritual conquest of the United States through Spanish, in order to impose the empire of a language that is now spoken by around thirty-five million persons there'.[57]

The notion of a 'conquest' has occurred frequently in similar speeches by writers asserting the unique claims of Spanish in the New World. In a speech in Madrid in 1987, Carlos Fuentes proclaimed that 'in the coming century, the Castilian language will be the dominant language in all the Americas, north, central and south'. In the Second International Conference of Spanish in Valladolid, Spain, in October 2001, he called for 'a silent reconquest[58] of the United States' as a new frontier for the language. The imperial dream, similar to that formulated by *Hispanismo*, is clear enough. And the number of people who are said to speak the language as their principal one has, it seems, no limits. The Spanish newspaper *El País* proclaimed confidently in the year 2000 that 'today close to four hundred million persons in the world speak Castilian'.[59] In the spring of 2007 a columnist in another newspaper, *El Mundo*, calculated that the real figure is five hundred million. The authors of the Spanish version of the online reference work Wikipedia do not doubt that Castilian is 'the second most widely used language in the world, after Chinese'.

It seems, therefore, that what began as a myth of imperial assertiveness, created in reaction to the loss of the Latin American territories in the early

1800s, evolved with time into a new imperial project, with the objective of subverting the nation which was responsible for the humiliations of 1898. As a Hispanic university professor in America has stated, 'Spain is mired in a symbolic battle with the United States'.[60] Sectors of the Spanish press await patiently the day when the number of Spanish speakers in the States catches up with the English speakers. That will be the moment when the 'language of Cervantes' achieves true universality, because it will be the majority tongue of the world's most powerful nation, and Spain will have achieved its sixteenth-century mission of civilizing the world by imposing its speech. It is of course unnecessary to comment that this symbolic battle has little in common with what really went on in the sixteenth century, a period when the languages of the peninsula coexisted in relative harmony and when nobody had any intention of linguistic imperialism. The imperialism came later, born out of the deep frustration suffered by Spain from the nineteenth century onwards. The minority non-Castilian languages of the peninsula were – and are – not exempt from this frustration. At least one of them has ambitions of replacing Castilian. As I write these lines in 2007, a nationalist minister of the regional government in Catalonia has announced the beginning of an expensive publicity campaign to encourage the other inhabitants of the peninsula to learn and speak Catalan.

CHAPTER SEVEN

THE MYTH OF
PERPETUAL DECLINE

From the year 1580 till now, everything that has happened in Spain has been decline and disintegration.

José Ortega y Gasset, *Invertebrate Spain* (1922)

'Griefs are of more value than triumphs'

The myth of decline is the most fundamental of all the myths in Spain's history, because it supplies a simple and universal explanation for every aspect of the country's development. It will survive for as long as the myth of Spain's greatness in the age of empire survives, since it is the exact reverse of it: a mirror image that contrasts present disasters with past successes.

Belief in the inevitability of decline was not peculiar to Spain. It can be found in Europe since classical antiquity, combined with the conviction that times of success are always followed by times of failure, ages of gold by ages of iron.[1] Poets of the Renaissance were familiar with the idea. Writers such as Gibbon in the nineteenth century and Spengler and Toynbee in the twentieth made their readers familiar with the ups and downs of civilizations. But it is the Castilians who seem to have been most influenced by this belief – which reflected a continuous insecurity. They were unique in insisting that their society was in decline before the age of empire, after the age of empire, and because of the age of empire, in an unending, obsessive saga of doom that stretched from the sixteenth down to the nineteenth centuries. As one of Philip II's officials commented in an unpublished private letter of 1590: 'the way we Spaniards function is this: however bad an event may be, we always imagine it to be worse'.[2]

What has made the notion of decline such an essential part of the Spanish mind? For an approximation to an answer, we need to go back to the first of the themes in this book: the myth of the nation. Every aspect of the myth of decline reflects a conviction that Spain had once achieved, or been in a position to achieve, greatness and success. The emphasis on decline was a kind of apology for the failure to rise to the heights of innate greatness demanded by the nation. As Ernest Renan pointed out long ago:[3]

A heroic past, great men, glory, this is the social capital upon which one bases a national idea. To have common glories in the past and to have a common will in the present; to have performed great deeds together, to wish to perform still more – these are the essential conditions for being a people. More valuable by far than common customs posts and frontiers conforming to strategic ideas is the fact of sharing, in the past, a glorious heritage and regrets, and of having, in the future, [a shared] programme to put into effect, or the fact of having suffered, enjoyed, and hoped together. Where national memories are concerned, griefs are of more value than triumphs, for they impose duties and require a common effort. A nation is therefore a large-scale solidarity, constituted by the feeling of the sacrifices that one has made in the past and of those that one is prepared to make in the future.

The acceptance of 'grief', however, was wholly unthinkable if it was not preceded by a profound conviction that there had been triumph. The distant past was therefore presented as an epoch of glorious achievement. The preceding chapters in this book have borne witness to the unending myths created around the nation, the empire and the faith. Spain was seen as the conqueror of the world, the reign of Ferdinand and Isabella became the legendary Golden Age. In his *Heterodoxos*, in 1880, Menéndez Pelayo permitted himself (as we have already seen) to eulogize the imagined past:

It was a happy age, one of signs and marvels, an age of youth and of vigorous life! Spain was or believed it was the people of God, and each Spaniard, like Joshua, felt within himself the faith and valour to demolish walls to the sound of trumpets or to stop the sun on its course. Nothing seemed or was impossible.

Some eighty years later, in 1962, the respected intellectual Pedro Saínz

Rodríguez published a study on 'decline' in which he began by apostrophizing the greatness that had once existed:

> Sixteenth-century Spain, full of religious idealism, a nation alive, a vibrant community united by a common ideal, anxious to do great things, conscious of the transcendence of its actions, created with its science and its art the highest type of culture that Christian civilization had produced in all its history.[4]

With the firm consciousness of past glory in mind, one could have no problem facing current troubles. As it was for Ortega y Gasset when he analysed what he called *Invertebrate Spain*, the cultivation of 'griefs' in the present diverted attention from the uncomfortable reality of failure and stressed that achievement was still possible somewhere in the future. An emphasis on decline was not, therefore, simply backward-looking. It was, in its own way, very positive, because it looked forward to the possibility of achieving again what had once been achieved in the past. The past became a pointer to future glory; decline was merely a passing (albeit somewhat extended) phase. That was the great contribution of the many writers, from the sixteenth to the nineteenth centuries, who seem to have been obsessed with national failure. I was preparing my doctoral thesis that same year of 1962, and did not have the advantage of the vision that Pedro Saínz enjoyed, but my admiration for Spain when I visited it was centred, like his own, on the culture that the sixteenth century had left behind. The poverty and backwardness of 1962 were of small moment when compared to what had gone before, four hundred years distant in time.

Was there a historical perception of decline?

For those who are accustomed to hear praises heaped on the sixteenth century as the great and successful age of power and culture, in contrast to the seventeenth, which was regarded as an age of problems, it comes as a shock to be confronted with the view that the sixteenth was also an age of disaster. The sentiments expressed by contemporaries were clear and firm. Writers may not have used the word 'decline' often, but they were in no doubt over the presence of continuous failure and missed opportunity. Indeed, in the writings of the Liberal historians and their successors, the entire history of Spain from 1516 to 1918 appeared as an epoch of never-ending decline. Four hundred years of uninterrupted collapse! Today, such a vision seems both exaggerated and unduly catastrophic. Were circumstances really so bad? Was there real evidence of decline? Are there historical data to support the catastrophic view? From what we have seen so far, there were of course factors to substantiate the image of decay. Moreover, every myth on which we have touched so far in this essay consolidated in some way the idea of decline and offered some degree of evidence to support it.

The myth of the 'nation', for example, reminded the Castilians that their country had been great but now was being ruined by foreigners. Hostility to all foreigners was a staple ingredient of nascent Castilian nationalism. In the early modern period, the fundamental enemy was France, antagonist in every war, century after century.[5] Books were written to demonstrate that the French and Spaniards were mortal enemies. An Aragonese noble in 1684 argued that 'God Our Lord created the Pyrenees as a barrier and protection to free Spaniards from Frenchmen'. The Italians fared no better. The *arbitrista* Martínez de Mata in the seventeenth century never ceased to insist that the Genoese had worked to destroy Spain.

The poet Francisco de Quevedo, in those same years, wrote a short tract, *Spain Defended* (unpublished until 1916), in which he presented Spain as the eternal victim of foreign villains. All of them (he omitted only the English from his invective) had schemed to destroy the paradise that Spain would have represented without them.

Would Spain have known the lustful offence against the laws of nature, had Italy not taught it to them? Would repeated drinking have raised the cost of meals in Castile, had the Germans not brought the custom with them? The Holy Inquisition would have had nothing to do had their Melanchthons, Calvins, Luthers and Zwinglis not challenged our faith.[6]

Quevedo's tract was an intemperate outburst of pure narcissistic nationalism,[7] in which Spain was doomed 'for our sins' to suffer decline at the hands of foreigners. Even while they admired and tried to imitate the world outside, many Spaniards – both progressives and traditionalists – became convinced that other Europeans did not understand them and were interested only in destroying them. Objections to the Habsburg and Bourbon monarchies (see Chapter 2 above) were only one facet of a general rejection of foreign culture. At the end of the War of Succession, in 1714, a pamphleteer complained that 'the principal reason for our lament is the innate hostility with which all foreigners have always looked on Spain'.[8] Despite all the contact with Europe, even progressive Spaniards refused to admit any superiority of others over Spain. The eighteenth-century traveller and memoir-writer Casanova concluded after a visit to the peninsula: 'Every Spaniard hates a foreigner simply because he is not a Spaniard.'[9] Ruin and decay (supposing that existed in Spain) could not have been the fault of Spaniards and therefore must have been a consequence of the way foreigners treated them. Why could foreigners not realize that Spaniards were no worse then they? The author of a *Literary History of Spain* (1769) complained: 'it hurts us to see that foreigners omit to mention our Spain when they list the nations with a culture'.[10] Under the Liberals in the later nineteenth century, hatred of foreigners became an essential ingredient of the history textbooks offered to schoolchildren.[11]

The most potent myth to substantiate the idea of decline was that of failed monarchy. With their gaze fixed on the Golden Age of a purely Castilian monarchy under Queen Isabella, the commentators lamented the ruin brought on Castile by foreign dynasties which spent the country's wealth, energy and manpower on enterprises alien to its interests, which were always run by foreigners. As we have seen in Chapter 2, the period of unsurpassed success in Spain's modern history was considered to have been the reign of Isabella the Catholic. When the young Charles of Burgundy became King of Spain in 1516, his spokesman at a meeting of the Castilian Cortes proclaimed that the Age of Gold had now arrived. He could not have been more wrong. It turned out to be the beginning of two centuries of complaint against Charles' Habsburg dynasty. The eyes of all men in Castile were fixed on what they felt had been the glorious reign of his recent predecessor, Isabella of Castile. 'Spain was, at the time of those blessed monarchs Don Ferdinand and Doña Isabella and while they reigned together, more triumphant and sublime, powerful, feared and honoured than it had ever been', wrote a chronicler of the time, Andrés Bernáldez.[12] 'That was a golden time and a time of justice', Gonzalo Fernández de Oviedo wrote a generation later.[13] 'Our Spain was never in a higher state of perfection than in those times', wrote Martín González de Cellorigo in his *Memorial on the Policy Necessary for a Restoration of the State of Spain* (Valladolid, 1600) 'when all the virtues of honour and glory shone in the Catholic Monarchs' and Spain reached 'the highest state of felicity and greatness, in which it continued until decline began'. Decline, for writers like Cellorigo, began with Charles V. The sentiment can also be found in Francisco Martínez de Mata, whose *Eighth Discourse* (1655) refers to 'the happy state of Spain, in both wealth and population, in the year 1518', after which decline occurred. Decline already in 1518? Martínez de Mata, who knew the history of his country well and was aware of its great moments of international success, had no hesitation in affirming that, after 1518, despite the capture of Mexico three years later, the battle of St Quentin forty years later , and the glory of Lepanto half a century on, Spain entered on an irreversible path of decay which was visible in his own time.

Can we take these writers and commentators seriously? Was the sixteenth century the epoch of disaster in Spain? What can be said for them is that, since they lived in those times, surely they knew what they were talking about. As all historians agree, Spain was a poor country. In 1512, during the much vaunted reign of Ferdinand and Isabella, a Venetian ambassador could report that 'poverty is great here, and I believe it is due not so much to the quality of the country as to the nature of the Spaniards'.[14] Emigrants to the New World, to take one case, were in no doubt as to what they were fleeing from: 'that wretched country, because it is only for people who have a lot of money', 'that poverty and need which people suffer in Spain'.[15] These declarations of poverty came from the country's great period of success under Philip II; they seem to bear incontrovertible testimony to the fact that Spain was then as poor as ever, despite its apparent rise to prominence in Europe.

Indeed, were we to believe only the testimony of contemporaries, we would end up with a picture of Spain in which all times were bad times. We may think of the country as being at the height of its military power under Philip II, but throughout his reign there were continuous complaints of distress, and the fault did not lie exclusively with the government. In military terms, Spain indeed suffered its greatest defeat in the early modern period at the beginning of the reign of Philip, namely in 1560, when the Turks destroyed half of the Christian fleet at the island of Djerba, off the North African coast and captured over ten thousand men, led in triumph through the streets of Istanbul a few days later. In 1562 the Council of War blamed the 'peace that has reigned here for so many years' for the defenceless state of the realm, and in 1566 the writer Jerónimo de Urrea deplored 'the decline of the martial arts in the Spanish infantry of our time'. Thirty years later, there seemed to be no improvement. By the end of that reign, when Spain had spent a fortune on armies and navies and seemed to be the supreme power in the world, Baltasar Álamos de Barrientos could write, in 1598, of 'our realms defenceless, infested, invaded; the Mediterranean and Atlantic lorded over by the enemy; the Spanish nation worn out, prostrate, discontented and disfavoured; reputation and honour laid low'. In short, we cannot entirely dismiss the testimony of contemporaries when they lamented that the sixteenth century was an age of failure and disaster. But we also need to adopt a sense of perspective, for few of us are capable of assessing correctly the age in which we live, and the vision of commentators of that time may have been seriously askew.

The nineteenth century invents decline

Despite the persistent complaints of bad times, the myth of decline did not take shape in the period – the sixteenth and seventeenth centuries – to which it referred. There were innumerable and interminable complaints for two centuries or more, with constant expressions of yearning for Ferdinand and Isabella, but no systematic statement of 'decline' appeared. Writers used the word very seldom; they spoke rather of lost opportunity and frustrated potential. Occasionally, a political figure might slip the word 'decline' into his reflections, as did the Count Duke of Olivares and Philip IV,[16] but there was no detailed elaboration of its significance. Only in 1650 did Juan de Palafox, an Aragonese bishop, first of Puebla in Mexico then of Osma in Aragon, put forward a firm argument, with dates, to the effect that 'our empire lasted barely thirty years from its completion (in 1558) to its decline. Its ruin began after 1570, and after 1630 it began to decline with more force. This is all the more remarkable when we consider the long life of other empires.'[17] He was referring, presumably, to the history of the country in its relations to others, rather than to its internal evolution. The change of dynasty in 1700 also brought biting commentaries on the depths to which Spain had sunk, but most such reflections were an attempt to extol the new Bourbons at the expense of the Habsburgs. Not until the end of the eighteenth century did the crucial word 'decline' begin to be applied systematically to Spain. One of the writers in whose head the idea took shape was José Cadalso, in an unpublished essay of around 1780, 'Defence of the Spanish Nation' (see Chapter 2 above). Living in a century when the Bourbon dynasty directed the country, he had no doubt that decline was a legacy of Habsburg rule:

The total decline of sciences, arts and military capability, trade, agriculture and population annihilated Spain at the same time as other European nations began to construct their greatness on top of our ruins.[18]

There was a hidden component to this argument. Criticism of the Habsburg inheritance (see Chapter 2) was a favourite theme of Spanish disciples of the French Enlightenment. They insisted on the failure of the Habsburgs to rise to the heights of glory achieved by Isabella of Castile. Cadalso, in common with many others, had no doubts about the failure of the Habsburgs, as contrasted to the successes of the Bourbons. However, at least one contemporary, the Catalan economist Capmany, felt that it was absurd to yearn for the past instead of working for a better present. He commented that 'those who are incapable of profiting from the present become apologists of past times, because they can find no other way to overcome their inferiority'.[19] Spaniards were, according to Capmany, lagging behind other peoples. Some foreign observers thought so too. In 1782, when the *Encyclopédie méthodique* was published in Paris, the entry on Spain, by Masson de Morvilliers, contained the statement: 'What do we owe to Spain? In two centuries, in four, in ten, what has she done for Europe?'[20] It was not an unjust question,[21] for Frenchmen and other Europeans had not yet discovered many positive aspects of peninsular culture (literature, art, music), but they were conscious that Spanish contributions to science and the latest philosophy were notably absent. It was Spain's record in the sciences that Masson was specifically referring to, not its general cultural showing (Masson was in fact open-minded enough about Spain to ask: 'Who knows to what heights this superb nation may rise?') The views of the *Encyclopédie* were shared by many. Liberals in Spain, as well as the disciples of the *philosophes* both in France and Spain were unanimous in condemning all aspects of traditional culture in the peninsula, which seemed to them decadent.

When the French invaded Spain in the early nineteenth century, they too were concerned to present the same picture of a nation in decay. Napoleon ordered that documents be sought in the archives, 'in order to publish one day and make known the state of decadence into which Spain had fallen'.[22] He wished to pose as the saviour of Spain. Paris became the centre of the 'decline' myth. It was there that, in 1826, the Spanish exile Juan Sempere y Guarinos chose to publish a seminal work on 'decline'.[23] Others, too, were publishing in Paris on the same subject in those years.[24] The historical presuppositions which we have encountered in the case of Masson and of Napoleon were rooted in the highest circles of the French government itself. When I was doing research for my doctoral thesis many years ago in the archives of the French Foreign Office, I came across an entire volume in manuscript (still, to this day, unpublished) bearing the date 1835 and devoted to an analysis of Spain's *décadence* in the seventeenth century.[25] This fascinating volume contains all the essentials of the decline myth. In those same years, French scholars began to devote themselves to studying the theme. Perhaps the most significant product was that of the historian Charles Weiss, whose doctoral thesis on the causes of Spanish *décadence* was later summarized in the two volumes, published in Paris in 1844, of his *Spain from the Reign of Philip II to the Coming of the Bourbons* (*L'Espagne depuis le règne de Philippe II jusqu'à l'avènement des Bourbons*).[26] Weiss presents the 'decline' myth in one of its forms. He accepts the idea of a successful sixteenth century: under Philip II, 'Spain was dominant abroad by its arms, and internally flourishing in agriculture, industry and trade'. By contrast, he states, the reign of Charles II brought complete ruin in all these respects. It is not surprising that works like this had an influence on what was to become a classic study in Spain: the essay by the statesman Cánovas del Castillo on *History of the Decline of Spain from the Succession of Philip III to the Death of Charles II*, which first emerged in 1854 as articles and saw book form only in 1910.[27] We shall return in a moment to the work of Cánovas.

The reason why 'decline' became an idea with a future was because, like all myths, it was ideologically charged. Various groups had strong motives for promoting the theory of decline in order to support the idea that Spain was backward and needed the reforms they backed. These men, dedicated reformers and progressives, had to flee later on when the army of Spain's French king (Joseph I, brother of Napoleon) was defeated in 1813 by the British forces under Wellington. The progressives became known as *afrancesados* (that is, 'pro-French'), and in time they came to form the core of the Liberal party. They numbered among their ranks the historian of the Inquisition, Llorente (see Chapter 5). The Liberals also included other politicians, who opposed Joseph but, even more firmly, opposed the national favourite king, Ferdinand VII. This latter group, most of whose members went into exile in the 1820s and 1830s and made Paris their effective home, included leading nobles, who were to head Spain's government in later years. Although they differed on political strategies when they came into power, all of them were agreed that Spain's history needed to be re-written in order to define what had gone wrong in the past.

From approximately the 1830s on, the exiles used their leisure hours to read up on what had been written in French and English in order to create a new history of their country. The conclusion, repeated in all their books, was wholly in line with the views on which we have already touched in Chapters

1 and 2. The great, the glorious, period of success and freedom had been the reign of Queen Isabella. That reign was followed, according to a prominent deputy in the Cortes of Cadiz in 1810, Argüelles, by 'a new era in which the nation began to decline rapidly', despite a short-lived period of 'the false glitter of expeditions and conquests'.[28] The impact of Prescott's version of the past (his *History of Ferdinand and Isabella* came out in English in 1838, but was not available in Spanish until 1845) must have reinforced the impressions of Spanish writers. The Liberal version of the past, as expressed by Modesto Lafuente in 1850, repeated the emphasis on false glories, although without committing itself wholly to the *concept* of decline.

Another author of that period, Adolfo de Castro, broached the issue in his *Philosophical Study of the Principal Causes of the Decline of Spain* (1851). The title suggested already, as various later writers would make plain, that one was dealing with a moral concept rather than a historical phenomenon. The historical dimension came later, with the revisions that conservatives made to Lafuente's picture. As we have seen, there was at first little disagreement over fundamentals: both Liberals and conservatives emphasized the fight for liberty and national unity as fundamental, together with distrust of foreign kings. However, Liberal attacks on the Church and religion were seen by conservatives as unacceptable. In the same way, the negative attitude of Liberals to the great age of empire began to be called into question. In his contribution to the final volume of Lafuente's history, issued in 1882 to bring the work up to date, the writer and politician Juan Valera was already committed to a different view. 'If in political terms', he wrote, 'this nation was a corpse when the house of Bourbon began to rule it, we should not forget that it owed important administrative reforms to the first three kings of this dynasty.'[29] Surveying the early modern period, he observed that Spain 'at the dawn of the sixteenth century found itself at the head of civilized nations, but that same period was also the beginning of our decline'.

The word decline – *decadencia* – became the cornerstone of a new, conservative vision of history, which began with Cánovas del Castillo and continued down to our own day. Antonio Cánovas del Castillo (1828–97) was the most prominent statesman of Spain's nineteenth century. During the critical period from 1868 to 1874, he supported moves to restore the Bourbon monarchy and was prime minister several times. He helped to introduce the Constitution of 1876, which created a conservative parliamentary monarchy, and he pioneered a political arrangement that seemed to secure stability by alternating power between his conservatives and the Liberal party.

After two decades in office, however, Cánovas began to experience serious problems with the rise of working-class opposition and, after 1895, with the insurrection against Spanish rule in Cuba. During a vacation trip to a spa near San Sebastian, he was assassinated by an anarchist. A proficient man of letters, he probably did more than any other to revise the prevailing Liberal interpretation of history and to give it a definitive conservative flavour.[30]

Cánovas was not, like Lafuente, a professional scholar, and his historical writings were not often backed up by the research that Lafuente conscientiously employed to arrive at his conclusions. Cánovas' history-writing consisted of disquisitions on the past made by a cultured gentleman, whose judgements were deemed to carry weight precisely because he was a gentleman. The technique worked amazingly well, and his interpretations have dominated historical scholarship. He accepted the broad lines of Lafuente's exposition, down to what he (or they) identified as the two main causes of Spain's failures in its great imperial age: royal absolutism and the Holy Inquisition. Like the Liberals, he believed that royal power must have its limits, and he opposed religious extremism. But his political views obliged him to shift the emphasis in all other respects. His new version had an important sequel, always tied up with political events. Half a century before, intellectuals of virtually all shades of opinion had agreed on accepting the myths of the nation, of medieval freedom, of the greatness of Isabella, and of the destruction wrought by the House of Austria. However, as the Liberal hold on power turned, after 1835, into revolutionary violence directed against Catholics, conservatives and dissenting Liberals, the victims of violence became disillusioned with a myth that seemed to be serving only one cause.[31] They therefore came up with a new version of history.

The concept of 'decline' became the vehicle employed to explain how the country had arrived at its present ills. Those responsible for bad policy were no longer the early Habsburgs, who now became, to conservative minds, the defenders of Spain's true values. So, while the Liberals blamed the first two Habsburgs, Charles V and Philip II, as being entirely responsible for the prostration of Spain, Cánovas looked on the later Habsburgs as a more direct cause. His *History of the Decline of Spain* expressly devoted itself to the period *after* the reigns of Charles V and Philip II. On the latter, Cánovas commented: 'Some have blamed Philip II for our decline, when in fact he strengthened the resources and enhanced the springs of the power of Spain.'[32] In his subsequent *Historical Sketch of the House of Austria in Spain* (published initially as a long article in 1869, then as a book in 1911), he admitted that there was a sombre side to the reign of Philip II, such as 'the expenditure, the penury, the losses of men and money, long and costly rebellions, schemes to rid himself of his enemies, terrible decisions that are difficult to justify'. But all of that, he felt, was significant in comparison with the methods of 'those [the Liberals] who in this century have employed violence to promote their principles'. Moreover, he argued, the bloodshed caused by Spaniards in the Netherlands was as nothing compared with the bloodshed caused in Spain by Napoleon and his Liberal supporters.[33]

The culprits, in Cánovas' eyes, were the later Habsburgs and, above all, the foreign Bourbon dynasty, which had distorted the path of Spain's evolution. Cánovas' relegation to oblivion of those who came to be known as 'the lesser Habsburgs' was so successful that, ever since, the story of 'decline' has been associated almost exclusively with the last kings of the house of Austria: Philip III, Philip IV and Charles II. Cánovas stated: 'If the Catholic Monarchs had had the successors that Philip II had, the prosperity of Spain would have lasted a century less.'[34] The conservative vision was transmitted in its entirety to American and British historians (including, inevitably, myself), who for the next century repeated confidently Cánovas' vision of success in the sixteenth century and failure in the seventeenth. The political and economic collapse in the seventeenth century, Cánovas argued, was matched only by the moral collapse under the early Bourbons, who were responsible for bringing in new ideas that corrupted Spain's character. That was the true decline of Spain.

History presents no example of such an immense dismemberment of territories as Spain has suffered in the reigns of the House of Bourbon. What can never be sufficiently lamented is the profound deterioration in the national character. Something that without doubt arose from the indirect importation of foreign laws, customs and habits, which undermined our traditions, overturned our sentiments, uprooted our ancient faith and enfeebled the ancient dignity of our race.[35]

Cánovas felt strongly that Spain had emerged as 'a permanent nation' by the time of Ferdinand and Isabella, and that the early Habsburgs had strengthened this 'communal Hispanic nationality'. Ideally, the bonds within this *nación* or *patria* had to be preserved and the role of the monarchy reaffirmed. Unfortunately, little had been done to further unity. Cánovas felt that 'one begins to doubt if the idea of national unity ever existed in the minds of the great kings of the Golden Century',[36] with the result that the community fell apart in the centuries that followed. The fact of decline thus pointed the way towards a necessary political solution. In the programme that he drew up for the restored monarchy of 1874, Cánovas emphasized the need for a centralized administration, focused on a sovereign crown with a parliament to support it and a state in which the regions would be bound together by common responsibilities. Everything he had read about decline confirmed him in his convictions about the future. He felt, for example, that Catalonia had learnt its lessons from the failure of separatism in 1640, and that its future was as a region 'indissolubly united to Spain'.[37]

Both Liberals and conservatives arrived in this way at the vision of a Spain that had been great up to the dawn of the sixteenth century but afterwards had gone downhill in terms of wealth, power, culture and aspirations. Someone, somewhere, had sabotaged the Spanish dream, and they disagreed only about the culprits. Although the two versions of the myth of decline focused on different targets, they coincided impressively in their agreement on two major points: first, there had been corruption of Spain's true character; second, that corruption had been brought in from outside, either by foreign absolutist dynasties or by foreign alien ideologies. The interpretation of both versions included every aspect of the themes that we have looked at in preceding chapters. All those mistakes, both Liberals and conservatives insisted, condemned Spain to a decadence that only an enlightened policy could reverse. Interpretation of the past had a clear political agenda and became a weapon in the hands of politicians and administrators. This was the vision transmitted to generation after generation, in book after book, down to the texts used in schools and colleges.[38] Insistence on the theme of decline was so persuasive that it influenced all Spanish university teachers and all foreign historians. In some foreign universities today, the history of Spain is being taught with reference to one single topic: its alleged decline.

The theme of decline had another fruitful consequence: it gave Spanish intellectuals a theme to which they could dedicate thousands of pages of debate, without always having much acquaintance with the historical facts. As Juan Valera pointed out in 1887, foreign scholars were now not the only ones able to give opinions on Spain and its problems:[39]

It was a most lamentable situation. In order to explain our decline we had either to imagine that there really had existed a monstrous deviation or aberration in the progress of our civilization and that it was necessary to renounce the past and condemn it by taking the principles of civilization from outside,[40] or we had to understand our past better, rehabilitate what was good in it, purify it of any corrupting elements and pursue our upward movement. In order to do this, it was necessary to examine our past with more exquisite care and a more acute and impartial criticism, and it is just and consoling to say that in these matters there has been a fruitful renaissance in recent times. For our political history, Lafuente, Cánovas and Ferrer del Río; for the history of our laws and institutions Colmeiro, Pidal and Cárdenas; for the history of our civilization in general Tapia and Gonzalo Morón; and for the history of our letters, sciences and arts Amador de los Ríos, Valmar, Gayangos, both the Guerras, Canalejas, Milá y Fontanals, Aribau, Menéndez y Pelayo and many others who have written studies and published books, by virtue of which we can now say that it is not only amiable foreigners who come to teach us what we are and what we have been.

After the Disaster of 1898, writers came back with morbid intensity to the theme. The myth served the same purpose for them as in the mid-nineteenth century. Decline was the concept through which they proposed to regenerate Spain and solve its problems. By analysing the phenomenon, they could reverse its course and find a way back to a better Spain. A typical reaction was that of Menéndez Pelayo, who in 1910, just over a year before his death, contemplated bleakly the ruin of his country:

We witness today the slow suicide of a people that, deceived a thousand times by wordy sophists, impoverished, run down and laid waste, employs its little remaining strength in destroying itself and running after the hollow fraud of a false and artificial culture instead of cultivating its own spirit (the only one that ennobles and redeems races and peoples), carries out a frightful liquidation of its past, at every step mocks the shades of its forefathers, flees from every contact with their thinking, renounces everything in history that made them great, scatters to the winds its artistic riches and contemplates with stupefied gaze the destruction of the only Spain that the world knows, the only Spain in whose past there is virtue enough to delay our agony.[41]

Unamuno was another of those who argued that there had once been an age of success (presumably the mythical sixteenth century) that had now turned sour. In *On Authenticity* (*En torno al Casticismo*) he argued:

> The qualities that in another age could have given us primacy, have laid us low. . . . The Castilian soul was great when it exposed itself to the four winds and spread throughout the world; later it turned off the valves and we have not yet woken up. Is everything dying? No, the future of our society awaits us within the society of our past history, in intra-history, in the unknown people, and it will not recover strength until awoken by the winds and breezes of the European environment. . . . Spain waits to be discovered, and only Europeanized Spaniards will discover it.[42]

Later, Unamuno changed his opinion as to whether Europe had anything to offer at all. It is interesting to note that, in the one hundred years after the Liberals set down their vision of Spain's decay, no serious historical research in Spain attempted to study the circumstances supposed to have provoked the disaster suffered by the country. The story of 'decline' was plucked out of the air, rather than arrived at on the basis of evidence. In 1927, the author of a new history of Spain, Mario Méndez Bejarano,[43] was still citing Lafuente and other sources from a hundred years earlier as his source of information. His conclusions had a familiar ring, and they deserve extensive quotation because they represent a vision that is still widely believed and actively taught in some educational centres:

> On the basis of the powerful wisdom, the Herculean vitality of the fifteenth century, reinforced spiritually by the Renaissance and the invention of printing, and geographically and politically by the discovery of a New World, the sixteenth century flourished and excelled, but this glorious century, called Golden because of the virtues of the preceding century, did not know how to administer its rich inheritance and sowed the seeds of the decline that thrived in its second half and bore bitter fruit in the seventeenth century. The Catholic Monarchs, without many scruples as to how they did it, carried out a peninsular unification that was incomplete and badly put together, and because of its defective structure, continued to be contentious, since they damaged trade with the expulsion of the Israelites and stifled thought with the terror of the Inquisition.
>
> Charles V turned us away from a future in the colonies by committing the country to useless wars of religion, and by crushing the nobility he

destroyed the rights and liberties of the cities and enthroned his personal power. Philip II, the least prudent of kings, chose the wrong path, shut his eyes to the providential destiny of the Peninsula and wasted rivers of Spanish blood on behalf of alien ideals. That ruler, who used up all the vital forces of the nation, which should have gone on agriculture and industry, opened the gates to the greatest epoch of misery Spain has ever known, since its people even 'went begging door to door for alms for the king of two worlds' (Lafuente, *History of Spain*, vol. XV, p. 29). More concerned for faith than for culture, he banned professors and students from studying at foreign universities, isolated the monarchy from the nation, and died covered in ulcers and worms, leaving as his image the Escorial, a gigantic pantheon of Spanish power, and as his testament the agony of a people who, thanks to its king, became hated throughout Europe. Wholly dedicated to fanaticism, when he returned from the Netherlands to take up the throne of Spain, his first act as ruler was an auto de fe. His reason was the absurd principle that 'it is better not to reign than to reign over heretics'. Application of this principle explains the killings in the Netherlands, the extermination of the Moriscos, the autos de fe, the repugnant murder of Montigny, the confiscations, the ruin of the most prosperous and flourishing provinces in the world.

In the first half of the seventeenth century Spain still lived on the prestige gained in better days. 'There were, it is true, no great philosophers, no distinguished men of state, though one among them may have achieved an uncommon reputation as a thinker and writer, despite the pressure exercised upon knowledge in these fields by the severe tribunal of the Holy Office, and despite the isolation from the European intellectual movement in which Spain lived since the time of Philip II' (M. Lafuente). Thus the second half of the century, void of ideas, plunged into unstoppable decline. During the reign of Philip III and of the insane Philip IV, Catalonia, Portugal and Roussillon were lost, autos de fe increased, there were more men in the 10,000 monasteries of religious orders than in the field and the factory, and in the sad days of the miserable Charles II the trade of America was destroyed by pirates and the country became depopulated. On this slide towards collapse and corruption, the soul of the country showed no regret. An inconceivable passivity, an incomprehension bordering on insanity and reinforced by apathy, paralysed all healthy action. The seventeenth century lacked any scientific or literary substance, drawing its learning and its soul only from the preceding century. Religious intolerance stifled all free thought. Whatever my revered friend Menéndez Pelayo may claim, he cannot deny that fear of error led to a fall into ignorance, and that Spanish thinkers had to learn to print their books outside the country, and there hardly remained any man of merit who did not, to greater or lesser degree, suffer persecution from the hateful tribunal of the Inquisition.

This amazing passage, in which almost every phrase is pure fantasy, unsupported by any information beyond the authority of Lafuente, reveals the degree to which many Spaniards, on the eve of a long civil war (1936–9) in which tens of thousands would lose their lives, were still relying for their ideas and their hopes for the future on a vision of the past that had been totally distorted by ideology and by a complete lack of serious historical research.

Decline criticized

The myth of a ruined country continued to survive, but for several different reasons. Some Spaniards objected strongly to a view that seemed to question not only the achievements of the past, but also their own character and capacities. The cumulative assertions of decline irritated them because they seemed not to be based on any serious analysis of what had happened. By a strange coincidence, the country's only two Nobel Prize-winners of that period, who also happened to be men of science, had grave doubts about the myth of decline.

One of them was José Echegaray (1832–1916), a Basque dramatist, mathematician, economist and cabinet minister who, in 1904, had shared with a French writer the Nobel Prize for literature. Forty years before that event, he had asserted that 'it is grossly unjust and a rank calumny to suggest that our Spain is fundamentally and innately incapable'.[44] But when he came to consider why Spain had produced no scientists of the calibre of Pascal, Descartes, Newton and Leibniz, he was driven to accept the reality of 'our lamentable decline since the Renaissance, which for Spain was more a time of dying than of being born again'. Similar comments on the notion of decline were made by the next Spaniard to win the Nobel Prize. Santiago Ramón y Cajal (1852–1934), who in 1906 shared with an Italian the Nobel Prize for medicine, was taking a peaceful walk out in the country with a friend, when he heard the news of the sinking of the Spanish fleet off Cuba and of the surrender of the city of Santiago to American troops. Some of his reflections on the Disaster were published in 1913, under the title *Advice on Scientific Research*. His argument in that tract was that the United States had won because it was a modern society that had embraced science, whereas Spain was still living in its past. 'We were defeated by the United States', he wrote, 'because we were ignorant and weak. We need to regenerate ourselves through work and study.' 'We need to re-write the history of Spain and cleanse it of all these exaggerations which instil in children an inflated vision of the valour and virtue of their race. It is an ill way to prepare young people to serve their country by painting it as a nation of unequalled heroes, intellectuals and artists.' He called in particular for the teaching of science to be given a central role in the university syllabus. In response to the stock affirmation that Spain had once been great and was now merely weakened, in a state of decline, he affirmed roundly that the excuse of 'decline' was false. 'Is it acceptable', he asked, 'to claim that we have degenerated in comparison with our forefathers of the sixteenth and seventeenth centuries?' The real problem, in his view, was that Spain had never been a modern country: 'Spain is an intellectually backward country, not one in decline', and had never emerged out of its medieval backwardness.[45]

In the same vein, Juan Valera had pointed out two decades before that:

Spain has been the nation most belittled and denigrated in general histories and in the histories of civilization that are now being written. The contempt has been so contagious that foreigners have succeeded in implanting it in the mind of many Spaniards. On seeing how ephemeral our predominance was, and on contemplating the depths to which we have fallen from so great a height, some have been seized with the suspicion that our rise was purely accidental or that our character and mind contain defects and vices which did not permit the rise to endure. To this disdain that we have induced in ourselves, ignorance and sloth were added, with the consequence that the idea we formed of ourselves became more and more wretched, and we felt ourselves more and more humiliated when we compared ourselves with England, Germany and France.[46]

For these writers, decency and pride demanded that the very idea of 'decline' be rejected as hurtful. However, there were powerful reasons to keep holding on to the myth. How else would it be possible to explain what had happened to Spain?

There were, broadly, three main phases in the evolution of the obsession with decline, and all three were associated with disappointment at Spain's inability to live up to the dream of success. Statements of 'decline' were statements of frustration. The first phase of disappointment occurred towards the end of the sixteenth century, when people realized that contact with America and Europe had brought nothing but negative returns. The writings of the earlier *arbitristas* and of propagandists like Álamos de Barrientos fall into this category. We have touched on them elsewhere in this book. The second phase occurred a century later, when, after repeated military and naval failures in every corner of the empire, it was obvious that Spain had become a political and economic wreck. 'The present state of the realm', wrote a Castilian grandee to Louis XIV in 1700, 'is the saddest in the world, for the feeble government of the last few kings has produced a horrible disorder in affairs: justice is abandoned, income spent, resources sold, the people oppressed, and love and respect for the sovereign lost.' A few years later, in 1714, another writer commented:

> Many talented pens have been worn out describing the root of our ills. Some say the cause is the union with the Habsburgs and with the Netherlands, that graveyard of Spaniards and ruin of their treasure; others claim it is the conquest of America, which has taken our sons and wearied our bodies in extracting its riches; others identify it with the expulsion of the moriscos, who supported our agriculture, that producer of soldiers and population. . . .[47]

The third phase took place shortly after 1800, as a result of the Peninsular War, when Spanish writers in exile were able to compare their country with the rest of Europe and discovered that they were indeed a social, economic and cultural backwater. Prescott's brilliant *History of the Reign of Ferdinand and Isabella* stated the issue clearly:

> The inhabitant of modern Spain or Italy, who wanders amid the ruins of their stately cities, their grass-grown streets, their palaces and temples crumbling into dust, their massive bridges choking up the streams they once proudly traversed, the very streams themselves, which bore navies on their bosoms, shrunk into too shallow a channel for the meanest craft to navigate – the modern Spaniard who surveys these vestiges of a giant race, the tokens of his nation's present degeneracy, must turn for relief to the

prouder and earlier period of her history, when only such great works could have been achieved; and it is no wonder that he should be led, in his enthusiasm, to invest it with a romantic and exaggerated coloring. Such a period in Spain cannot be looked for in the eighteenth, still less in the seventeenth century, for the nation had then reached the lowest ebb of its fortunes; nor in the close of the sixteenth, for the desponding language of the Cortes shows that the work of decay and depopulation had then already begun. It can only be found in the first half of that century, in the reign of Ferdinand and Isabella.[48]

Prescott's verdict leaves us with an insoluble problem. How was it possible for a good historian to state that what was commonly regarded as the Golden Age was really a period of 'decay'? Prescott's sources were reliable ones, for nearly every significant writer of the sixteenth and seventeenth centuries also shared this view. And that was the view that continued to prevail. We have seen in Chapter 2 that the Liberal and conservative historians of the 1820s were unanimous in their claim that the Habsburg monarchy had brought disaster to Spain. Therefore they identified decline with the 'foreign' despotism imposed on Spain, and from that period on the entire period of Habsburg rule, including the much vaunted sixteenth century, became associated with decline. At no point did any of the studies give any evidence to demonstrate 'decline', nor indeed could they, for was this not the great age of Spain's imperial success? That detail was no obstacle. One after another, historical studies adhered to the argument that the age of greatness had really been an age of decline.

We might assume that this thesis was so contradictory that it would soon collapse. Far from it. Human ingenuity can find a way round the most difficult of concepts. Depending on the criterion each writer adopted, 'decline' could be made to coexist happily with 'success'. Indeed, one man's decline could be another man's success, and vice versa. Behind this strange duality of approach, we may rightly suspect that there was a duality of ideology. What one man (a traditionalist conservative) might view as the great age of glory of the Inquisition, for example, might be regarded by another (say, a revolutionary Liberal) as the most profound era of national disgrace. 'Decline' ceased to have any specific meaning, and became a mere label applied according to one's individual political preferences. A good example is that of Catalonia. The nationalist Prat de la Riba proclaimed in 1894 that Catalonia had been in continuous decline since the late fifteenth century, when Castile, beginning with Ferdinand the Catholic, set about dominating the principality and ruining its culture, language and commerce.[49] The historical data used by Prat to support his contention were completely spurious, but did not impede him from arriving at his principal contention: that Castilians had brought Catalonia to its knees, and that this condition of decline would form the basis for the rebirth of the Catalan nation.

America as the ruin of Spain

One of the most ironic aspects of Spain's great triumph was that its centre-piece, the possession of America, was instrumental in that triumph being turned on its head. Since Spain's problems – in the view of patriotic analysts – could not be blamed on Spain, they had to be blamed on America. It was a point of view expressed vigorously by commentators during the three hundred years following Columbus' voyages. The list of complaints was a long one, but it boiled down to Spain's inability to benefit from the riches offered by the New World. During the 1500s the drawbacks were not so apparent, and indeed in the middle years of the century both government and people were basking in the warm sunshine of promise from the riches of America. By the end of that century, however, it was clear that the colonies and their wealth were in large measure out of Spain's grasp. Silver imports into Spain aggravated inflation and debt. González de Cellorigo stated in 1600: 'our Spain has looked so much to the Indies trade that its inhabitants have neglected the affairs of these realms . . . wherefore Spain from its great wealth has attained great poverty'. In 1619, Sancho de Moncada devoted a whole section of his *Political Recovery of Spain* to the uncompromising thesis that 'the poverty of Spain has resulted from the discovery of the Indies'.[50] In 1631, Olivares told a meeting of the Council of State that 'if its great conquest has reduced this monarchy to such a miserable condition, one can say reasonably that it would have been more powerful without the New World'. 'What use is it', a Castilian writer protested in the 1650s, 'to bring over so many millions worth of merchandise, silver and gold in the galleons, at so much cost and risk, if it comes only for the French and Genoese?'[51] A state official wrote in a private letter in 1688: 'America, instead of being our salvation, has become our perdition, for no nation profits from it less than we.'[52] In 1743, the chief minister José de Campillo blamed America for causing Spain's poverty, because 'when we should have applied ourselves to agriculture and learned how usefully to employ human labour', Spaniards instead preferred the easy wealth from America's mines. A subsequent minister, Campomanes, in his famous *Discourse on Public Education* (1775), argued that American silver had gone not to Spain but to its enemies, deceived Spain into waging expensive wars and failed to be invested in agriculture and industry. The result had been to precipitate decline.[53] It was an impressive verdict, insisted upon unremittingly from the sixteenth to the eighteenth centuries.

Spaniards blamed America not only for bringing wealth but also for luring away manpower. The departure of thousands of people for the New World had been a constant complaint of writers from the seventeenth century onwards, and by the eighteenth century not a single commentator disagreed with the thesis that emigration (and foreign wars) had ruined Spain. When Lafuente wrote in 1850, he judged that around thirty million Spaniards had left for America in the course of the period 1500–1700.[54] The figure was a grotesque exaggeration, but it reveals the importance Lafuente attached to the phenomenon. His views about the role of America as a cause of decline were shared by Cánovas, who stated: 'The discovery of America was fatal to our demography, and to the spirit of labour and production'.[55] There were, he said, two main reasons. Emigration to the New World drew away the peninsula's labour force and commercial vitality; and the promise of easy wealth sapped the productivity of Spaniards in their own country. Spain's most promising entrepreneurs had preferred to go to the New World to make their fortunes. This had made it impossible for Spain to develop into a proper nation. Instead of becoming an energetic and vigorous country, Spain had lapsed into decay.

> We abandoned every class of labour, and were soon forced to import from foreign countries even the most necessary consumer articles, which we paid for with the treasures that came from America. It was said with good reason that Spain was no more than a bridge over which these treasures passed to other more industrious nations.

Consequently, in the wake of the 1898 Disaster, he felt that there was no need to shed tears for the loss of the American colonies. Spain had lost its way since the seventeenth century, 'sidetracked from the general course of ideas in Europe'. However, not everyone could contemplate the tragedy with such equanimity. After 1898, Spaniards saw that the dream they had once harboured in their minds, created three centuries before, through the image of three small vessels that set out bravely across the ocean and brought a whole new world within the ambit of Hispanic civilization, was reduced to dust and ashes. America may have been a negative influence, but at least it had given glory and dignity. Now none of that was left.

'There has never been any decline'

There continued to be a school of thought which rejected the idea of decline, because it went against all the observed facts and constituted an offence to the pride of Castilians and a denial of their undoubted achievements. Decline, for this school, was a product of the imagination. It simply did not happen. Spain may have had a few dark moments, but it was always on the road to success, on which it would have continued but for the plots of its enemies. The most extreme form of this view was adopted by the regime of General Franco (1939–75), when publicists proclaimed that virtually the entire history of Spain since the Catholic Monarchs was a success story punctuated by a few reverses, which were amply compensated by great achievements. This optimistic approach, taken up by historians and clergy of the Franco years, was meant to present the regime as a fulfilment of all the aspirations of the Spanish people. If there had been failure, it was because the classic enemies of Spain were responsible. The version of this thesis offered by a historian, Luis Suárez Fernández, is interesting:

> Spain's struggle was a battle of giants. We Spaniards struggled for what was right, and we lost. For nearly two centuries it appeared that Spain was going to close in on itself, as if it had lost its initial energy and the capacity to fight. Spain was the great loser. So much so that it accepted foreign kings, and foreign formulas for its institutions. It is true that from time to time it sprang a surprise, with gestures like those of 1808 or 1833, but these, however, were like the outbursts of a wounded wild animal, which turns on its own sons because it refuses to die. For the minority political leaders there appeared to be no other solution than to imitate what we were told from outside. In imitating, we were irredeemably condemned to arrive late, losing slowly what little remained of our enormous national heritage. From the depths of their feelings, some raised their voices in warning. Voices like that of don Marcelino Menéndez Pelayo, who discovered and proclaimed that the unity of Spain rests on a central pivot, one of flesh, blood and spirit, above all of spirit, Roman and Christian, and reminded

us that if one day this were to be lost and we were to revert to primitive cantonalism Spain would disintegrate definitively, as it seemed to be doing. In the midst of this madness, a man dressed in civilian clothes out of respect for the territory over which he was flying made his way to Tetuan. When he arrived at the airport, a lieutenant colonel received him with a salute: 'All quiet in Morocco, General.' That man was Francisco Franco, who took on himself the responsibility of re-establishing the unity of Spain. And he succeeded.[56]

In the same vein wrote another historian, Manuel Fraga, author of a fine study of how Spain faced its great year of trial, 1648, when it lost a huge slice of its European empire. Fraga went on to become a distinguished minister, diplomat and head of regional government. Analysing the ups and downs of Spain's imperial career, Fraga concluded that Spain did not decline. 'It was defeated by a European conspiracy led by France and England, and viciously kicked as it lay on the ground prostrate.' Spain remained where it was, with all its energies. The other powers had merely gained a temporary advantage.

The optimistic view was also shared in the post-Franco years by many who were in the opposing political camp and bitterly against the dictatorship, yet felt that the notion of decadence was unacceptable. For them decline was demeaning, while optimism was a question of dignity. To adopt Renan's terms, as cited above, the triumphs were what counted, the griefs were passing shadows. 'Decline' was a subjective illusion, not a reality. It was 'a myth, a history that is only a mist drifting through an ocean of paper'.[57] The author of those words, one of Spain's most widely read historians, is the latest commentator on the theme. Through the centuries (according to his view) there were always pessimistic writers who, for one reason or another, with just cause or because of their own disillusion, picked on factors which they felt were responsible for present problems. All found reasons to criticize or apportion blame. According to them, 'economy, government, monarchy, people, science, art, literature, everything in Spain at the beginning of the twentieth century had been reduced to a non-stop collapse into the abyss'. All sighed for a vanished Eden and for lost opportunities, which left Spain in the rear of other nations. But, he says, their laments were misplaced. The so-called decline was overstated, and for three main reasons.

First, he argues, Spain did not fail but in fact triumphed, above all in America. 'The Spanish empire was never greater than in the year 1780' (when it took over parts of Louisiana and Florida). Spain's control of the New

World reached its peak in that decade, when it constructed 'entire cities, universities, churches, enormous cathedrals, palaces, fortifications, ports, navigation techniques, printing presses, trade'. Someone disagreeing with this statement might comment that Spain gained little in 1780 except a new imaginary frontier which it quickly abandoned, and that few of the other alleged achievements took place. Indeed, a Spanish official on the spot concluded in 1783 that Spain's 'spirit of aggrandizement is now a thing of the past'.[58] But the New World has always, among many prominent writers, been looked on as a sort of ultimate frontier. The vision of that frontier in America provoked the essayist Azorín to state: 'So-called decline never existed. When is it supposed to have existed? It is supposed to have occurred at the exact moment when Spain discovered a New World and populated it. There has never been any decline' (*Spain's Hour*, 1924).[59]

The second reason offered by optimists was that Spain always bounced back. If there were ups and downs in Spain's history, they were a consequence of temporary natural events. They by no means affected the fact that Spain had been mighty, had conquered, had evangelized and civilized. It was inevitable that weak points would develop, that enemies would undermine, that in some respects there would be greater progress elsewhere. But reverses of fortune were never fatal. Even in the mid-seventeenth century, Spain possessed 'the most powerful war machine that Europe had ever experienced'. There were, of course, times of disaster, but 'we should not make the mistake of falling into fatalism, for the military defeats were never decisive'. Spain remained supreme at sea throughout the centuries until its defeat at Trafalgar in 1805.[60]

Third, Spanish culture triumphed everywhere. 'Literature, painting, architecture, religious thought, music, treatises of international law are by themselves enough to sweep aside part of the shadow cast by the complaints of the *arbitristas* and the comments of foreign ambassadors. The Spaniards of the Golden Age accomplished a staggering cultural achievement.'[61]

The denial of decline, it can be seen in these quotations, is based on a wholly optimistic appraisal of Spain's past and its universal power, its mighty armies, its undefeated strength at sea, and its capacity to conquer, populate and civilize both Europe and America. The optimistic view, as we shall see, is particularly vulnerable at several points but notably so in its vindication of 'America', because it relies on a wholly unreal vision of the American experience and of what exactly Spaniards achieved there. In some sense, the optimism can also be viewed as an expression of nationalist pride in the achievement of Castile. In his 1985 study *España inteligible* (*Understanding Spain*), the writer Julián Marías insisted that 'decline' was invented by the enemies of Spain, a nation that had never failed to be true to its religious and civilizing mission, which other nations did not understand or even envied.

It is easy to see why many Spaniards, faced by an interminably sombre view of their past, reject the myth of decline as wholly unacceptable. No self-respecting nation can put up with such persistent pessimism. As a result, García Cortázar's optimism shines bravely through the gloom. Even after 1898, he says, Spain recovered. Within a decade, 'culture was flourishing with a fullness it had not enjoyed since the seventeenth century'. A generation later, in 1936, 'Spanish culture was at the highest peak of its entire history: from mathematics to physics, from philology to philosophy, from architecture to music, levels of creative originality were achieved that equalled those of advanced Europe'.[62] The skylark of the new spring, however, all too soon had its wings clipped, for Spain's glory was cut short by the Franco regime. Destiny turned, once again, unfavourable.

As this summary demonstrates, the relentless myth of 'decline', as a method of interpreting Spain's Golden Age, has become so ideologically pervasive that it refuses to go away. The attempt to reject it wholesale, however, ends up only in creating a mirror myth, one not of failure this time but of success. Both presentations are, from the point of view of a historian of early modern Spain, difficult to justify. They end up equally as myths, in the sense that they are necessitated by ideology, and their justification lies not in any facts – for the facts give no support to either – but in the apparent solution they offer to the painful story of Spain's difficult struggle to survive.

Decline in historical perspective

Trapped between fantasy and fact, it is difficult to emerge from underneath the mass of contradictory affirmations. The maze remains there, a delight to professional scholars, who refuse to let it go because they can entertain themselves with its concepts,[63] a nightmare to students, who continue to struggle with its tortuous ingenuity, and a solace to ideologists, who believe that it explains what happened to their country.[64]

Those who uphold the idea of decline have a powerful and valid argument. There may have been a myth, they would say, but the facts antedate it and it is the facts that are the chief matter, not the myth. The facts, as set out in

Cadalso's image of a 'total decline of science, arts, militia, trade, agriculture and population', are (they would say) irrefutable. To attempt to deny them would be a clear attempt to defend the great criminals of Spain's history, from Charles V and Philip II and their associates, the Inquisition and the Catholic Church, to those other guilty parties, the nefarious foreign powers and the insidious Jews, who, together, succeeded in destroying Spain. It is irrelevant that a political myth was constructed later. The facts speak for themselves.

The problem is that the 'facts' can be presented in different ways. That is what made it so easy for Cánovas to shift the weight of decline from Charles V to the last Habsburg kings. And we historians have not resolved the question, even though we seem not to differ about the facts. Purveyors of decline, whether they saw it in their own day or in some past age, were seeking refuge from their griefs. On the other hand, the optimistic view shrugged off the griefs and clung to the triumphs. But what were the relevant triumphs? What were the griefs? Writers who touched on the theme tended to have a specific political agenda and often confused the issues. The debate went off in different directions, and commentators ended up speaking about entirely different things. This was no problem for men such as Ortega y Gasset, who confessed in *Invertebrate Spain* that he knew little history but had an intuitive feeling for getting to the heart of the problem, which was that 'the roots of national decay lie in the soul of our people'. There is undoubtedly room for 'soul' in the debate, but there are also other fundamental issues that merit attention.

What was in decline? Spain? That was the first and biggest of the confusions. For the great myth-makers, notably Lafuente and Cánovas, the primary fact was the dissolution of Spain's world power. It is obvious that the rich tapestry of territories, brought together by inheritance under Ferdinand of Aragon and the early Habsburgs, began to fall apart until by the seventeenth century it was in evident decay. Driven by the conviction that Spain, or Castile, had created that tapestry, fashioned that empire – financed its expenses, won its battles and populated its colonies – and that Castilian writers of the seventeenth century seemed to agree with them, the myth-makers had no hesitation in affirming that the decline of empire was a consequence of a decline in Spain's own capacity. There was, in short, no difference between the decline of Spain and the decline of its empire. The view was, of course, intensely nationalist, because it identified Spain with the growth of empire. The myth of an all-conquering Spain (Chapter 2) was a central component. An immense number of conclusions followed from this simple premiss, but the most important one was this: Spain wasted its manpower and great riches on fruitless wars, instead of spending those riches on improvement, art, science and culture.

We may object, of course, that Spain was always poor, never rich; that it conquered no empire but rather inherited it; that it could not waste resources it did not have; that the imperial programme functioned thanks to the mines of Potosí and to the soldiers and bankers of Italy; and that the territories it 'lost' (like the Netherlands) had never really 'belonged' to it in any political or economic sense. Such objections would be fruitless in the face of a determined conviction that Spain was once the most powerful nation in Europe, indeed in the world, and that its achievements have been frustrated by a combination of reckless rulers (Philip II and his successors) and inveterate enemies (Protestants, Jews, the English). The interminable chain of international treaties which robbed Spain, relentlessly, of 'its' territories was irrefutable proof.

Solving the problem of why Spain lost its empire was child's play compared to solving the related problem of Spain's internal decline. The two problems were normally linked in historical studies, for it seemed logical that if Spain crumbled it was because it had been reduced internally from wealth to poverty, with the attendant consequences. When had that period of wealth come to pass? When did it crumble? Curiously enough, up to the early twentieth century not a single historical study attempted to document the disintegration. All writers agreed that the government of Castile faced terrible debts, which only got worse. Government debt, they seemed to assume, plunges a whole country into poverty. They did not realize, as economic historians now know, that debt and poverty are not necessarily related, and that it is often the most flourishing countries that have the biggest debts.

In the event, Spanish historians made no attempt to analyse the material dimensions of the phenomenon of alleged decline. Like Adolfo de Castro, they were content to look at the 'philosophical' aspect only, or to explore, like Ortega, 'the soul'. The first scholars to document decline happened to be Americans. Prescott's conclusion in 1838 (quoted above in Chapter 2) was that Spain was in total decay, a picture that helped him set the contrast with the glory of Ferdinand and Isabella. Then in 1898 Henry Charles Lea, the future historian of the Inquisition, published in the *Atlantic Monthly* an article, 'The Decadence of Spain', and wrote to a correspondent that he felt that Spain was 'a most deplorable picture of degradation in both public and private life'.[65] This happened to be the year of the Spanish–American war, which ended badly for Spaniards. Not until 1938, when the Chicago economic historian Earl J. Hamilton published his essay, 'The decline of Spain',[66] was a systematic attempt made to analyse the sixteenth-century reasons for this decline. Hamilton was author of three fundamental studies on prices of goods in Spain between the middle ages and the nineteenth century, and his article was a brilliant analysis of the information then available. Looking back from our moment in time, we can see that almost every conclusion at which he arrived in his essay was wrong. Hamilton's great contribution, however, was his attempt to bring some order to the debate. What declined? Where? When? Enough historical research has now been done on the issues to allow some firm perspectives.

We know, for instance, that Spain was a poor country that found it difficult to keep up with imperial commitments. Throughout the early modern period there were writers – the famous *arbitristas* – who complained about problems and put forward solutions. Their claims did not necessarily mean that Spain had collapsed, but the *arbitristas* were correct in pinpointing problems. One of the big issues was the way in which the Spanish textile market, formerly quite sufficient for domestic needs and a good sector for employment, was swamped by foreign textiles destined both for Spain and for America. The development took place precisely because Spain, thanks to its political importance and to the silver it received from the New World, was changing its market status. It was a sign of success, but also a sign of trouble. Success and trouble were two sides of the same coin. Ups involved downs. The same type of problem occurred in many other sectors, because Spain had changed aspects of its lifestyle. People were buying more because more money was available (thanks, in part, to American silver); but that pushed prices up, so they also suffered in the long run. As we go through other sectors of economic and cultural life in the Spain of that time, we can see that the ups and downs were constant. There is no convincing evidence to show that the nation suddenly became great and rich, and then suddenly declined.

For the same reason, it is difficult to put a firm date on economic decline. Was the sixteenth century the great age of success? The *arbitristas*, as we have seen, did not think so. In contrast to their views, however, a reliable scholar has concluded that 'for the first three quarters of the sixteenth century Castile's population multiplied, arable land was extended, agriculture and production increased, the level of urbanisation rose, the manufacture of silks and woollens flourished, wool exports remained buoyant until the 1560s, foreign trade until the 1590s, traffic with the Indies until the 1610s'.[67] If the sixteenth century, then, was not one of disaster, can we follow those historians who claim that the great age of decline was the seventeenth century, and especially its last fifty years? The answer is not easy to give, for experts appear to have come to the rescue of those last fifty years of the century. They argue on good evidence that, after the 1680s and despite a spate of serious reversals, the population figures rose, inflation levelled out, the government lowered taxation, production and trade began to expand, grain and wool output increased.[68] If anything, the internal condition of Spain was remarkably good, and it could be argued that there was no overall deterioration. In 1580 the Spain of Philip II was supposed to be still at the peak of its power, and in 1680 the Spain of Charles II was supposed to be at the nadir of its alleged decline. Yet in 1580 population was falling, and in 1680 it was rising. In 1580 agriculture was stagnating, in 1680 it was booming. In 1580 silver imports from America were falling, in 1680 they had never been higher. In 1580 inflation was soaring, in 1680 it was coming to an end. In 1580 the state budget was in ruins, in 1680 the government was reducing taxes. In 1580 Spain was spending its income and men on wars, in 1680 the wars were diminishing. The economic recovery of the 1680s, therefore, offers good reason for not confusing the international situation of the monarchy, which was disastrous, with internal evolution, which was positive.

In short, a little attention to the facts shows how difficult it is to impose a model of 'decline' on the country. Spain's success as an imperial power was always shaky, and in any case depended heavily on the resources of its allies. Measuring its rise and fall as an empire in terms of the territories it theoretically controlled is a wholly meaningless exercise, since each territory had a different relevance and its role as a possession was not always advantageous. Internally, in economic terms the country had a period of difficulties from around 1580 to around 1680. Those difficulties were to some extent related to a century of imperial power which covered roughly the same period, from the 1580s to approximately the 1680s. Unfortunately, the debate over decline always – until Hamilton's pioneering article of 1938 – remained indifferent to economic questions, and preferred to concentrate on two other themes: Spain's greatness as a world power and its cultural achievement. And even within the compass of these themes there were ample grounds for confusion and contradiction. For example, did the loss of its European empire (at the Treaty of Utrecht in 1713) mean that Spain had reached the lowest point of its fortunes? The reverse is true. The loss of the famous empire in Europe had a wholly beneficial effect on Spain, which exhibited remarkable signs of energy, made an attempt to modernize itself, improved its international contacts and recovered economically. Throughout the early modern period, in bad times and in good, the monarchy staggered along, but survived. There were never any reasons for imperialist triumphalism, but neither were there reasons for total pessimism.

The permanence of decline

Whichever way we look at the long story of unmitigated 'decline', it is clear that historical myth always had a political or cultural agenda. Those who wished to present a special version of the past, as the Liberals notoriously did, were second to none in their drive to create a national history that would explain their own stance. When their programme failed, or at least fell victim to forces they were unable to resist, the myth was given a new twist by their opponents, who chose instead to fix the blame for decline on persons and policies associated principally with the French Enlightenment. In all this maze of myth and counter-myth, several other historical fictions were also brought into play, which identified Spain as a medieval home of democracy, a coherent nation of free peoples, a land of unlimited natural riches, a haven of cultural tolerance. The purveyors of myth – both in the 1820s and the 1890s – tended for the most part to be not historians, but poets, dramatists and politicians who felt that visions of the past could reflect their own historical theories, without the need for unnecessary information produced by research into facts.

A typical 'progressive' view of decline was expressed as follows by the Marxist activist Joaquín Maurín (1896–1973) in 1930:

> The period of intellectual splendour in Spain from the middle of the sixteenth century to the end of the following, was a shadow from the days of Empire. When the latter disappeared – after the loss of the Netherlands, Italy, Portugal etc. – the spiritual activity of Spain vanished. The eighteenth century in Europe was one during which the bourgeoisie dedicated itself with passion to philosophy and the economic sciences, in order to discover the path that would lead to their definitive predominance. But Spain passed it by in silence. The same happened during the entire nineteenth century. It was terrible. The descending slope after the feudal epoch, the extermination of the bourgeoisie carried out in every possible

way, left no possibility of artistic expression. Spain became a feudal wasteland. The unrelenting terror of the Inquisition weighed on it for three hundred years. Life was destroyed. Croce in his *History of Aesthetics* mentions hundreds of thinkers and artists who contributed to the development of art. In this overview Spain occupies a tiny spot.[69]

The same picture was given by other writers of the same generation who touched on problems pertaining to science and industry. Spain was judged to be a backward country, having made few relevant contributions in these areas. Who was responsible for this dismal performance? A commentator writing in 2003 had few doubts about Spain's decline, whose origins he also traced to the Inquisition:

> Until well into the nineteenth century the Hispanic world remained excluded from modern development, and since then it has struggled with mixed results to modernize its economy, its society, its politics, and of course to develop its science. Because it was industrialized late, its dependence on the outside in economic matters was overwhelming, and its social structure continued to be marked by an enormous gap, inherited in part from the past. Despite the advance made in the last few decades, democracy has not taken root in all the Hispanic countries. In the same way, philosophy and modern science have not penetrated the social fabric, so that we continue to be mere recipients of science and technology.[70]

This writer is probably typical of the powerful tradition of a Castilian generation of elite intellectuals who used the distant past as a way of giving substance to their present concerns. The myth-makers of the nineteenth century, among them Lafuente and Cánovas, had a real political programme behind their delineation of the story of decline. In the same way, the generation that had to come to terms with Spain's loss of its New World empire in 1898 clung to the notion of decline as if it were medication. It is significant that Ortega y Gasset used medical analogies in his *Invertebrate Spain* (1922). His choice of words is interesting:

> The abnormality of Spain's history has been too long-lasting to be explained by temporal causes. Fifty years ago it was believed that national decline dated from only a few decades back. Costa and his generation began to suspect that decline was two centuries old. Some fifteen years ago

I attempted to demonstrate that decline permeated the entire early modern period of our history. One is always struck by the clear fact that in our past the abnormal has been normal. We arrive, then, at the conclusion that the entire history of Spain has been a history of decline.

At first sight, these words appear wholly meaningless, because they represent a judgement based on no evidence or rational thinking. They are simply absurd, the uninformed fantasy of a mature writer, thirty-nine years of age. However, they reflect faithfully a pessimism that can be found in generation after generation of Spain's thinkers. As Ortega went on to state, the basic problem was not the illness (*decadencia*) of the patient (Spain); the problem was the patient. 'Decline is a concept that refers to a state of health, but if Spain has never been healthy one cannot say that it has declined.' Generation after generation, beginning with the dawn of contemporary Spanish historiography in the 1850s, Spanish historians down to the twentieth century have tended systematically to perform ideological postmortems on their country without attempting to analyse the reasons for its demise or to discover whether any life was left in the body. If anyone was responsible for the patient's illness, it was invariably someone or something that had its origins in the sixteenth century. A French scholar pointed out some years ago that 'a neo-Manichean vision of the national past underlies the greater part of current Spanish history-writing'.[71]

One facet of this conservative outlook, which can be found in the works of a handful of Castilian writers starting with those of 1898, was the expression of the view that Castile's destiny was bound up with its special mission in the world. Other empires might seek material success, but that was not Spain's way. Other nations could surge ahead in science and wealth, but Spain had chosen a better path, seeking salvation through spiritual exaltation and poverty. It was, as we have seen, the point of view expressed by Unamuno when he penned the phrase 'Let others invent!' One hundred years later, the same attitude was alive and well in Madrid. An article expressing an identical point of view was published in the socialist newspaper *El País* on 12 April 2003. According to the author, Spain's great empire was based on a 'humanism' preached by 'our mystics and our thinkers' and 'drew its inspiration from a rejection of the will to power, which is a sentiment basic to the Anglo-Saxon nations'. Unlike the materialist-inspired civilizations of the British and Americans, Spaniards preferred the 'Spanish spirit', which was a 'rejection of the religion of success' and preferred failure, because that was

'Spanish humanism'. 'This has been the core of our culture, and has given character and personality to the Spanish people throughout the centuries.'[72] On this view, failure rather than material success was the Spanish way. Decline, for those who thought along these lines, became a permanent and necessary part of Spain's role in the world. The myth became elevated into a cultural faith.

MYTH AND THE EROSION
OF IDENTITY IN SPAIN

The main purpose of myth-making at a political level was to outline a common past that would explain the present and also define the future. People would be brought together because they would recognize what they shared. The intellectuals who gave support to myths were not passive in attitude, but wished to use the sense of the past in a creative way as part of a positive contribution to public life. The various strands of the myths mentioned in the previous chapters were therefore, from the nineteenth century onwards, integrated into the visions offered by political and cultural leaders. It is a common mistake to think that backward-looking myths were a hallmark only of conservatives, laying emphasis on sixteenth-century themes such as Catholic religion and imperial glory. On the contrary, related constructs about nation, language and empire were an integral part also of so-called 'progressive' thought, and were defended with equal tenacity. There has been continued loyalty to the myths across the whole political spectrum, left and right alike. In a 2007 review of the Spanish version of the present book in the socialist newspaper *El País*, which enjoys the country's widest circulation, a journalist objected with some feeling:

> The author argues that there was no conquest of America because that was the work of the hordes of Indians who helped Cortes and Pizarro, when by the same token one could say that neither did the British conquer India, because of all the native auxiliaries Clive had at the battle of Plassey. Spanish is not a universal language because, the author writes, nobody should claim that it is spoken by a fifth of the human race, when (he suggests) everybody knows that it is spoken by only a seventh, a trifle less than 400 million people out of six thousand millions. Of course, nobody

in their right mind should deny that the only language on the planet is English. Moreover, there was no decline of Spain because it never rose to greatness and the Iberian peninsula appeared in the world by, no doubt, a freak conjunction of the stars. The empire was not Spanish because it was paid for by Genoese and German bankers. And Spanish soldiers were always a minority in the armies of the empire, even though Castile paid the costs out of its own pocket.[1]

From these sentiments – whose accuracy can be checked against what the text of the present book actually says – it is apparent that a version of the past that reigned supreme over a century ago is still defended tenaciously today. This hold of the mythical past on the imagination was broken decisively at only one point in time, during the Popular Front government of the Second Republic in 1936. The cultural agenda of the writers and artists who supported the social revolution that year excluded completely any looking back. Inspired in part by the programme of the Soviet Union, they threw overboard religion, monarchy, empire and all the other paraphernalia of the past. Through activists like Federico García Lorca, they went directly to the people with literature, poems and plays, in an effort to change traditional culture.[2] This effort collapsed when the Civil War broke out, and Franco's victory assured the triumph of the most radical traditionalism, which became the official cultural doctrine of the state. By way of rebelling against it, opponents of the dictatorship eagerly lapped up Marxist thought, which, however, never came to play any significant role after the end of the Franco regime and was never capable of providing any alternative cultural constructs. During the 1980s, in Spain, Marxism – and with it the Communist Party – melted away like snow, as though it had never been.

Since the 1960s the experience of democracy in Spanish politics has brought into being new ways of looking at the past which, inevitably, have pushed the sixteenth century into the background and caused many to re-examine their ideological attitudes from newer standpoints. In general, Spaniards became more open to outside ideas[3] and less obsessed with the mistakes or achievements of their past. A case in point was the widespread acceptance of and respect for the institution of monarchy, seen now (as I have commented in Chapter 2) as a serious contributor to political stability after the years of dictatorship. In the same way, obsession with the glorious religious role of Spain almost disappeared, an inevitable development in a country where religious belief and practice have shrunk to minute dimensions. A study carried out in 1992 reported: 'until the 1970s one could say that being a practising Catholic was the norm among Spaniards. Nine out of ten practised their religion. A generation later the proportion has fallen to one out of two. One can state that Spain is ceasing to be Catholic.'[4] Many of the myths to which ideologues clung stopped being relevant matters of dispute. The reality or otherwise of Spain's decline, to take one example, has become a theme on which Spanish scholars obviously disagree, but can usually disagree without anger. It seemed that there was room for debate within the broad field of historical research, and that myths could be accepted as harmless contributions to learned discourse. In these and other respects, some of the themes of this book are no longer a relevant part of cultural experience. They are preserved only in the attitude of those, whether 'conservatives' or 'socialists', who grew up in a past generation or are heirs to its outlook. In normal circumstances, therefore, it would seem that the historical myths outlined in preceding chapters can coexist peacefully with basic agreement concerning the main outline of the historical past, since details and interpretations are always and validly open to debate.

The early modern period, however, continues to occupy a central role in myth-making because it supplies material for new conflictive attitudes in a country which has not yet achieved a stable national identity. The core problem remains that of the nation, or 'Spain'; but beyond it lies a real minefield, which affects many aspects of the past. The replacement of a single central government in Spain by a number of autonomous governments, which all lay claim to their separate identities, has encouraged the systematic rewriting of history along ideological lines. This book has already touched on problems affecting the historical past of the largest political component of Spain, Castile. In the same way, the early modern period had to be ideologically reshaped in order to create an officially approved past for the autonomous regions of Catalonia, Valencia and Aragon. As a consequence, there are historical themes that have begun to be politically untouchable. In Aragon, for example, there is only one disseminated version of the intervention, in pursuit of Antonio Pérez, by the troops of Philip II in the year 1591. When some years ago a medical foundation in Madrid planned to hold a conference in Saragossa to commemorate Gregorio Marañón's biography of Pérez, grants for holding it in the city were withdrawn by Aragonese groups, with the excuse that any conference touching on the role of Philip II would arouse popular indignation and could not be risked. Thirty years after the end of the Franco dictatorship, it became politically unwise to speak about events which happened four hundred years previously. The urge to create a valid historical past has ended up in numerous other incidents of this type, reaching of course down to the history of our own times.[5] A well-known literary figure relates how a friend was asked by a Barcelona publisher to write an account of the fall of the city to Nationalist forces at the end of the Spanish Civil War. When the author produced his text, the publisher found that it contained references to how thousands of Catalans cheered Franco when he made his victorious entry into the city in 1939. Since this image was at variance with the official view that no Catalans could possibly have cheered Franco, the publisher refused to proceed with the book.[6]

A deliberate manipulation of facts about the past seems to be an inevitable political consequence of the search for identity.[7] All nations rely on a variety of historical myths, disseminated through textbooks, popular literature and cultural pastimes, in order to consolidate appreciation of the past (national achievements) and of the present (national character). In the case of Spain, the myth-building seems, regrettably, to have been of little use in achieving the lineaments of a national identity. The governing elites of the nineteenth century gave their support to many educational texts about history,[8] but were unable to arrive at a definition of what the country of their own day was. For one hundred years after Modesto Lafuente, governments attempted to define their past (hence the emphasis on the sixteenth century) but correspondingly failed to define their present or to arrive at any consensus of attitude and sentiment about the reality of Spain. Profound disagreements arose between Castilian intellectual elites and their own government, as well as between regional elites and the Castilian centre. In this way, 'diverse historical memories and traditions provided fertile soil for a regional cultural production',[9] but the end result was a fragmentation of the past that everyone should have been able to share without disagreement. 'Over the last century', observes a leading American historian, 'a succession of political regimes has largely failed in attempts to instil a common understanding of national history.'[10] The early modern period, generally enthused over rather than researched into by Spanish historians before the mid-twentieth century, became swept up in this failure. In 2002 the country's leading historical society, the Royal Academy of History, denounced the collapse of national history. 'Many of us', stated the president of the Academy, Gonzalo Anes, a distinguished expert on the eighteenth century, 'are professors and are aware of the collapse at university level. Every year we receive students who either know no history or know only about local matters that are incorrect and deliberately distorted.' The conclusion we can draw is evident. Myth-making about the early modern history of Spain will persist because it is a direct consequence of the failure to create a homogeneous national identity and a coherent, commonly shared historical memory.

NOTES

Preface

1. Arturo Pérez-Reverte is a writer of popular novels in Spain. In an interview on his books in *El País*, 15 Nov. 2003, he commented: 'I wanted to narrate Golden Age Spain, which is not so distant from the Spain of today. It was an age that marked us deeply . . . I wrote my books to explain our history.'
2. Claude Lévi-Strauss, 'The structural study of myth', in *Structural Anthropology*, New York 1963, p. 202.
3. For references and bibliography, see my *Early Modern European Society*, London 2000.
4. Robert Walinski-Kiehl, 'Reformation history and political mythology in the German Democratic Republic, 1949–89', *European History Quarterly*, 43: 1 (2004).
5. Perhaps the best survey of the Comuneros from this point of view is the one by J. A. Maravall, *Las Comunidades de Castilla*, Madrid 1979.
6. Cf. Antonio Mestre, 'La Historiografía española del siglo XVIII', *Actas. Coloquio Internacional Carlos III y su siglo*, 2 vols, Madrid 1990, vol. 1, p. 21.
7. To take one example, an article by Pedro Ruiz Torres, 'Political uses of history in Spain', *Mediterranean Historical Review*, vol. 16, no. 1 (June 2001), seems to see bias only in those who do not share his own views.
8. Ramiro de Maeztu, *Defensa de la Hispanidad*, Madrid 1934.
9. J. N. Hillgarth, *The Mirror of Spain, 1500–1700. The Formation of a Myth*, Ann Arbor 2003.

Chapter 1: The myth of the historic nation

1. Raymond Carr, *Spain 1808–1939*, Oxford 1966, p. 105.
2. Charles J. Esdaile, *The Spanish Army in the Peninsular War*, Manchester 1988, pp. 96–102. Esdaile has updated his whole presentation of the war in *The Peninsular War: A New History*, New York 2003.
3. Carr, p. 106.
4. In some Spanish school and university textbooks on the Peninsular War, the word 'Bailén' appears, but not the word 'Wellington'.
5. Cf. Charles J. Esdaile, *Fighting Napoleon: Guerrillas, Bandits and Adventures in Spain 1808–1814*, New Haven and London 2004. Despite the definitive work of Esdaile, the year 2008 is seeing the publication in Spanish – to celebrate the bicentenary of 1808 – of a large number of popular works that ignore current research and revert implacably to the nationalist myths of the nineteenth century.
6. Cf. Juliá, pp. 44–5.

7. José Álvarez Junco, 'The formation of Spanish identity', *History and Memory*, vol. 14, no. 1/2, Fall 2002.
8. Quoted in Juliá, p. 25. The references, one will recall, are to the execution of the *comunero* leader Padilla in 1521, on the field, after the battle of Villalar; to the execution of the Justiciar of Aragon in 1591; and to the death (in tranquillity, in his own bed) of the man who had led the secession of Catalonia to France in 1641.
9. Samuel A. Dunham, *The History of Spain and Portugal*, 5 vols, Philadelphia 1832.
10. J. S. Pérez-Garzón, *Modesto Lafuente, artífice de la Historia de España*, Pamplona 2002, p. 70.
11. Pérez-Garzón, *Modesto Lafuente*, p. 79.
12. A good introduction is A. L. Macfie, *Orientalism*, London 2002. It is usual to cite the work *Orientalism*, by Edward Said, as an exposition of the cultural trend, but a more scholarly look at the topic is offered by John Mackenzie, *Orientalism, History, Theory and the Arts*, London 1995.
13. Richard L. Kagan, 'Prescott's paradigm', *American Historical Review*, vol. 101, no. 2 (April 1996).
14. *Bosquejo histórico de la política de España*. Available in the Biblioteca de Autores Españoles, in *Obras de Don Francisco Martínez de la Rosa*, vol. 8, Madrid 1962.
15. Álvarez Junco, 'Formation of Spanish identity', p. 26.
16. Boyd, p. 76.
17. For Tolstoy, see *War and Peace*, Epilogue, Part II. For Lafuente, see vol. I: i of the 1877 edition.
18. Cf. Nicholas Henshall, *The Myth of Absolutism. Change and Continuity in Early Modern European Monarchy*, London 1992, p. 209. It would be superfluous to mention that historians argued over the word 'absolutism' for much of the twentieth century. Spanish scholars refused to give up the concept and continued to write about the 'absolutism' of Ferdinand and Isabella or the 'absolutism' of Philip II. One more flexible and perceptive Spanish approach may be found in José Antonio Maravall, *Estado moderno y mentalidad social*, 2 vols, Madrid 1972, vol. 1, pp. 295–310.
19. Among the numerous studies which are of relevance for pre-industrial nations, see E. J. Hobsbawm, *Nations and Nationalism since 1780: Programme, Myth, Reality*, Cambridge 1990; and Benedict R. Anderson, *Imagined Communities: Reflections on the Origin and Spread of Nationalism*, London 1991. For Spain, there is a short work by Inman Fox, *La invención de España. Nacionalismo liberal e Identidad nacional*, Madrid 1997.
20. Gustavo Bueno, 'Legitimidad y Estado autonómico', *El País*, 29 January 1993.
21. Quoted by Adrian Hastings, 'The construction of nationhood', in Philip Spencer and Howard Wollman, eds., *Nations and Nationalism: A Reader*, New Brunswick, NJ 2005, p. 35.
22. L. Brockliss and D. Eastwood, eds, *A Union of Multiple Identities: The British Isles, c.1750–c.1850*, New York and Manchester 1996.
23. Cf. A. G. Dickens, *The German Nation and Martin Luther*, London 1974, ch. 2.
24. *The Prince*, various editions, ch. 21.
25. Fernand Braudel, *L'Identité de la France*, Paris 1986; English version, *The Identity of France*, London 1988; Spanish version, *La Identidad de Francia*, 3 vols., Barcelona 1993.
26. When I gave a talk in 1998 to an elite dining group in Madrid on the theme of the identity of Spain in the time of Philip II, and followed the schema outlined by Braudel, I was solemnly warned by a senior bureaucrat 'never to speak in such terms again', because the terms did not apply to Spain, which had never experienced diversity and had always been a united nation.
27. Baltasar Gracián, *El Político don Fernando el Católico*, Saragossa edn 1985.
28. A recent look at local consciousness in pre-industrial Spain and America is offered by

Tamar Herzog, *Defining Nations. Immigrants and Citizens in Early Modern Spain and Spanish America*, New Haven and London 2003, ch. 2. She looks in particular at the word *vecindad*, which she translates as 'citizenship'.

29. Cited in Thompson, p. 128, n. 10.

30. Maravall, *Estado Moderno*, vol. 1, p. 483.

31. Cited in René Quatrefages, *Los tercios españoles (1567–77)*, Madrid 1979, p. 282.

32. Quoted in Maravall, *Estado Moderno*, vol. 1, p. 488.

33. Maravall, *Estado Moderno*, vol. 1, p. 475ff, has a good brief survey.

34. A. Alvar Ezquerra, *Isabel la Católica*, Madrid 2002, p. 77.

35. Baltasar Cuart Moner, 'La larga marcha hacia las historias de España en el siglo XVI', in R. García Cárcel, ed., *La Construcción de las Historias de España*, Madrid 2004, p. 110.

36. Kathryn A. Woolard, 'Is the past a foreign country? Time, language, origins and the nation in early modern Spain', *Journal of Linguistic Anthropology*, vol. 14, no. 1, p. 73.

37. There is a good account of the context of Mariana's work by Enrique García Hernán, in García Cárcel, *La Construcción de las Historias de España*.

38. Peter Sahlins, *Boundaries. The Making of France and Spain in the Pyrenees*, Berkeley 1989, p. 113.

39. Benzion Netanyahu, *The Origins of the Inquisition*, New York 1995 , pp. 995–6, from whom I take the examples that follow.

40. Cited in Kamen 1993b, p. 42.

41. *Excellences of the Jews*, cited in Y. H. Yerushalmi, *From Spanish Court to Italian Ghetto. Isaac Cardoso: A Study in Seventeenth-Century Marranism and Jewish Apologetics*, New York 1971.

42. Miriam Bodian, '"Men of the nation": The shaping of converso identity in early modern Europe', *Past and Present*, 143, 1994, p. 70–2.

43. Philip II to duke of Osuna and Cristóbal de Moura, 30 June 1579, *Colección de Documentos Inéditos para la Historia de España* (cited hereafter as *CODOIN*), 6, 519–20.

44. For Valencia, the towns were Valencia and Peñíscola; for Aragón, they were Saragossa, Tarazona, Calatayud, Borja, Fraga; see P. Molas, 'Las Cortes de Castilla y León en el siglo XVIII', in the collected volume *Las Cortes de Castilla y León en la Edad Moderna*, Valladolid 1989.

45. Hugh Seton-Watson, *Nations and States: An Enquiry into the Origins of Nations and the Politics of Nationalism*, London 1977.

46. Horst Pietschmann, 'El problema del "nacionalismo" en España en la edad moderna. La resistencia de Castilla contra el Emperador Carlos V', *Hispania*, no. 180 (1992).

47. Juan Maldonado, *La revolución comunera*, p. 41, cited by Thompson, p. 133.

48. Cited in Thompson, p. 135.

49. Antonio de Herrera, *Historia general de los hechos de los Castellanos*, Madrid 1601, pp. 6, 265.

50. Prudencio de Sandoval, *Historia de la vida y hechos del Emperador Carlos V*, Biblioteca de Autores Españoles, Vol. 80: 1, Madrid 1955, p. 20.

51. Ruth Pike, *Enterprise and Adventure. The Genoese in Seville and the Opening of the New World*, Ithaca, NY 1966, p. 195.

52. *España invertebrada*, Madrid 1975, p. 50.

53. *Epistolario de Pedro Martir*, Madrid 1953, *CODOIN*, 9, p. 123.

54. Maravall, *Estado Moderno*, vol. 1, pp. 472, 478.

55. Tamar Herzog, 'Private organizations as global networks in early modern Spain and Spanish America', in L. Roniger and T. Herzog, eds, *The Collective and the Public in Latin America. Cultural Identities and Political Order*, Brighton 2000, p. 121.

56. Isabelo Macías and Francisco Morales Padrón, eds, *Cartas desde América 1700–1800*, Seville 1991, p. 65.

57. Cf. Michael Kenny, '"Which Spain?" The conservation of regionalism among Spanish emigrants and exiles', *Iberian Studies*, vol. 5, no. 2, (1976).
58. Jonathan I. Israel, *Race, Class and Politics in Colonial Mexico 1610–1670*, Oxford 1975, p. 115.
59. Juan Javier Pescador, *The New World inside a Basque Village*, Reno 2004, p. 126.
60. Luis de Avila y Zúñiga, *Comentarios de la Guerra de Alemania hecha de Carlo V*, Antwerp 1549, fo. 66v.
61. *Crónicas del Gran Capitán*, ed. Antonio Rodríguez Villa, Madrid 1908 (Nueva Biblioteca de Autores Españoles, vol. 10), p. 375.
62. Maravall, *Estado Moderno*, vol. 1, pp. 464, 475.
63. David Brading, 'Patriotism and the nation in colonial Spanish America', in Luis Roniger and Mario Sznajder, eds, *Constructing Collective Identities and Shaping Public Spheres*, Brighton 1998.
64. Cited by Antonio Mestre, 'La historiografía española del siglo XVIII', *Coloquio Internacional Carlos III y su siglo. Actas, tomo I*, Madrid 1990, p. 39.
65. This process is a matter of nineteenth-century history, and hence falls outside the scope of the present short study.
66. For all this, see e.g. Clare Mar-Molinero and Angel Smith, 'The myths and realities of nation-building in the Iberian peninsula', in Mar-Molinero and Smith, p. 16.
67. Cf. Chapter 7 of Llobera, *Foundations of National Identity*.
68. Cited by James Casey, 'Patriotism in early modern Valencia', in Kagan and Parker, p. 208.
69. By far the most balanced and readable essay on the Catalan problem is by J. L. Llobera, *Foundations of National Identity*.
70. Quoted by Juliá (above, n. 6), p. 116.
71. Juliá, p. 117.
72. Xavier Trias in *El Mundo*, 11 September 2004.
73. Benedict Anderson, *Imagined Communities*, rev. edn, London 1991, p. 6.
74. David Miller, *On Nationality*, Oxford 1995, p. 35. One must also, of course, respect the view which holds that historical fictions are unhealthy. A good discussion of this view is given by Arash Abizadeh, 'Historical truth, national myths and liberal democracy: On the coherence of liberal nationalism', *Journal of Political Philosophy*, vol. 12, no. 3 (2004), pp. 291–313.
75. By this treaty, a section of northern Catalonia, including the city of Perpignan, was surrendered to and permanently integrated into France.
76. In a subsequent referendum for regional autonomy held on 18 February 2007 in Andalusia, only 31 per cent of the electorate voted in favour.
77. An excellent summary is given by Isidro Sepúlveda Muñoz, 'De intenciones y logros: fortalecimento estatal y limitaciones del nacionalismo español en el siglo XIX', *@mnis*, September 2002.
78. National anthems were created very recently in the history of modern nations. One example is interesting: the Japanese national anthem was composed in 1870 by a British soldier who was director of the emperor's court orchestra.
79. The term 'Iron Century' is a reference to my study of early modern Europe, *The Iron Century*, first published in 1971.
80. 'Legitimidad y Estado autonómico', *El País*, 29 January 1993.
81. *El País*, 15 January 1978.
82. My note: 1474 was the date of the marriage between Ferdinand and Isabella.
83. Interview with Bueno, *La Nueva España* (Oviedo), 6 November 2005.
84. Manuel Fernández Álvarez, *La Sociedad española del Renacimiento*, Madrid 1974, p. 62.
85. For the king's visits to these provincial cities, see my *Philip of Spain*, New Haven, CT and London 1997.

86. José Luis Abellán, 'España contra sí misma', *El País*, 12 April 2003.

87. Quoted in Santoveña, p. 95.

88. Lafaye, p. 440.

Chapter 2: The myth of the failed monarchy

1. Angus MacKay, 'Ritual and propaganda in fifteenth-century Castile', *Past and Present*, 107 (1985).

2. Cf. Helen Nader, *The Mendoza Family in the Spanish Renaissance 1350–1550*, New Brunswick 1979, p. 19.

3. See the seminal study by Teofilo Ruiz on 'Unsacred monarchy. The kings of Castile in the late Middle Ages', reprinted in his *The City and the Realm: Burgos and Castile 1080–1492*, Aldershot 1992, ch. 13.

4. Spain is notably absent from the essays edited by János Bak, *Coronations. Mediaeval and Early Modern Monarchic Ritual*, Berkeley 1990. The kings of Spain were not crowned and did not have a coronation ceremony.

5. The care taken at their deaths could still be complex: see the rituals for Philip II described in Carlos M. Eire, *From Madrid to Purgatory. The Art and Craft of Dying in Sixteenth-Century Spain*, Cambridge 1995.

6. The idea of comparing Philip II with Louis XIV was first mooted in the nineteenth century by French republican intellectuals who viewed Louis as a Spaniard (his mother and his wife were from Spain's royal family, which made him a direct blood relative of Philip II) and considered his absolutism an alien Spanish import. The classic statement on this was made by one of France's great historians, Ernest Lavisse. See Jean-Frédéric Schaub, *La France espagnole. Les racines hispaniques de l'absolutisme français*, Paris 2003, p. 31. There were many antecedents to this idea, perhaps the first being the publication by an exiled French Protestant, Quesnot de la Chesnée, of *Parallèle de Philippe II et Louis XIV sur le renversement de la Monarchie Universelle*, Cologne 1709.

7. Parker 1998, p. 95.

8. Fernando Bouza, 'La majestad de Felipe II. Construcción del mito real', in J. Martínez Millán, ed., *La Corte de Felipe II*, Madrid 1994, p. 55.

9. Parker 1998, p. 286, believes that Philip felt he was Moses.

10. Kamen 1997, pp. 194–199.

11. Maravall, I, 382–5.

12. Cf. Kamen 1997, p. 231.

13. Cited in Alvar, p. 310.

14. The following comment by a colleague of Vicens is relevant: 'Vicens himself saw this as a vital contribution to the construction of the Catalunya of the post-Franco era, because he believed that myths were an unstable foundation for national identity. It was not enough simply to blame Castile for the historical misfortunes of Catalunya. One must also look deep into Catalan society itself, and into the whole historical conjuncture at any given moment. This approach, which did not endear Vicens to some of his colleagues of an older generation, seemed to me eminently sensible. As far as I was concerned, Vicens brought a breath of fresh air to an enclosed historical world. His enthusiasm and engagement gave additional excitement and meaning to my work, and confirmed me in my conviction of the importance of relating the history of seventeenth-century Spain and Catalunya to the broad sweep of European history, in an attempt to break free from the isolationist approach of so much Spanish historiography.' Taken from John H. Elliott, 'In search of 1640', *Journal of Catalan Studies*, 2001.

15. Egido, p. 59.

16. Cf. Alvar, p. 266.

17. Castro, p. 264.
18. Cited by Castro, p. 265.
19. In Juliá, p. 35.
20. Lafuente, I, xxii.
21. Lafuente, II, 430, 435.
22. Juliá, p. 383.
23. Luis Suárez, 'España, unidad de destino', *Arbil*, no.100 (2005). This is a reprint of a lecture apparently given in the 1950s.
24. Spanish historians of that time passed over in silence the matter of the demographic impact of the discoveries, and considered depopulation to be a lie invented by Las Casas and other enemies of Spain. However, now that research has made the fact of depopulation incontrovertible, the current argument – to be found in very many writings today – is that the Spanish conquistadors and settlers were wholly blameless, all the negative aspects of conquest being due to epidemics alone.
25. Cited in Juliá, p. 28.
26. Cf. J. A. Maravall, *La oposición política bajo los Austrias*, Barcelona 1972.
27. Egido, p. 64. This was part of a text pinned up on several churches in Valladolid, probably around 1519.
28. Cited in H. Kamen, *The War of Succession in Spain, 1700–15*, London and Bloomington IN 1965, pp. 25–6
29. Schmidt, p. 84.
30. In Juliá, p. 36.
31. Lafuente, III, 214.
32. Lafuente, I, xxiii, xxx.
33. In Juliá, p. 42.
34. Cf. Martina Fuchs, *Eine populäre Figur? Zur Rezeption des Kaisers in deutschsprachiger Belletristik*, Münster 2002.
35. For the reputation of Philip outside Spain, a theme we shall not broach, see e.g. W. S. Maltby, *The Black Legend in England*, Durham, NC 1971.
36. His reign is correctly dated from 1556 to 1598, which makes 42 years, but he was also supreme governor of Spain from 1543, which adds 13 years to the total.
37. The leaflet was discovered by a graduate of Saragossa university, Pilar Sánchez.
38. Except in the eyes of commentators three centuries later, who felt that Cervantes was a hero of the struggle against the tyranny of the king, and thought it necessary to twist the meaning of his words. For a balanced and interesting discussion of this sonnet, see E. C. Graf, '*Escritor/Excretor*: Cervantes's 'Humanism' on Philip II's Tomb', in *Cervantes: Bulletin of the Cervantes Society of America*, 19.1 (1999), pp. 66–95.
39. In Egido, p. 21.
40. Cf. Hillgarth, *The Mirror of Spain*, chapter 14.
41. Cf. Kamen 1997, pp. 33, 61.
42. The quotations and a further discussion come from François Mignet, *Antonio Pérez y Felipe II*, introduction by Henry Kamen, Madrid 2001.
43. Quoted in Vicente Llorens, *El Romanticismo español*, Madrid 1989, p. 144.
44. Quoted in Pierre L. Ullman, *Mariano de Larra and Spanish Political Rhetoric*, Madison WI 1971, p. 25.
45. Francisco Martínez de la Rosa, *Bosquejo histórico de la política de España*, in Biblioteca de Autores Españoles, *Obras de Francisco Martínez de la Rosa*, vol. 8, Madrid 1962, pp. 180, 187.
46. Lafuente, I, xxv.
47. 'Were our father a heretic we would carry the faggots to burn him': *Calendar of State Papers, Venice*, London 1890, VI, ii, no. 1067.

48. The king in fact attended five *autos de fe* in Spain in his lifetime, or one every fourteen years, hardly the zeal of a fanatic. At none of them did he witness any executions. His last attendance at an *auto de fe* was in 1591; prior to that he had not been at one in nearly thirty years (since 1564).
49. Cited in Juan-Sisinio Pérez Garzón, *Modesto Lafuente, artífice de la Historia de España*, Pamplona 2002, p. 94.
50. Cánovas del Castillo, *Bosquejo Histórico de la Casa de Austria en España*, Madrid 1911, pp. 78–9.
51. Fernand Braudel, *La Méditerranée et le monde méditerranéen à l'époque de Philippe II*, Paris 1949.
52. Geoffrey Parker, *Philip II*, Boston 1978 (reprinted Chicago 2002); and my *Philip of Spain*, New Haven CT and London 1997 (and subsequent editions). A passionate attack on *Philip of Spain* by a professor of history at a Spanish university claimed that the book had been financed by, and written for, the conservative government that had just come to power. In reality, it had been largely completed in the epoch of the previous socialist government! Unknowingly, in writing the book I had strayed into the century-old battleground between nineteenth-century ideologues.
53. A. García Sanz, in *Historia*, vol. 16, no. 270 (1998), p. 23.
54. Gregorio Colas, 'Felipe II y el constitucionalismo aragonés', *Manuscrits*, no. 16 (1998).
55. The best survey of Philip's decision-making is Hugo de Schepper, 'Ensayo sobre el modelo del proceso de decisión política en los Países Bajos de Felipe II', in the collective work *Tussen twee culturen*, Nijmegen 1991, pp. 173–98.
56. For the king's role in government, cf. Kamen 1997, pp. 218–19.
57. For the long process of consultation which led eventually to intervention in Aragon, see my *Philip of Spain*.
58. Cited in Kamen 1997, pp. 286–7.
59. L. P. Gachard, *Carlos V y Felipe II a través de sus contemporaneos*, Madrid 1944, p. 114.
60. Written in the monastery of San Jerónimo, Madrid, 15 October 1578, archive of the Instituto de Valencia de Don Juan, file 51, no. 180.
61. Geoffrey Parker, *The World is not Enough: The Imperial Vision of Philip II of Spain*, Waco TX 2001, p. 27.
62. Egido, p. 85.
63. Egido, pp. 117–18.
64. For a discussion, see my *Philip V of Spain. The king who reigned twice*, London and New Haven CT 2000.
65. Archivo Histórico Nacional, Madrid, Estado leg. 2530, no. 139.
66. Cf. Egido: 'The loss of respect for King Philip, who had been sacred till then, was the central fact marking the change of direction in criticisms made against the government', in *Opinión pública y oposición al poder en la España del siglo XVIII (1713–1759)*, Valladolid 1971, p. 148.
67. Egido, p. 259.
68. Quoted in Juliá, p. 28.
69. Boyd, p. 76.
70. Volker Sellin, 'The breakdown of the rule of law: A comparative view of the depositions of George III, Louis XVI and Napoleon I', in Robert von Friedeburg, ed., *Murder and Monarchy. Regicide in European History 1300–1800*, London 2004.
71. Quoted in Juliá, p. 223.
72. José María Valverde, *Azorín*, Barcelona 1971, p. 361.
73. The most recent analysis of the downfall of the Republic is by Stanley G. Payne, *The Collapse of the Spanish Republic, 1933–1936. Origins of the Civil War*, New Haven CT and London 2006.

74. Cited in Juliá, p. 395.
75. Carlos Seco Serrano, 'Nuestra monarquía: vigente y necesaria', *ABC*, 10 July 2004.
76. Javier Tusell, 'La monarquía, en peligro', *El País*, 27 December 2004.
77. Ortega published the article in the Madrid paper *El Sol*, 15 November 1930.

Chapter 3: The myth of a Christian Spain

1. Saínz Rodríguez, p. 91.
2. Álvarez Junco, p. 16.
3. Lecture on 'España y su Futuro. La Iglesia Católica', in the Club Siglo XXI, Madrid, on 27 October 2005.
4. Quoted in Orlando Figes, *Natasha's Dance. A Cultural History of Russia*, London 2002, p. 319.
5. Carlos Carrete Parrondo, *Fontes Iudaeorum regni Castellae, vol. II: El Tribunal de la Inquisición en el Obispado de Soria (1486–1502)*, Salamanca 1985, pp. 37, 79. The statement, attributed to a priest, went on to state: 'and have a nice woman friend and eat well'.
6. Felipe de Meneses, *Luz del alma Christiana* (1554), Madrid 1978 edn, pp. 317, 321.
7. Cited by J. L. González Novalín in *Historia de la Iglesia en España*, ed. R. García-Villoslada, Madrid 1979, vol. 3. 1, p. 369.
8. Kamen 1993[a], p. 82.
9. For what follows, cf. Kamen 1993[a].
10. Cf. Richard L. Kagan, *Lucrecia's Dreams. Politics and Prophecy in Sixteenth-Century Spain*, Berkeley 1990.
11. For the late arrival of this belief among Catholics in Europe, see J. Le Goff, *The Birth of Purgatory*, London 1984.
12. M. Angeles Cristóbal, 'La Inquisición de Logroño', in *Inquisición española: Nuevas aproximaciones*, Madrid 1987, p. 141.
13. However, one expert on religious sociology believes that, despite profanity, excess and ignorance, the villagers he studies were Christian by the nineteenth century: Carmelo Lisón Tolosana, *Belmonte de los Caballeros. A Sociological Study of a Spanish Town*, Oxford 1966, p. 281.
14. J. M. García Fuentes, *La Inquisicion en Granada en el siglo XVI*, Granada 1981, p. 445.
15. There is a good recent discussion of this by Nicholas Griffiths, 'Popular religious scepticism and idiosyncrasy in post-Tridentine Cuenca', in Lesley Twomey, ed., *Faith and Fanaticism. Religious Fervour in Early Modern Spain*, Aldershot 1997.
16. For these references and the whole context of post-Reformation religion in Europe, see Henry Kamen, *Early Modern European Society*, London and New York 2000, chapter 3.
17. Among the very few studies on it, three are basic: Kamen 1993[b]; Sara T. Nalle, *God in La Mancha. Religion, Reform and the People of Cuenca 1500–1650*, Baltimore 1992 (e-book); and Allyson M. Poska, *Regulating the People. The Catholic Reformation in Seventeenth-Century Spain*, Boston 1998.
18. Philip II to the Count of Luna, 12 May 1563, *CODOIN*, vol. 98, p. 438.
19. Maureen Flynn, *Sacred Charity: Confraternities and Social Welfare in Spain, 1400–1700*, London 1986.
20. William A. Christian Jr, *Local Religion in Sixteenth-Century Spain*, Princeton 1981; see also his *Apparitions in Late Medieval and Renaissance Spain*, Princeton 1981 (e-book).
21. William J. Callahan, *Church, Politics and Society in Spain, 1750–1874*, Cambridge, MA 1984, p. 155.
22. The quotations that follow are taken from Alvar, pp. 274–85.
23. There are very many editions of the *Heterodoxos*, including a complete version available

on-line. In general, I have used the eight-volume edition published in Buenos Aires in 1945, but have refrained from giving specific page references because the texts are easily accessible to those who wish to consult them.

24. Antonio Domínguez Ortiz, in the publication *Saber Leer*, no. 114 (1998), p. 2.

25. The recent claim by Teofilo F. Ruiz, in *Spanish Society 1400–1600*, Harlow 2001, p. 84, that 'one can certainly speak of a reformed Church in Spain before the Reformation' and that abuses had been 'met and redressed in Spain a quarter of a century before Luther', is pure fantasy and bears no relation to any available evidence. Abundant research done in recent years demonstrates quite the reverse. Cf. Helen Rawlings, *Church, Religion and Society in Early Modern Spain* (New York 2002), p. 51: 'Ferdinand and Isabella did little more than establish the foundations for a long-term reform.'

26. Figures from Pedro Borges, *El envío de misioneros a América durante la época española*, Salamanca 1977.

27. Cardinal Isidro Gomá Tomás, 'Apología de la Hispanidad', *Acción Española*, vol. 11, nos 64–5 (Nov. 1934).

28. Luis Nicolau d'Olwer, *Fray Bernardino de Sahagún (1499–1590)*, Salt Lake City 1987, p. 121. This is a translation of a work published in Spanish in Mexico in 1952.

29. Eric Thompson, ed., *Thomas Gage's Travels in the New World*, Norman 1958, p. 234.

30. Nicholas Griffiths, *The Cross and the Serpent. Religious Repression and Resurgence in Colonial Peru*, Norman, OK 1996, p. 263.

31. Lance Grahn, '"Chicha in the chalice": spiritual conflict in Spanish American mission culture', in Nicholas Griffiths and Fernando Cervantes, eds, *Spiritual Encounters. Interactions between Christianity and Native Religions in Colonial America*, Lincoln 1999, p. 261.

32. The standard study is Herbert E. Bolton, *Ruin of Christendom. A Biography of Eusebio Francisco Kino*, Tucson 1984 (reprint of 1936 edn).

33. Quoted in Edward H. Spicer, *Cycles of Conquest. The Impact of Spain, Mexico and the Unites States on the Indians of the Southwest 1533–1960*, Tucson 1962, p. 310.

34. Grahn, '"Chicha in the chalice"', p. 268.

35. John J. TePaske, ed., *Discourse and Political Reflections on the Kingdoms of Peru*, Norman OK 1978, p. 118.

36. Michel Vovelle, *Piété baroque et déchristianisation en Provence au XVIIIe siècle: Les Attitudes devant la mort d'après les clauses des testaments*, Paris 1973.

37. Both quoted in M. A. Fernández García, *Inquisición, comportamiento y mentalidad en el reino de Granada (1600–1700)*, Granada 1989, p. 247.

38. Quoted in Emilio la Parra López and Manuel Suárez Cortina, eds, *El anticlericalismo español contemporáneo*, Madrid 1998, p. 157.

39. In Parra and Suárez, p. 176.

40. Both quotes in Juliá, p. 276.

41. Quotation from Juliá, p. 281.

42. In Juliá, p. 294.

43. Juliá, p. 305.

44. Juliá, p. 322.

45. Quoted in Juliá, p. 356.

46. Andrés-Gallego et al., p. 65.

Chapter 4: The myth of an empire

1. Pagden 1990, p. 3.

2. J. H. Elliott, 'A Europe of composite monarchies', *Past and Present*, 137 (Nov. 1992), pp. 48–71, deals with the case of Spain. Prof. Conrad Russell has identified the union between

Scotland and England as similar to that between Castile and Aragon.

3. B. J. García García and A. Álvarez Osorio, eds, *La Monarquía de las naciones: Patria, nación y naturaleza en la Monarquía de España*, Madrid 2005.

4. Pagden 1995, p. 49.

5. Cf. the quotation from Vázquez de Menchaca in Pagden 1995, p. 58.

6. John M. Headley, *Tommaso Campanella and the Transformation of the World*, Princeton 1997.

7. Luis Ortiz to the king, Valladolid, 15 October 1558, Archivo General de Simancas, Consejo y Juntas de Hacienda, leg. 34, f. 437.

8. López Madera, *Excelencias de la Monarquía y Reyno de España*, Madrid 1625, p. 79.

9. These pages touch only on aspects of the question as it relates to early modern Spain. For a good guide to the nineteenth-century context, see Sebastian Balfour, *The End of the Spanish Empire, 1898–1923*, London 1997.

10. Enric Ucelay-Da Cal, *El imperialismo catalán. Prat de la Riba, Cambó, D'Ors y la conquista moral de España*, Barcelona 2003.

11. *España invertebrada*, p. 51.

12. Peter Rassow, *Die Kaiser-Idee Karls V dargestellt an der Politik der Jahre 1528–1540. Historische Studien*, Berlin 1932, p. 217.

13. Perhaps the best recent biographies of the emperor are those by Alfred Kohler, *Karl V. 1500–1558. Eine Biographie*, Munich 1999, and Wim Blockmans, *Emperor Charles V, 1500–1558*, London 2002.

14. Menéndez Pidal, *Idea Imperial de Carlos V*, first published in the *Revista Cubana* of 1937. I quote from the Madrid 1955 edition. It was first published in 1940 in Madrid, a sign of the welcome given to the idea by the Franco regime.

15. Joseph Pérez, *La Révolution des Comunidades de Castille (1520–1521)*, Bordeaux 1970, p. 155.

16. Pidal's reading is not shared by Pérez, who says: 'We cannot give to the 1520 speech the special importance given it by Pidal', p. 159.

17. The two authors were Antonio de Guevara and Alfonso de Valdés.

18. Carande's definitive work on Charles' Spanish finances, *Carlos V y sus banqueros*, 3 vols, 2nd edn, Madrid, 1965–7, helped to confirm, in the minds of Spanish scholars, that Spain was the financial mainstay of the empire. For a more rounded survey, which places the Spanish contribution within its international context, see James D. Tracy, *Emperor Charles V, Impresario of War*, Cambridge 2002.

19. Yona Pinson, 'Imperial ideology in the triumphal entry into Lille of Charles V and the crown prince (1549)', in *Assaph: Studies in Art History*, vol. 6, p. 205; also J. Jacquot (ed.), *Les Fêtes de la Renaissance*, Vol. 2: *Fêtes et cérémonies au temps de Charles Quint*, Paris 1960. The imagery of arches should, however, be interpreted with caution. In most cases, this imagery reflected the ideas of those who built the arches (i.e. the cities), not of those who were the honoured guests (the emperor).

20. Scott Dixon, p. 116.

21. Horst Rabe, ed., *Karl V. Politische Korrespondenz. Brieflisten und Register*, 20 vols, Konstanz 1999.

22. Quoted in Juliá, p. 330.

23. Santiago Juan Navarro, 'Between El Dorado and Armageddon: Utopia and apocalypse in the films of the encounter', *Delaware Review of Latin American Studies*, vol. 6, no. 2 (2006).

24. I quote at random from a book in my library, W. L. Schurz's *This New World*, London and New York 1956, p. 116, writing about the conquistadors: 'The essential fact is that they were Spaniards of the sixteenth century and therefore superb fighting material. As Spaniards, they were the end product of centuries of preparation for some collective effort

of the human will. A .concurrence of circumstances furnished the setting for the great adventure for which everything else had been a preparation. . . . To a superlative degree the conquistadors epitomized the peculiar genius of Spain.' Schurz was an eminent scholar, author of the best study we have on the Manila galleon.

25. John Lynch, *Spain 1516–1598*, Oxford 1991, p. 212.
26. Pagden 1995, p. 43.
27. Elliott, p. 63.
28. The myths of the Spanish empire are effectively rebutted in the useful book by Matthew Restall, *Seven Myths of the Spanish Conquest*, Oxford 2003, esp. chs 1 and 4.
29. Elliott, p. 63.
30. The quotation comes from a version in *artehistoria.com*. The current version of events given on this web page, which is financed by the regional government of Castile and Léon, is even more triumphalist, and explains that 'fifty years after the voyage of Columbus, what came to be Spanish America was already conquered'.
31. Cieza de León, *Obras completas*, vol. 1, p. 2.
32. Bernardo de Vargas Machuca, *Milicia y descripción de las Indias*, Madrid 1599 (my citation is from the two-volume 1892 edition, volume 1, p. 102).
33. One popular novelist, Arturo Perez Reverte, who uses his special vision of (and special vocabulary about) Spain's history as the basis of his novels, says: 'We were the great world power. Spain had Europe by the balls so Europe turned against Spain. The English and Americans write novels and make films about pirates and colonial settlers, we Spaniards do not. We have kept on constructing a solidly based achievement. They have made us feel guilty about it, something that happens in no other country in Europe. But looking at the past through politically correct glasses is just shit. You can't look at the conquest of America or the war in Flanders through those glasses. The world was different and you can't apply the politically correct criteria of the twenty-first century to the fifteenth, sixteenth and seventeenth centuries.' Interview in the newspaper *El País*, 15 November 2003.
34. Blanco White, *Autobiografía*.
35. Cf. Boyd, p. 85.
36. Quoted in Saínz Rodríguez, p. 119.
37. Eloy Benito Ruano, 'La participación extranjera en la guerra de Granada', *Revista de Archivos, Bibliotecas y Museos*, vol. 80, no. 4 (Oct.–Dec. 1977).
38. Juan de Narváez, cited in Otis H. Green, *Spain and the Western Tradition. The Castilian Mind in Literature from El Cid to Calderón*, 4 vols., Madison 1968, vol. III, p. 99.
39. The best summary of the context in which accusations were made against the emperor is in chapter 3 of Bosbach.
40. In a speech to Parliament in 1656, Cromwell pronounced the words: 'Your great enemy is the Spaniard.' (W. C. Abbott, ed., *The Writings and Speeches of Oliver Cromwell*, 4 vols, Cambridge, MA 1947, vol. 4, p. 261).
41. Cf. Henry Kamen, *The Duke of Alba*, New Haven, CT and London 2004, chapter 7.
42. 'Anti-Spanish propaganda employed concepts and contexts which were made applicable to the Spanish kings': Bosbach, p. 73.
43. Parker 1998, p. 166.
44. Parker 1998, p. 93.
45. Kagan and Parker, eds, p. 259.
46. Parker 1998, p. 95.
47. Some of his reactions are mentioned in Kamen 1997, chapter 10.
48. Geoffrey Parker, *The World is not Enough: The Imperial Vision of Philip II of Spain*, Waco TX 2001, p. 30, sees 'at least three related layers of messianic vision. First, Philip believed that God had chosen him to rule expressly to achieve his purpose for the world. Second,

he was equally convinced that God held him under special protection, to enable him to achieve these goals. Third, he felt certain that if necessary God would intervene directly in order to help him succeed.'

49. Cf. Peer Schmidt, *Spanische Universalmonarchie oder 'teutsche Libertet'. Das spanische Imperium in der Propaganda des Dreissigjährigen Krieges*, Stuttgart 2001, p. 102.

50. Schmidt, p. 117.

51. This paragraph could have been expanded into a book, but documentary support for its statements can be found in my studies on Philip II and on Alba.

52. Pedro de Ribadeneira to Quiroga, 16 February 1580, *Monumenta Historica Societatis Jesu: Ribadeneira*, Madrid 1923, vol. 1, p. 22.

53. Pagden 1990, p. 6.

54. Fernando de Alva Ixtlilxochitl, *Ally of Cortes*, trans. Douglass K. Ballentine, El Paso 1969, p. 23.

55. And, indeed, of most empires, as a number of recent studies have tended to emphasize.

56. Marcos de Isaba, *Cuerpo enfermo de la milicia española*, Madrid 1594, modern edition 1991, pp. 66–7. The French army consisted of an estimated 17,000 infantry and 6,500 cavalry; Isaba's account omits to mention that the rest of the anti-French forces with whom the Spanish troops served consisted of over 22,000 men. A recent study of the battle is Angus Konstam, *Pavia 1525: The Climax of the Italian Wars*, Oxford 1996.

57. D. Aedo y Gallart, *Viage, successos y guerras del Infante Cardenal Don Fernando de Austria*, Madrid 1637, pp. 130, 195.

58. The career of Xavier (who died in 1552 and was declared a saint in 1662) is an interesting historiographical case. The members of Xavier's family were strongly anti-Spanish and fought against the Spanish occupation of their country. Xavier went into exile from Navarre and studied in Paris, where he met Ignatius Loyola and helped to found the Jesuits. His outstanding career as a missionary was spent wholly within the ambit of the Portuguese empire, not the Spanish. The first exhaustive study of his career was written between 1955 and 1971 by a German Jesuit, Georg Schurhammer. Not until 1992 was this immense work published in Spanish.

59. I take the list of Spanish 'victories' given by J. P. Fusi, *España. La evolución de la identidad nacional*, Madrid 2000, p. 109.

60. I. A. A. Thompson and Geoffrey Parker, 'Lepanto (1571): The costs of victory', in I. A. A. Thompson, *War and Society in Habsburg Spain*, Aldershot 1992.

61. March, J. M., *Don Luis de Requeséns en el gobierno de Milán*, Madrid 1943, p. 57.

62. Menéndez Pidal, *Idea Imperial*, p. 35.

63. 'Observaciones críticas sobre las biografías de Fray Bartolomé de las Casas', Ramón Menéndez Pidal, in Cyril A. Jones and Frank Pierce, eds, *Actas del Primer Congreso Internacional de Hispanistas : Celebrado en Oxford del 6 al 11 de septiembre de 1962*, 1972. Also Ramón Menéndez Pidal, *El Padre Las Casas: Su doble personalidad*, Madrid 1963.

64. Cesar Vidal, 'El primer imperio moderno', *Muy Especial*, no. 62 (summer 2003).

65. *El Basilisco*, no. 24 (April–June 1998).

66. Review of *España frente a Europa* by Felipe Giménez Pérez, in the online right-wing Spanish publication *Cuaderno de Materiales* (www.filosofia.net/materiales/).

67. In what follows, I rely on the excellent outline by Ilan Rachum, 'Origins and historical significance of the Día de la Raza', *Revista Europea de Estudios Latinoamericanos y del Caribe*, 76 (April 2004).

68. Online article by Sebastian Balfour, 'The Spanish Empire and its Dissolution: a Comparative View in Nineteenth- and Twentieth-Century Europe'.

69. A reference to the voyages of Columbus and Sebastián Delcano.

70. Isidro Gomá Tomás, 'Apología de la Hispanidad', published in the paper *Acción Española*, vol. XI, no. 64–5 (Nov. 1934), Madrid.

Chapter 5: The myth of the Inquisition

1. Vicente Llorens, *El Romanticismo español*, Madrid 1989, p. 71.
2. In Spanish there is a recent photostatic edition, published in 1988 in Barcelona; my quotations are from it.
3. Puigblanch, p. 487.
4. For Montano, see my *The Disinherited*, London and New York 2007, chapter 3.
5. Outlined usefully by Edward Peters, *Inquisition*, Berkeley 1989.
6. See the introduction by Gerard Dufour to his edition of the *Memoria histórica*, Paris 1977.
7. *The History of the Inquisition of Spain*, London 1827, Preface.
8. Cánovas del Castillo, *Historia de la decadencia*, p. 21.
9. My impression is that there is not a single textual reference to Lea in any of the books published on the Inquisition in Spain before 1983, when a Spanish translation of his work was finally brought out in Madrid.
10. Vicente Palacio Atard, *Razon de la Inquisición*, Madrid 1954.
11. Leopold von Ranke, *The Ottoman and Spanish Empires*, Philadelphia 1945 (translated from the German version of 1827).
12. Menéndez Pelayo, *Heterodoxos*, Buenos Aires 1945, VI, 18–19.
13. *Heterodoxos*, V, 482.
14. John E. Longhurst, *The Age of Torquemada*, Lawrence KN 1962, Introduction, p. xi.
15. Cited in Gil Fernández, p. 476.
16. Lafuente, III, 212.
17. 'Crisis de Imperio', *El País*, 17 January 1998; 'El error del Rey Prudente', *El País*, 28 November 1998.
18. Cited in Kamen 1993[b], p. 520 of the Spanish edn.
19. For some bits of evidence, see, for example, S. d'Irsay, *Histoire des universités françaises et étrangères*, 2 vols, Paris 1933–5 ; F. Eulenberg, *Die Frequenz der deutschen Universitäten*, Leipzig 1904 ; F. de Dainville, 'Collèges et fréquentation scolaire au XVIIe siècle', *Population*, 1957 ; H. Schneppen, *Niederländische Universitäten und deutsches Geistesleben*, Münster 1960. Adequate matriculaton lists do not begin until the later sixteenth century, which makes it difficult for us to identify the presence before that period of Spaniards at Paris, a centre they certainly attended in some number.
20. Report of January 1585, quoted in Kamen 1993[a], chapter 6.
21. Archivo de la Corona de Aragon, Barcelona, leg. 358, document by Dr Geronimo Tamboni, 16 April, 1616.
22. David E. Vassberg, *The Village and the Outside World in Golden Age Castile*, Cambridge 1996, p. 129.
23. Quoted in Ramón Menéndez Pidal, *The Spaniards in their History*, trans. Walter Starkie, London 1950, p. 204.
24. Menéndez Pidal, p. 132.
25. Cánovas del Castillo, *Bosquejo Histórico de la Casa de Austria en España*, Madrid 1911, p. 156.
26. 'El español ¿lengua de pensamiento?', *Anuario del Instituto Cervantes* (2003).
27. Castro, pp. 596–9.
28. In Spain today (2006), one adult in two never opens a book, according to official statistics. In the village where I live in Catalonia, the majority of households do not possess one single book.
29. F. J. Norton, *Printing in Spain 1501–1520*, Cambridge 1966, p. 125.
30. T. S. Beardsley Jr, 'Spanish printers and the classics 1482–1599', *Hispanic Review*, 47 (1979), p. 30.
31. Jaime Moll, 'Problemas bibliográficas del libro del Siglo de Oro', *Boletín de la Real*

Academia Española, 59 (1979); also his 'Valoración de la industria editorial española del siglo XVI', in *Livre et lecture en Espagne et en France sous l'Ancien Régime*, Paris 1981.

32. Law of 1569, text in Instituto de Valencia de Don Juan, Madrid, envío 21, caja 31, doc. 230.

33. Paul F. Grendler, *The Roman Inquisition and the Venetian Press, 1540–1605*, Princeton 1977, p. 162.

34. Alfred Soman, 'Press, pulpit and censorship in France before Richelieu', *Proceedings of the American Philosophical Society*, 120 (1976), p. 454.

35. J. Pardo Tomás, *Ciencia y Censura. La Inquisición Española y los libros científicos en los siglos XVI y XVII*, Madrid 1991, however, feels that 'the efficiency of systems of control was very high' up to the seventeenth century (p.269). His view is based exclusively on the Inquisition's own papers, which were generally optimistic about the success achieved (because officials were reporting to superiors).

36. Angel Alcalá, in 'Inquisitorial control of writers', in his *The Spanish Inquisition and the Inquisitorial Mind*, Highland Lakes NJ 1987, p. 321, places emphasis on the word 'control'. Elsewhere (same volume, p. 617) he makes the bizarre statement that 'the inquisitorial system kept Spain in chains for three hundred and fifty years'. This is the language of the Liberal zealots of the 1820s.

37. The phrases come from Virgilio Pinto Crespo, 'Thought control in Spain', in Stephen Haliczer, ed., *Inquisition and Society in Early Modern Europe*, London 1987, p. 185.

38. Some years ago I addressed a meeting of university professors in Spain, one of whom felt that I was underestimating the impact of the Inquisition on freedom of thought. As an example of repression, he cited the (temporary) ban in the 1560s on a catechism published by a Catalan bishop. I explained that the Inquisition issued the ban because the bishop had maintained, in a manual intended for parish clergy, that a couple is not married in the eyes of the Church unless their union is sanctioned by the bishop. When I asked the professors to explain why the bishop was wrong (in Church law, the bishop has no role, because marriage needs only the consent of the two participating parties in order to be valid), none of them was able to do so. They felt that, quite simply, any act of censorship by the Inquisition must be wrong.

39. Antonio Domínguez Ortiz, *Los judeoconversos en la España moderna*, Madrid 1993.

40. José María Blanco White, *Cartas de España*, trans. Vicente Llorens, Madrid 1972, p. 55. My text in English is translated from this translation, since I have not been able to access the original work that White wrote in English.

41. A fuller treatment of blood purity can be found in chapter 11 of Kamen 1993[a].

42. Elliott, pp. 220–1.

43. Among several recent surveys of anti-Semitism in Spain, one may mention Pere Joan i Tous and H. Nottebaum, eds, *El Olivo y la Espada. Estudios sobre el antisemitismo en España (siglos XVI–XX)*, Madrid 2003.

44. The president of Castile was Hernando Niño de Guevara. All documents referred to here are in the Archivo General de Simancas, Cámara de Castilla leg. 291 f. 1.

45. L. Cabrera de Córdoba, *Filipe Segundo, rey de España*, 4 vols, Madrid 1876–7, vol. 1, p. 47.

46. Kamen 1993[b], VII, 7.

47. The captain was Julián Romero: see Cabrera de Córdoba, vol. 2, p. 429.

48. Linda Martz, 'Pure blood statutes in sixteenth-century Toledo: Implementation as opposed to adoption', *Sefarad*, 64: 1 (1994), pp. 91–4.

49. P. L. Lorenzo Cadarso, 'Oligarquías conversas de Cuenca y Guadalajara (siglos XV y XVI)', *Hispania*, 186 (1994), p. 79.

50. C. Carrete Parrondo, *El judaismo español y la Inquisición*, Madrid 1992, p. 155; Gil Fernández, p. 470.

51. Cited in Gil Fernández, p. 476.
52. Cf. Ruth MacKay, *'Lazy, Improvident People'. Myth and Reality in the Writing of Spanish History*, Ithaca NJ 2006, p. 185: discrimination was 'a placeholder for power and status, not race or religion'.
53. A good recent study of the subject is Juan Hernández Franco, *Cultura y Limpieza de Sangre en la España Moderna*, Murcia 1996.
54. Menéndez Pelayo, *La Ciencia española*, 3 vols, Santander 1953, vol. 1, p. 84. The three volumes make up vols 58–60 of the Edición Nacional of the Obras Completas, Santander 1953. The author of the quotation was Manuel de la Revilla.
55. Cited in Santoveña, p. 116.
56. Compare this statement with the fact (noted below, chapter 6) that in Holland alone more than 1,500 editions of Spanish books could be found on the bookshelves during the period referred to.
57. Since Ortega never entered the debate over Spanish science, the word 'decisive' apparently implies that a word from him was sufficient to expose the hollowness of Menéndez Pelayo's exposition.
58. A more critical vision of Ortega's links with the dictatorship is given in Gregorio Morán, *El Maestro en el Erial. Ortega y Gasset y la Cultura del franquismo*, Barcelona 1998.
59. Cf. John Gascoigne, 'A reappraisal of the role of the universities in the Scientific Revolution', in David Lindberg and Robert Westman, eds, *Reappraisals of the Scientific Revolution*, Cambridge 1990, p. 250.

Chapter 6: The myth of a universal language

1. Quoted in Pagden 1990, p. 58.
2. Cited in Otis H. Green, *Spain and the Western Tradition*, 4 vols, Madison, WI 1968, vol. 3, p. 84.
3. For an overview of the low level of Latin in Spain, see Gil Fernández, *Panorama social del humanismo español*.
4. Cited in Kamen 1993[b], p. 355.
5. Cf. the diagram of Castilian books published abroad, in Kamen 1993[b], p. 404.
6. Henry Thomas, 'The output of Spanish books in the sixteenth century', *The Library*, 1 (1920), p. 30.
7. Cf. Dale B. J. Randall, *The Golden Tapestry. A Critical Survey of Non-Chivalric Spanish Fiction in English Translation (1543–1657)*, Durham, NC 1963.
8. Jan Lechner, *Repertorio de obras de autores españoles en bibliotecas holandesas hasta comienzos del siglo XVIII*, Utrecht 2001, p. 10. I am grateful to Dr Lechner for making this very useful work available to me.
9. Lechner, p. 309.
10. Carlos Gilly, *Spanien und der Basler Buchdruck bis 1600*, Basel 1985, pp. 155–273.
11. For France, see the summary in Fernand Braudel, *The Identity of France*, London 1988, pp. 96–7. On Italy, it is interesting that one of the biggest obstacles to translating the Bible into Italian in early modern times was the absence of any general Italian language into which it could be translated.
12. Cf. Clare Mar-Molinero, 'The role of language in Spanish nation-building', in Mar-Molinero and Smith, eds, p. 72.
13. Elliott, p. 128.
14. Alan Patten, 'The humanist roots of linguistic nationalism' (online article, Jan. 2006 version), p. 2.
15. Dr Diego Cisteller, cited in Kamen 1993[b], p. 365.

16. My wife remembers how her grandmother, in the days when television first arrived in Catalonia, used to watch the screen happily for hours even though she did not understand a word of the Castilian being spoken.

17. Puigblanch, p. xxvii.

18. Juan de Valdés, *Diálogo de la Lengua*, Mexico 1966, p. 78.

19. J. V. Polisenský, *War and Society in Europe 1618–1648*, Cambridge 1978, p. 32.

20. See the pioneering study by Otto Brunner, *Neue Wege der Sozialgeschichte*, Göttingen 1956.

21. 'En Francia ni varón ni muger dexa de aprender la lengua castellana', in his *Persiles*. A surprising proportion of the cultural elite spoke the language at that period, but they were 'a tiny minority': Alexandre Ciorănescu, *Le Masque et le visage. Du baroque espagnol au classicisme français*, Geneva 1983, p. 145.

22. 'Cet enthousiasme est bien mitige': Alain Hugon, *Au service du Roi Catholique. 'Honorables ambassadeurs' et 'Divins espions'. Représéntation diplomatique et service secret dans les relations hispano-françaises de 1598 à 1635*, Madrid 2004, p. 60.

23. *L'Age d'Or de l'Influence espagnole. La France et l'Espagne à l'époque d'Anne d'Autriche 1615–1666*, Paris 1991, p. 51.

24. Serge Gruzinski, *The Conquest of Mexico. The Incorporation of Indian Societies into the Western World, 16th to 18th Centuries*, Cambridge 1993, p. 91.

25. What follows is derived from Kamen 2003.

26. Mercedes López-Baralt, *Icono y conquista: Guamán Poma de Ayala*, Madrid 1988, p. 303.

27. C. R. Boxer, *The Portuguese Seaborne Empire 1415–1825*, Harmondsworth 1973, p. 128.

28. J. S. Cummins, *A Question of Rites. Friar Domingo Navarrete and the Jesuits in China*, Aldershot 1993, p. 210.

29. P. Van der Loon, 'The Manila incunabula and early Hokkien studies', *Asia Major*, 12 (1966), p. 30.

30. Quoted in Edward Glaser, *Estudios Hispano-Portugueses. Relaciones literarias del Siglo de Oro*, Madrid 1957, pp. v–vii.

31. Vicente L. Rafael, *Contracting Colonialism. Translation and Christian Conversion in Tagalog Society under Early Spanish Rule*, Ithaca NJ 1988, p. 26.

32. The study by Vicente Rafael is a brilliant exposition along these lines.

33. My experience of childhood life in British India and Burma offered a comparable experience. The British learnt to speak a pidgin language, called Hindustani, which established a basic communication but was deficient as a vehicle of social contact. For effective contact, my mother used her fluent Nepalese and my father his fluent Burmese.

34. Cf. Miguel Angel Ochoa Brun, *Historia de la diplomacia española*, 6 vols, Madrid 1999, vol. 4, p. 502.

35. In reality, the Vatican had no domes, and the great dome of St Peter's was not constructed until fifty years later.

36. Menéndez Pidal, *Idea Imperial*, 1955 edn, p. 31.

37. Manuel Alvar, 'Carlos V y la lengua española', in his *Nebrija y estudios sobre la Edad de Oro*, Madrid 1997.

38. The context of the speech is discussed in Vicente de Cadenas y Vicent, *El Saco de Roma de 1527*, Madrid 1974.

39. The phrase can be traced, apparently, to a French source of 1671.

40. Though Italian by family, Farnese was brought up at the Spanish court, where he was one of Prince Philip's companions.

41. Alan Freeland, 'The people and the poet: Portuguese national identity and the Camões tercentenary (1880)', in Mar-Molinero and Smith, p. 54.

42. Miguel de Unamuno to Angel Ganivet, in Miguel de Unamuno and Angel Ganivet, *El porvenir de España*, Madrid 1912. The letter to Ganivet was first published in a Granada newspaper in 1898.

43. E. Storm, 'El tercer centenario del *Don Quijote* en 1905 y el nacionalismo español', *Hispania*, no. 199 (1998).
44. Lucas Mallada, *La futura revolución española*, Madrid 1998, p. 104.
45. Cited in *Cervantes. Bulletin of the Cervantes Society of America*, 22 (2002), p. 207.
46. M. J. Martínez Alcalde, *Las ideas lingüísticas de Gregorio Mayans*, Valencia 1992, pp. 243–4.
47. John C. Landreau, 'José María Arguedas: Peruvian Spanish as subversive assimilation', in Valle and Gabriel-Stheeman, p. 171.
48. Leslie E. Bauzon, 'Language planning and education in Philippine History', *International Journal of the Sociology of Language*, 88 (1991), pp. 101–19; Antonio Quilis, 'Historia de la lengua española en Filipinas', *Hispanic Linguistics*, 5: 2, no. 1 (1985), pp. 133–52.
49. Vicente L. Rafael, *The Promise of the Foreign. Nationalism and the Technics of Translation in the Spanish Philippines*, Durham NC 2005.
50. In Valle and Gabriel-Stheeman, p. 113.
51. In Valle and Gabriel-Stheeman, p. 6.
52. *El Mundo*, Madrid, 18 November 2004.
53. José del Valle, 'Menéndez Pidal, national regeneration and the linguistic utopia', in Valle and Gabriel-Stheeman, p. 79.
54. This passage comes from his *Defensa de la Hispanidad*.
55. Marqués de Tamarón, *El peso de la lengua española en el mundo*, Valladolid 1995, p. 15.
56. Address in the III Congreso Internacional de la Lengua española, printed in *El País*, 12 January 2004.
57. 'Español conquistará a Estados Unidos', in the 26 November 2004 issue of the online journal *El News Hispano*.
58. Since no previous conquest took place, the word 'reconquest' is clearly a reference to the medieval conquest of the Iberian Peninsula from its non-Christian occupiers.
59. *El País*, 9 July 2000.
60. Ilan Stavans, 'The *gravitas* of Spanglish', *Chronicle of Higher Education*, 13 October 2000.

Chapter 7: The myth of perpetual decline

1. Henry Kamen, 'Golden Age, Iron Age: A conflict of concepts in the Renaissance', *Journal of Medieval and Renaissance Studies*, Fall 1974.
2. Juan de Silva to Esteban de Ibarra, Madrid, 12 July 1590, Biblioteca Casanatense, Rome, 2417 f. 74.
3. Ernest Renan, 'Que-est ce qu'une nation?', in Geoff Eley and Ronald Grigor Suny, eds, *Becoming National: A Reader*, New York and Oxford 1996, pp. 41–55.
4. Saínz Rodríguez, p. 98.
5. Asensio Gutiérrez, *La France et les français dans la littérature espagnole. Un aspect de la xénophobie en Espagne (1598–1665)*. St-Etienne 1977.
6. Schmidt, p. 43.
7. The phrase is used by Schmidt, p. 37.
8. Cited in Henry Kamen, *The War of Succession in Spain 1700–15*, London 1969, p. 392.
9. Quoted in Jean Sarrailh, *L'Espagne éclairée de la seconde moitié du XVIIIe siècle*, Paris 1954, p. 373.
10. Antonio Mestre Sanchis, *Apología y Crítica de España en el siglo XVIII*, Madrid 2003, p. 60.
11. Boyd, p. 76.
12. Biblioteca de Autores Españoles, Madrid, vol. 70, p. 722.
13. Alvar, p. 314.
14. Francesco Guicciardini, *Viaje a España*, Valencia 1952, p. 56.

15. James Lockhart and Enrique Otte, eds, *Letters and People of the Spanish Indies: The Sixteenth Century*, Cambridge 1976, pp. 119, 136.
16. Cf. the references gathered in the index to J. H. Elliott, *The Count Duke of Olivares*, New Haven, CT and London 1986, p. 715.
17. See my *Spain 1469–1714. A Society of Conflict*, 3rd edn, London 2005, chapter 4.
18. Quoted in Schmidt, p. 91.
19. Quoted in Mestre, *Apología y Crítica* (cited above in note 10), p. 65.
20. Nicolas Masson de Morvilliers, 'Espagne', in *Encyclopédie méthodique ou par ordre de matières*, ser. 'Géographie moderne', i, Paris 1783.
21. J. N. Hillgarth, *The Mirror of Spain, 1500–1700*, Ann Arbor 2000, p. 6, writes: 'What did Spain give non-Spaniards in the centuries that preceded Bayle? The answer is by no means easy.'
22. *Correspondance de Napoléon I*, 32 vols, Paris 1858–69, vol. 17, p. 221.
23. Juan Sempere y Guarinos, *Considérations sur les causes de la grandeur et de la décadence de la monarchie espagnole*, 2 vols, Paris 1826.
24. Saínz Rodríguez, p. 74.
25. 'Tableau de la décadence de l'Espagne pendant le XVII siècle, par M. De la Porte, redacteur aux archives, 1835': Archives du Ministère des Affaires Etrangères, Paris, Mémoires el Documents (Espagne), vol. 41.
26. Charles Weiss, *L'Espagne depuis le règne de Philippe II jusqu'à l'avènement des Bourbons*, 2 vols, Paris, 1844.
27. Antonio Cánovas del Castillo, *Historia de la decadencia de España desde el advenimiento de Felipe III al trono hasta la muerte de Carlos II*, Madrid 1910.
28. Juliá, p. 36, quoting Argüelles, *Examen histórico*.
29. Lafuente VI, ii.
30. For an excellent sketch of Cánovas and decline, see Juliá, pp. 38–41.
31. I owe this valuable point to Juliá, p. 45.
32. *Decadencia*, p. 8.
33. Cánovas del Castillo, *Bosquejo Histórico*, pp. 78–9, cited above in Chapter 2.
34. *Decadencia*, p. 11.
35. *Decadencia*, p. 758.
36. *Decadencia*, p. 34.
37. Cf. Fusi, pp. 181–5.
38. Cf. Boyd, *Historia Patria*.
39. Juan Valera, *Obras completas*, vol. 3, Madrid 1958.
40. Valera is referring to the standard Liberal view on the question.
41. Quoted in Antonio Santoveña, 'Menéndez Pelayo y la crisis intelectual de 1898', *Anuario Filosófico*, 31 (1998).
42. *Obras completas*, pp. 282–303.
43. *Historia de la Filosofía en España*, Madrid 1927, pp. 295–305.
44. Quoted by Juliá, p. 40.
45. See J. M. Sánchez Ron, 'Más allá del laboratorio: Cajal y el regeneracionismo a través de la ciencia', in his *1898: Entre la Crisi d'Identitat i la Modernització*, Montserrat 2000, pp. 350, 353.
46. Valera, *Obras completas*, vol. III, Madrid 1958.
47. 'Respuesta de un amigo a otro que le pregunta por el fin que vendrán a tener nuestros males en España': Biblioteca Nacional, Madrid, MS. 10818/7; cited in Kamen, *The War of Succession in Spain*, p. 392.
48. Prescott, p. 731.
49. Cf. Juliá, pp. 115–18.
50. Martín González de Cellorigo, *Memorial de la política necessaria y útil restauración a la*

república de España, Valladolid 1600, p. 15v. Sancho de Moncada, *Restauración política de España*, Madrid 1619, p. 22.

51. Francisco Martínez de Mata, *Memoriales*, ed. Gonzalo Anés, Madrid 1971, pp. 149–50.
52. Duke of Montalto to Don Pedro Ronquillo, 15 December 1688, in *CODOIN*, vol. 79, Madrid 1882.
53. Cited in Pagden 1995, p. 71.
54. Lafuente, III, 217.
55. *Decadencia*, p. 44.
56. Luis Suárez, 'España, unidad de destino', *Arbil*, no. 100 (2005).
57. García de Cortázar, p. 81.
58. Quoted in David J. Weber, *The Spanish Frontier in North America*, New Haven CT and London 1992, p. 273.
59. In García de Cortázar, p. 99.
60. All the quotations are from García de Cortázar, pp. 87–96. Spain in reality had never been a significant naval power, and quite apart from the Armada disaster (1588) its death rattle at sea occurred nearly two hundred years before Trafalgar, at the battle of the Dunes (1639).
61. García de Cortázar, p. 100.
62. García de Cortázar, p. 112.
63. A balanced examination of what Spanish decline may have been is given in chapter 6 of J. K. J. Thomson, *Decline in History. The European Experience*, Oxford 1998.
64. My comments here may be seen as an extension of what I wrote many years ago in Henry Kamen, 'The decline of Spain: A historical myth?', *Past and Present*, 81 (1978).
65. Jo Tollebeek, *Writing the Inquisition in Europe and America. The Correspondence between Henry Charles Lea and Paul Fredericq (1888–1908)*, Brussels 2004, p. 86.
66. Earl J. Hamilton, 'The decline of Spain', *Economic History Review*, 8 (1938), p. 2.
67. I. A. A. Thompson and B. Yun Casalilla, eds, *The Castilian Crisis of the Seventeenth Century*, Cambridge 1994, p. 2.
68. See the summary in Henry Kamen, *Spain 1469–1714: A Society of Conflict*, London and New York 2005, pp. 284–5. Pere Molas, *Comerç i Estructura Social a Catalunya i València als segles XVII i XVIII*, Barcelona 1977, discusses the economic renewal on the Levant coast. See also James Casey, 'Spain: A failed transition', in Peter Clark, ed., *The European Crisis of the 1590s*, London 1985.
69. *La Nueva Era*, Año I, núm. 1, October 1930.
70. Ignacio Sotelo, 'El español, al margen de la modernidad', *Anuario del Instituto Cervantes* (2003).
71. Lafaye, p. 440.
72. J. L. Abellán, 'España contra sí misma', *El País*, 12 April 2003.

Postscript: Myth and the erosion of identity in Spain

1. M. A. Bastenier, in *Babelia* of *El País*, 10 February 2007. The writer seems to be suggesting that the present book has the aim of putting down the Spanish empire in order to elevate the glory of the British empire and its language.
2. The subject is explored magnificently in Sandie Holguin.
3. 'In general', because sections of the state bureaucracy, including educational and research institutions, remain firmly closed to outside ideas and personnel, despite attempts to introduce change.
4. Cited in Andrés-Gallego et al., p. 260.
5. The urge to convert myth into fact can be consulted by anyone who has access to the Internet. In Wikipedia, which allows surfers to create and modify encyclopaedia entries,

the Spanish option has allowed a group of Spanish surfers to create a very special version of their country's history.

6. *El País*, 27 January 2007.
7. A case in point is the foundation of the state of Israel, which relies heavily on myths to give substance to national identity: see Zeev Sternhell, *The Founding Myths of Israel: Nationalism, Socialism, and the Making of the Jewish State*, Princeton 1998.
8. Boyd, p. 76.
9. Mar-Molinero and Smith, p. 7.
10. Cf. Boyd, p. 307. There is a useful brief essay on the relation between historians and Spanish nation-building in the nineteenth century by Juan Sisinio Pérez Garzón, 'Memoria, historia y poder. La construcción de la identidad nacional española' (http://www.uclm.es/profesorado/juansisinioperez/investigacion/IDENTIDAD%20NACIONAL%20ESPA%C3%91OLA.pdf).

SELECT BIBLIOGRAPHY

of items cited several times in the text

Alvar Ezquerra, Alfredo, *Isabel la Católica*, Madrid 2002

Álvarez Junco, José, 'The formation of Spanish identity and its adaptation to the age of nations', *History and Memory*, vol. 14, no. 1/2 (2002)

Andrés-Gallego, José A. M. Pazos and L. de Llera, *Los Españoles entre la religión y la política. El franquismo y la democracia*, Madrid 1996

Bosbach, Franz, *Monarchia Universalis. Ein politischer Leitbegriff der frühen Neuzeit*, Göttingen 1988 (*Schriftenreihe des Historischen Kommission bei der Bayerischen Akademie der Wissenschaft*, Band 32)

Boyd, Carolyn, *Historia Patria. Politics, History and National Identity in Spain, 1875–1975*, Princeton NJ 1997

Cánovas del Castillo, Antonio, *Historia de la decadencia de España desde el advenimiento de Felipe III al trono hasta la muerte de Carlos II*, Madrid 1910

Cánovas del Castillo, Antonio, *Bosquejo Histórico de la Casa de Austria en España*, Madrid 1911

Castro, Américo, *España en su historia. Cristianos, moros y judíos*, Barcelona 1984

Egido, Teófanes, *Sátiras políticas de la España moderna*, Madrid 1973

Elliott, J. H., *Imperial Spain 1469–1716*, London 1963

Fusi, Juan Pablo, *España. La evolución de la identidad nacional*, Madrid 2000

García de Cortázar, Fernando, *Los mitos de la historia de España*, Barcelona 2005

Gil Fernández, Luis, *Panorama social del humanismo español (1500–1800)*, Madrid 1981

Holguin, Sandie, *Creating Spaniards. Culture and National Identity in Republican Spain*, Madison WI 2002

Juliá, Santos, *Historia de las dos Españas*, Madrid 2004

Kagan, Richard L. and Geoffrey Parker, eds, *Spain, Europe and the Atlantic World*, Cambridge 1995

Kamen, Henry, *The Spanish Inquisition. A Historical Revision*, New Haven, CT and London 1993.

Kamen, Henry, *The Phoenix and the Flame. Catalonia and the Counter-Reformation*, New Haven CT and London 1993.

Kamen, Henry, *Philip of Spain*, New Haven, CT and London 1997

Kamen, Henry, *Empire. How Spain Became a World Power 1492–1763*, New York 2003 [English edn: *Spain's Road to Empire. The Making of a World Power 1492–1763*, London 2002]

Lafaye, Jacques, 'La imagen del pasado en la España moderna', in *Actas del Sexto Congreso Internacional de Hispanistas* (Toronto, 22–6 August 1977), Toronto 1980

Lafuente, Modesto, *Historia general de España desde los tiempos primitivos hasta la muerte de Fernando VII*, 6 vols, Barcelona 1877–82

Llobera, Josep R., *Foundations of National Identity*, New York 2004

Maeztu, Ramiro de, *Defensa de la Hispanidad*, Madrid 1934

Mar-Molinero, Clare, and Angel Smith, eds, *Nationalism and the Nation in the Iberian Peninsula. Competing and Conflicting Identities*, Oxford 1996

Maravall, José Antonio, *Estado Moderno y Mentalidad social*, 2 vols, Madrid 1972

Menédez Pidal, Ramón, *Idea Imperial de Carlos V*, Madrid 1941

Menéndez Pelayo, Marcelino, *Historia de los Heterodoxos españoles*, 3 vols, Madrid 1880–2

Ortega y Gasset, José, *España invertebrada*, Madrid 1921

Pagden, Anthony, *Spanish Imperialism and the Political Imagination*, New Haven, CT and London 1990

Pagden, Anthony, *Lords of All the World. Ideologies of Empire in Spain, Britain and France, c.1500–c.1800*, New Haven, CT and London 1995

Parker, Geoffrey, *The Grand Strategy of Philip II*, New Haven CT and London 1998

Pérez Villanueva, Joaquín, *Ramón Menéndez Pidal, su vida y su tiempo*, Madrid 1991

Pike, Fredrick B., *Hispanismo 1898–1936. Spanish Conservatives and Liberals and their Relations with Spanish America*, Notre Dame IL 1971

Prescott, William H., *History of the Reign of Ferdinand and Isabella the Catholic*, London 1841

Puigblanch, Antonio, *La Inquisición sin Máscara*, Barcelona 1988 (original edn 1811).

Saínz Rodríguez, Pedro, *La evolución de las ideas sobre la decadencia española*, Madrid 1962 (original edn 1924)

Santoveña Setién, Antoni, *Marcelino Menéndez Pelayo. Revisión crítico-biográfica de un pensador católico*, Santander 1994

Schmidt, Bernhard, *El problema español de Quevedo a Manuel Azaña*, Madrid 1976

Scott Dixon, C., 'Charles V and the historians: Some recent German works on the emperor and his reign', *German History*, vol. 21, no. 1 (2003)

Thompson, I. A. A., 'Castile, Spain and the monarchy: the political community from *patria natural* to *patria nacional*', in R. L. Kagan and G. Parker, eds, *Spain, Europe and the Atlantic World*, Cambridge 1995

Ucelay-Da Cal, Enric, *El imperialismo catalán. Prat de la Riba, Cambó, D'Ors y la conquista moral de España*, Barcelona 2003

Valle, José del, and Luis Gabriel-Stheeman, eds, *The Battle over Spanish between 1800 and 2000. Language Ideologies and Hispanic Intellectuals*, London 2002

INDEX

INDEX

Descartes xiv, 166, 188
Diada of Catalonia 29
Disaster of 1893, 162–3, 185, 189, 193
Domínguez Ortiz, Antonio 144, 146
Don Carlos 56, 58

Echegaray 188
Elizabeth of England 41, 44
Emerson, Ralph W. xiv
empire xi, xii, 9, 18–19, 21–2, 24, 28–9,
    45, 89, 91, 96–122, 151, 165, 170,
    172, 178, 190, 195, 199, 207
  as benevolent 120, 169
  as collaboration 110, 115, 116, 117
  as conquest 107–9, 112, 118–19, 124,
    199
  idea of 100, 102, 105, 121, 122
  and language 156–7, 159
  myth of 102, 104, 106, 173, 201, 206,
    Chap. 4 *passim*
  theories on 97
Encyclopédie 94, 179
Erasmians 94
Erasmus 87
Escobedo, Juan de 55

Falange 47
Farnese, Elizabeth 66–7, 116, 161
Feijoo 24
Ferdinand and Isabella 4, 6, 8, 12, 15, 22,
    33, 46–8, 56, 58, 60, 70, 72, 80, 100,
    105, 110, 173, 177, 178, 181, 183,
    190–1, 199
  legend of 43, 45–7, 65, 69, 87
Ferdinand the Catholic 9, 11, 18, 39, 43,
    45, 100, 101, 104, 192, 198
Ferdinand VII 4, 5, 27, 28, 39, 49, 57–8,
    68, 71–2, 130–1, 180
Fernández de Oviedo, Gonzalo 176
Fita, Fidel 133
Flanders *see also* Netherlands
foreign dynasties, as cause of ruin of Spain
    3, 9, 50, 176
foreigners, as cause of ruin of Spain 48, 68,
    70, 175–6
founding myths xi–xii
Fraga, Manuel 195
Francis I of France 59, 160
Franco, General ix, 29, 33, 38, 44–5, 47,
    61–2, 73, 75, 83, 94, 104–6, 131,
    149, 166, 194–5, 197, 207–8

French Revolution 10, 67, 92
Fuentes, Carlos 167, 170
fueros 25–7, 29, 30, 59, 69
Furió Ceriol, Fadrique 97

Gachard, Louis-Prosper 7, 56
Gage, Thomas 90
Galicia 17, 20, 79, 101, 154
Ganivet, Angel 51, 163
García de Cortázar, Fernando 197
García Lorca, Federico 207
Garcilaso de la Vega, Inca 157
Garibay, Esteban 13
Gattinara, Mercurino 102
Gibbon, Edward 4, 172
Golden Age ix, xii, 42, 46, 78, 83, 147,
    159, 162, 173, 176, 191, 196–7
Golden Century 75, 169, 184
Gomá, Cardinal 88, 123, 168
Góngora, Luis de 133
González de Cellorigo, Martín 176, 192
González Montano, Reinaldo 54, 128
Goya, Francisco 1, 129
Goytisolo, Juan 143, 144
Gracián, Baltasar 11, 15, 43, 133, 150
Granada 6, 14, 22, 18, 20, 23–4, 43, 57,
    79, 83, 89, 91–2, 103, 108, 110
Granvelle, cardinal 114
Great Captain 116
Guajiro people 91
Guaman Poma de Ayala, Felipe 156

Habsburg dynasty 17, 25, 35, 58, 60,
    65–6, 68–9, 70, 72, 111, 130, 147,
    154–5, 178, 179, 182, 183, 190, 191,
    198
  absolutism of 48
  as cause of ruin of Spain 50, 57–8, 68,
    191
  hostility to 48–50, 175–6, 179
Hamilton, Earl J. 200–1
Hanke, Lewis 120
Henry IV of Castile 38–9
Henry IV of France 44
Herder, Johann x, 153
Herrera, Antonio de 19
Hispanidad 105, 122–4
Hispanismo 166–7, 170
history, writing of 84

identity of Spain xii, xiv, 4, 11, 14, 18–20,

236